Big Ideas of the Bible

Mark Fackler, Ph.D.
General Editor

Big Ideas
of
the Bible

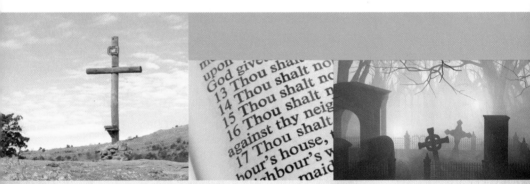

BARBOUR
PUBLISHING

Produced with the assistance of The Livingstone Corporation (www.livingstonecorp.com). Project staff include: Dana Niesluchowski, Dave Veerman, Linda Washington, Linda Taylor, Betsy Schmitt, Andy Culbertson, Ashley Taylor, Larry Taylor, Cheryl Blum, and Neil Wilson.

Published by Barbour Publishing, Inc., P.O. Box 719, Uhrichsville, Ohio 44683, www.barbourbooks.com

Our mission is to publish and distribute inspirational products offering exceptional value and biblical encouragement to the masses.

 Member of the
Evangelical Christian
Publishers Association

Printed in the United States of America.

Contents

Introduction

101 big ideas on any subject is a lot of ideas. My bird-watching journal has maybe four entries. My languages-learned file is thinner yet. Maybe you have a long way to go toward your 101st anniversary of anything. This book may give you a first.

"Big ideas" may sound like highway billboard ad-speak. We don't intend that—no puffery or sales hype here. These are the genuine articles—honestly significant, important ideas. They don't need a pitchman's quick patter. These 101 words/concepts/truths speak directly to the human condition: healing, resting, working, worshipping.

Moving through these big ideas you will see the Bible's core message. All the ideas focus on God's love and mercy, Jesus' resurrection power, and the promise of exhilarating life as God's work in people and in history unfolds.

These 101 summaries are not Methodist in orientation, or Presbyterian, Roman Catholic, or Baptist. Where church traditions have staked out different approaches, we mention them but leave the details for your further investigation in those churches and traditions. Our work here is introductory, not exhaustive. For the curious reader, each Big Idea offers much more to probe.

We take the Bible as God's truth, revealed through many inspired writers and supremely through Jesus Christ. The core message, then, is relevant to everyone. No one lives apart from God's gift of life, now or in heaven. The Big Ideas explore that gift in 101 dimensions.

Some of the "Bigs" are long, abstracted words, frankly. Count the letters in "Regeneration"—a word you may never have heard or read. Such words may seem intimidating the first time you confront them. But they will turn into friends by the end, when you yourself may be talking more about "regeneration" than you ever imagined.

Best case scenario: Use these Big Ideas to pray for and live the life God intends for you. Share the ideas at your family table. Work at their applications in your employment. In your television viewing or magazine reading, notice their appearance (or the consequences of their neglect).

(cont.)

We are delighted to present this book. If these Big Ideas help you discover the Big God who conceived and communicated them, that is good. More than a few readers will be drawn by the curiosity of childhood church memories long ago set aside. If that happens, then the effort of many people—from writing to design to reader checkers for the eradication of cliché and verbiage—will be vindicated. Did we say vindicated? Sounds like another Big Idea for the next book.

—*Mark Fackler, Ph.D.*

Adoption

Believers undergo a status change from children (or slaves) to sons and daughters of God.

Now you are no longer a slave but God's own child. And since you are his child, God has made you his heir. —Galatians 4:7 NLT

New Testament letters (Paul's writings) use *adoption* as a metaphor, borrowed from Roman and Greek law, to illustrate the difference faith makes in the believer's relationship to God. The status change is remarkable—more so when the role of first-century children and slaves is understood and applied. Both categories of people were subjects; that is, they had no rights of their own, no property, and no possibility of appealing their status. They were entirely under the thumb of their master, normally the male head of household. Paul compares that circumstance to a person outside the circle of faith, a slave to sin. Cynical indifference to God drives a sin-slave's heart and will. Worse, the devil himself may crush such a person with loss, pain, discouragement, or other harms. Absent faith, the slave has no legal appeal. He or she is trapped, as it were, in a world of chaos and lonely struggle, without standing before God's court (to extend the metaphor) to claim the right to be protected.

A man adopts one of his son and heir that does not at all resemble him; but whosoever God adopts for His child is like Him; he not only bears His heavenly Father's name, but His image.
—*Thomas Watson, poet*

Jesus Christ, by His death and resurrection, opens the courtroom door, as it were, enabling the status change from slave to son or daughter. Foremost among the changes signaled by adoption into God's family is the new name by which believers address the Master/Head of the household. That new name is a term of familiarity and love, gratefulness and kinship: *Abba* (Galatians 4:6). Some writers see this term as similar to "dad" or "papa." God now is the son's sure protector, the daughter's loving father.

The second major change signaled by adoption was also important during the Roman era as the legal means of securing family wealth: the appointment of heirs. By this device, a family's work and wealth would be preserved and distributed. For believers, becoming an heir means that all the benefits won by Christ in His death and resurrection—and intended by God for all of creation—are secure and available. These benefits include payment of the penalty of sin, the presence of God in one's life, the hand-in-hand relationship of believer to God, open channels of communication, and never-ending life with God in the eternal kingdom.

In the Old Testament, adoption is not mentioned. Nonetheless, the stories of Esther and Moses, Eliezer and Obed, speak of movement from outside one family to joining another. Psalm 2:7 (NLT), "You are my son. Today I have become your Father," is regarded as a formula for adoption that signals both status change and inheritance rights.

Adoption underscores a new, familial relationship to God, freedom from the oppressive evil of the devil, the gift of pardon, and a life of empowerment through God's presence. Adoption changes a person's role and relationship to God from outsider to child.

Additional scriptures

- **Romans 8:15**
- **Romans 8:23**
- **Ephesians 1:5**
- **John 1:12–13**
- **John 3:9–10**

Angels

Spiritual beings, often messengers of God, but sometimes agents of evil.

But when He again brings the firstborn into the world, He says: "Let all the angels of God worship Him." And of the angels He says: "Who makes His angels spirits and His ministers a flame of fire." —Hebrews 1:6–7 NKJV

Angels mean messengers and ministers. Their function is to execute the plan of divine providence, even in earthly things. —*St. Thomas Aquinas*

To the modern mind, angels may seem like fictional creatures best suited to adorning old stained-glass church windows. In the Bible, however, angels appear as messengers and agents of God, sometimes opposed to God and infrequently posing as God Himself. The regular mention of angels in both Old and New Testaments affirms that angels play a key, though mysterious, role in God's kingdom.

Angels (also called "cherubim" in some versions of scripture) first appear as guardians to the closed gates of Eden (Genesis 3:24). Other Old Testament terms often associated with angels are "gods," "sons of gods," and "holy ones." Angels visit Abraham, or is it

God Himself (Genesis 18)? An angel wrestles with Jacob, or is it the Lord Himself (Genesis 32:24–32)? An angel of the Lord (or God) speaks to Moses from a burning bush (Exodus 3). A named angel, Gabriel, appears to Daniel as a mentor (Daniel 8:16) and to Zechariah and Mary with special messages (Luke 1:19, 26). Another named angel, Michael, appears in Daniel's prophecy as a warrior (Daniel 10:21). Angels constitute God's heavenly council in Job 1–2.

Angels in the New Testament appear most publicly to shepherds on the night of Jesus' birth, singing (Luke 2:8–14). Angels help Jesus through His forty days of temptation in the wilderness (Mark 1:13). The book of Acts reports that angels open prison doors (Acts 5:19; 12:7).

Yet the situation is more complex. Angels are not always the messengers of God and, in some Bible instances, they even oppose God. In Paul's letters, fallen angels are the "principalities" and "powers" that wage spiritual warfare against believers (Ephesians 6:12). Jude mentions fallen angels as those who abandoned their home and surrendered their positions of heavenly authority (Jude 6).

Angels are prominent in the letter to Hebrews as a benchmark of Jesus' superiority, and humankind's giftedness. In Romans 8, often cited as the Bible's greatest statement on hope, angels and demons are described as powerless to separate believers from God, so strong is the bond of love established by Jesus Christ. The book of Revelation includes dramatic interventions of angels as the last days unfold and God's kingdom nears its fulfillment.

Clearly angels as described in the Bible are meant to be taken seriously. Their reputation in the life of the church has closely followed cultural changes, however. Thomas Aquinas, for example, wrote of the logical necessity of angels, who then gained huge popularity in the liturgy and architecture of medieval churches. The Reformers toned down angelic importance to recover the Bible's central person, Jesus, as Savior and God.

John Milton's epic poem *Paradise Lost* was the high point of angels in Western literature. But the Enlightenment and the modern era favored more material explanations for events. Thus, angels have been relegated to myth, often depicted as chubby and childlike. In the Bible, angels are not so described, and dismissive attitudes must reckon with the Bible's forthright description of angelic appearance and action.

Additional scriptures

- **Hebrews 1:14**
- **Hebrews 2:2**
- **Hebrews 2:9**
- **1 Peter 1:12**
- **1 Peter 3:22**
- **2 Peter 2:11**
- **Jude 6, 9**

Apostasy

Deliberate abandonment of faith in God.

Be careful then, dear brothers and sisters. Make sure that your own hearts are not evil and unbelieving, turning you away from the living God.
—Hebrews 3:12 NLT

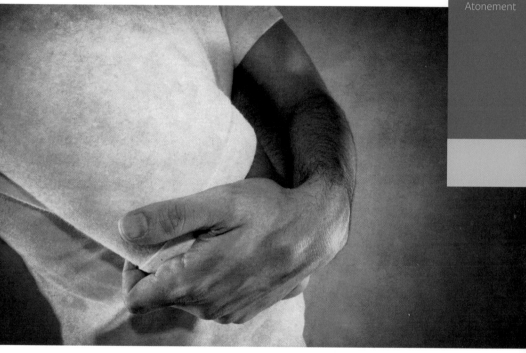

Everywhere the Bible urges believers to be strong in faith and patient during the inevitable challenges that strike every person's life. Many Bible stories feature people of weak faith caving in to temptations. Severe warnings are reserved, however, for people who have faith but consciously and publicly stop believing. Those who persist in repudiating the truth of God they once believed are said to be apostate.

Old Testament kings are often called unfaithful. Not only disobedient to the Torah (law), these leaders also actively work *against* the worship of God. Ahaz is one example (2 Chronicles 29:19). During the times of Isaiah and Jeremiah, the Hebrew nation is said to have abandoned God through steady and persistent indifference to the Torah (Isaiah 1:2–4; Jeremiah 2:1–9). In the New Testament, Paul cites Demas (2 Timothy 4:10), Hymenaeus, and Alexander (1 Timothy 1:20) as people whose faith not only suffered but seemed altogether gone by their own choice. Paul does not elaborate how this happened, only that it did, and that persons who abandon faith must be considered outside the church.

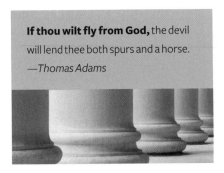

If thou wilt fly from God, the devil will lend thee both spurs and a horse.
—*Thomas Adams*

Warnings against such dangerous decisions are clear and consistent. The letter to the Hebrews is a long sermon to persecuted Christians. Its writer laments the irretrievable loss of prolonged abandonment of faith and urges readers/listeners toward loyalty to God despite painful circumstances.

Churches debate whether the Bible actually allows for apostasy. Churches that teach the "perseverance of the saints" (God keeps all His children safe) believe that no true believer is ever a casualty of apostasy. If no believer can be lost (John 17:12), then perhaps "believers" who repudiate faith were never true believers at all. Yet people who have formally confessed belief have been known to formally repudiate it. To deny the possibility flies in the face of lived experience. Why would the Bible warn against apostasy if it were not a real danger? Churches that teach a weak view of God's capacity to protect believers' faith emphasize the dangerous penalties of apostasy. These penalties serve as incentive to retain faith during periods of temptation or doubt.

The great apostasy is yet to come. Paul describes a "man of lawlessness" (2 Thessalonians 2:3) who will cause many to abandon faith. Don't be deceived by that charlatan, Paul warns without ever clearly identifying him. Did Paul mean a contemporary whose opposition to God most readers would know or a future figure not yet on the horizon? Churches divide on this question based on other teachings concerning the last days, the culmination of history.

Clearly, among heinous sins believers are urged to avoid, willful abandonment of faith is the most serious. To separate from God is to cut oneself off from the source of life and the only hope of eternal life. It is to choose to be an orphan, to live in God's world but not with God in any way. It is to choose to live apart from truth, in great loneliness, and without protection from evil.

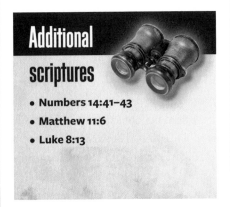

Additional scriptures

- **Numbers 14:41–43**
- **Matthew 11:6**
- **Luke 8:13**

Armor

A symbol for strong faith, especially during times of adversity and stress.

Put on the full armor of God so that you take your stand against the devil's schemes. For our struggle is not against flesh and blood, but against the rulers, against the authorities, against the powers of this dark world and against the spiritual forces of evil in the heavenly realms. Therefore put on the full armor of God, so that when the day of evil comes, you may be able to stand your ground, and after you have done everything, to stand. —Ephesians 6:11–13

The Christian life is not a playground; it is a battlefield.
—Warren W. Wiersbe

Actual armor in the ancient world consisted of defensive shields and helmets protecting against the blows of clubs and other offensive devices. The Bible uses armor as a metaphor for strong and enduring faith as well as for the strength of God to protect and serve.

The prophet Isaiah writes that God wears armor (Isaiah 59:17). Israel was under constant threat from ancient superpowers Egypt, Assyria, Babylon, and Persia. Its own army had its heyday during David's reign, but even then internal rebellion threatened to bring the kingdom down. Where could Israel and Judah turn for better defense? To their God, called Yahweh in the Old Testament, who is frequently described as the leader who alone can save His people. In that sense, Yahweh wears armor that no enemy can penetrate. Yet even then, the ancient superpowers still had their superior spears and chariots, and Israel often still felt threatened. Circumstances contradicted the promise of victory, even though victory was assured through the power of God. Trusting in the power of God is the people's responsibility. The crushing defeat of Israel to Assyria and Babylon, the Old Testament insists, was due to the people's (especially the leaders') loss of trust and faith.

In the New Testament, armor is everywhere associated with war against evil—spiritual warfare. Those who follow God, Paul writes, will encounter Satan's attacks; his sole purpose is to dissuade the believer and destroy the life that honors God. Jesus Christ has defeated evil on the cross, but intense skirmishes still hamper everyone's journey of faith. To ward off evil, temptation, and unbelief, the full armor of God includes truth, righteousness, the gospel of peace, faith, salvation, and finally, the one offensive weapon mentioned, the sword of the Spirit, the Word of God (Ephesians 6:14–18). Using this array of armor is strongly associated with prayer, though other disciplines are also intended, such as worship, the sacraments, personal appropriation of Bible promises, and moral watchfulness lest Satan detect a way around the armor.

The armor of God is essential to spiritual health. Satan's futile yet persistent "war" to derail faith requires spiritual readiness, alertness, and preparedness on the part of the believer. Paul warns of the evil day, which may point to an aggressive outburst of spiritual warfare at the end of time or to sudden shockwaves of evil in the life of the believer which will lead to questions of God's existence and care. ("How could a good God let this happen?") Failure to grow in the spiritual disciplines described by the metaphor of the armor make the believer vulnerable to doubt and despair. Many parts of the Bible assure that Satan is unable, no matter the intensity of the assault, to snatch a believer from God's hands.

Additional scriptures

- Matthew 4:1–11
- James 4:7
- 1 Peter 5:8–9

Atonement

The death of Jesus Christ on the Cross pays for all human sin, making us at-one with God again.

God presented him as a sacrifice of atonement, through faith in his blood. He did this to demonstrate his justice, because in his forbearance he had left the sins committed beforehand unpunished. —**Romans 3:25**

The original design of creation was that humans would walk with God in a luxurious garden. Before eating from the forbidden tree, Adam and Eve walked and talked with God. They were created for fellowship with Him.

Sin foiled all that. The penalty for eating the fruit was death, but Adam and Eve continued to live, though banished from Eden. The death of the body would come years later. But most importantly, their relationship with God had changed. No more walking and talking as friends. Disobedience had soiled the "goodness" of creation, and for that, God's holiness must be satisfied. The crown of creation (humankind) must be brought back to fellowship with God or the very heart of God would melt in grief and the purpose of creation would fade away.

Atonement (coming back to God) is a common theme in the Old Testament. The Hebrew word *kapar* is often translated to the English *atonement*. The Old Testament process took public form in animal sacrifices, for in the Hebrew world, the proper payment for sin was blood. To achieve any relationship with God, even temporary, blood sacrifice was required. An elaborate system of animal sacrifice developed. But just as clearly, God's holiness in the Garden of Eden and thereafter was not "made whole" (a legal term) by animals alone. Even in the Old Testament, strong hints of a final, complete, and all-sufficient sacrifice confront the believer. Especially in Isaiah's prophecy, a Servant of God will be "pierced for our transgressions. . .and by his wounds we are healed" (Isaiah 53:5 NIV)

That Servant was Jesus Christ, whose death paid for sin and brings humankind back to God (Acts 20:28). Jesus' death and resurrection fulfills

In the cross, God descends to bear in his own heart the sins of the world. In Jesus, he atones at unimaginable cost to himself. —*Woodrow A. Grier*

the work that animal sacrifice began but could never complete. Jesus is our High Priest (Hebrews 10) who came to do God's will, to fulfill God's intentions in creation, and to save humankind from the consequences of disobedience. Jesus' death gives life to all who believe as it permanently pays for all human sin. Fellowship is restored.

Several questions remain, however. If God wants human fellowship, why not simply order it? Why such a painful process of blood, including Jesus' crucifixion? Modern critics pose the issue in contemporary humanitarian terms: Why would a good God demand such a painful process of payment? Indeed, throughout Christian history, theologians have tried to fashion in words why and how atonement is achieved, and whether it must be re-enacted regularly to keep the penitent sinner in secure fellowship with God (as in the Roman Catholic tradition). Augustine set the stage for Luther and Calvin on this matter when he taught that Jesus accomplished "penal expiation." God's justice and holiness cannot dismiss evil as though it did not happen. Rather, divine holiness requires the full measure of payment for sin. All Christian churches believe that Jesus' death and resurrection secures the benefits of atonement. The Reformers taught that Jesus paid in full for all time. Clearly, many of these older answers are not satisfying to modern sensibilities.

Today, where biblical language and teaching is followed, atonement is achieved when the sinner (everyone, no exceptions) places trust in Jesus to bring him or her back into fellowship with God, who then declares that person free of guilt because of Jesus' obedience. The Bible presents no other way, yet this way is said to be "free" (all debts to God paid at the cross) and "by grace" (God Himself enables us to come). Here are mysteries that cannot be fully explained, but the heart of God is love, the message of God is "come," and the way of God (atonement) has been accomplished by Jesus Christ. This is the gospel, the Good News, the central theme of the entire Bible.

Additional scriptures

- **Exodus 30:10**
- **Leviticus 1:4**
- **Deuteronomy 32:43**
- **Ezekiel 16:63**
- **Hebrews 2:17**

Baptism

B

Baptism
Blessed
Body of Christ
Born Again
Bread of Life
Bridegroom

The application of water to signal new life through faith in Christ and membership in the church.

Go therefore and make disciples of all the nations, baptizing them in the name of the Father and of the Son and of the Holy Spirit. —Matthew 28:19 NKJV

Water baptism is done in all Christian churches to initiate people into membership. But the precise purpose of baptism varies from church to church, depending on what the rite is believed to mean. In churches believing that sacraments (church ceremonies) are powerful means of communicating divine blessing ("means of grace"), baptism is said to affect salvation. Where sacramental practice is believed to be secondary to the inner faith and outward life of the individual believer, baptism is regarded as a public profession of new faith. History and scripture are brought to the debate by both sides, but neither argument has persuaded the other. Some churches hold that a second, spiritual baptism of the Holy Spirit separates true disciples from nominal believers. In addition, one reference in Paul's writing to baptism for deceased persons (1 Corinthians 15:29) is likely a reference to a practice no longer recognized, except in the Mormon Church where genealogical research and subsequent baptisms are still performed.

Faith is essential to baptism. Sacramental churches insist that parents, godparents, or the church itself confess faith for a child being baptized; the surrogates are then obliged to lead the child to personal faith. In churches that restrict baptism to adult believers, faith of the one being baptized must be confessed before baptism is performed.

The Bible describes baptism in many ways: as a rite that pardons sin, as a rite initiating new birth in God's family, as the arrival of the Holy Spirit, as a Christian equivalent to Jewish circumcision, and as an essential element in discipleship—trusting one's life to God.

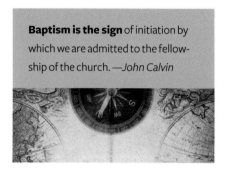

Baptism is the sign of initiation by which we are admitted to the fellowship of the church. —*John Calvin*

All churches baptize, but not all churches recognize the legitimacy of the others' rite. Christian baptism, commanded by Jesus as part of the mission of His followers, is to be done once to any person. But the failure of churches to find agreement on the means and meaning of baptism results in occasional re-baptisms. Re-baptism has been a disputed church practice since the Roman persecutions when baptized believers renounced faith and then later, as danger passed, sought re-entry into church membership.

The best-known baptism in the Bible, when John the Baptist applied water to Jesus, is also one of the most difficult to interpret. John likely drew his understanding of baptism from a community of Jewish priests called the Qumran, where believers were baptized daily for the forgiveness of sins. Repentance was the essential spiritual discipline associated with John's rite. Why then would Jesus, who did not need to repent, be baptized? The Gospels report that John begged Jesus to switch roles, as he (the Baptist) was the unworthy one, the subordinate. Yet Jesus insisted, and John baptized Him. At this baptism only, the Bible reports that heaven opened and a voice declared Jesus as God's Son while a dove flying over Jesus indicated that the Spirit of God was with Him. This baptism was unique, though Orthodox churches see it as normative for all believers: grace is bestowed, the heavens open to them, and God's power descends.

For all their varieties of practice and interpretation, Christian churches hold these elements in common: (1) water is a cleansing agent, symbolizing sin washed from the heart; (2) baptism is in the name of the Father, Son, and Holy Spirit, identifying the person baptized as now belonging to the Triune God; and (3) baptism is a step in discipleship—faithful living in the light of God's Word.

Additional scriptures

- **Matthew 3:5–6**
- **Matthew 3:13–17**
- **Mark 1:4–5**
- **Acts 2:41**
- **Acts 8:36–39**
- **1 Peter 3:21**

Blessed

The blessed person has received from God a confidence that life will be good, even in the face of difficulties or stress, because God is in control.

Blessed are the poor in spirit, for theirs is the kingdom of heaven.
—Matthew 5:3 NKJV

Santa Biblia

To be blessed, or feel blessed, goes beyond happiness, as the term is normally used. To feel blessed is first to know that the self and those close by (family, groups, nation) are living in God's favor, receiving from God the provision and security necessary to face tomorrow confidently. Beyond that, *blessed* connotes a solid sense of well-being that permits the one blessed to dream, to risk, to give freely and live "carelessly" since God is totally committed to the believer's care. To be blessed is to live fully, anticipating a delightful future, and to be confident that no matter the day's stresses, one will pull through with God's help.

In the ancient world, people assumed that the gods, who did not work and were not affected by fear or hunger, were blessed. Those who shared these godlike privileges were thought to be similarly blessed: the rich who had food, the wise who had foresight, and the seated who had rest. Aristotle used the Greek term for "blessed" to describe the person who is living at full human capacity, exercising virtue in a life free from labor and want.

The Bible both enriches the ancient

concept and radically alters it.

In the Old Testament, the blessed are those who live in covenant with God (Genesis 17:7). It is not a state to be earned but to be received as a gift from God. This blessing flows to the land (fruitful harvest), to the family (many heirs), and to the nation in its role of showing the world the truth of God by demonstrating blessedness. General material prosperity is part of the Old Testament's presentation of the blessed life (Deuteronomy 11:26–28). Often blessing is contrasted to its opposite: a declaration by God that the person, by his or her own decision, is outside the covenant and not available for blessing but rather is cursed, full of woe, very unhappy.

In the New Testament, a radically new vision of blessing emerges. In stark contrast to the ancients, the blessed are those who live at low economic levels yet who place hope in God for their daily needs. Fifty times in the New Testament, blessing is mentioned. On forty-four occasions, the blessing is a beatitude, an announcement of good hope to people who least expect it, the poor and powerless. In the Gospel of Matthew, for example, the blessed are the poor in spirit, the sorrowful, the meek, the hungry, and the persecuted. Why these? And how could blessedness possibly describe them? For two reasons, the Bible explains.

> **God is more** anxious to bestow his blessings on us than we are to receive them. —*Augustine of Hippo*

First, they are blessed because they are not self-satisfied, so not offended by a Savior who dies as a Roman criminal on a cross (a shameful execution). These blessed poor and hungry ones see Jesus properly, not like the rich and powerful who tend to reject Jesus as a misguided rabbi or failed prophet. Second, the poor and hungry are blessed because they are able to grasp the future that Jesus introduces. The kingdom of God has arrived, Jesus says. This is good news to those who enjoy few privileges, bad news to those already so comfortable that a new kingdom, much less a God-directed kingdom, would disrupt their successful lives.

To be blessed means to receive the spirit of God (Galatians 3:8), to receive forgiveness (Romans 4:7–8), and even to face trials with God's strength (James 1:12). In turn, those blessed are responsible to share the blessings of God with others (Romans 12:14–21).

Additional scriptures

- **Genesis 1:28**
- **Genesis 2:3**
- **Genesis 12:3**
- **Deuteronomy 28**
- **Matthew 5:3–11**

Body of Christ

In the New Testament, refers to people worldwide who confess Jesus Christ as Lord and Savior, and who are thereby obliged to share the Good News with all the world.

But you are a chosen people, a royal priesthood, a holy nation, a people belonging to God, that you may declare the praises of him who called you out of darkness into his wonderful light. Once you were not a people, but now you are the people of God; once you had not received mercy, but now you have received mercy. —1 Peter 2:9–10

Throughout history, God called certain people to obey His Word. Abraham, Isaac, and Jacob are the patriarchs, but the Bible tells of many more: Noah, Moses, Joshua, and David, to name a few. In each case, the order given to them created and nurtured a community that was intended to model the character of God and teach the ways of God. The Old Testament "chosen people" (Israel) were not favored for their own sake but as a witness to God's love for the entire world. But Israel often forgot God's Word, ignored it, or lost confidence in it. Yet the repeated failure of Israel did not mitigate God's choice of Israel to renew and transform all of creation.

The Bible speaks of Jesus Christ as the Messiah, the One sent by God, to initiate a new kingdom. Jesus became the most transparent witness to God's truth. So stunning is Jesus' person and work that angels celebrated His birth, old priests listened to His youthful wisdom, and the Jerusalem Sanhedrin eventually brought charges of blasphemy against Him. By His life of perfect obedience, Jesus became the perfect sacrifice for sin. (Old Testament worship required regular animal sacrifice for sin.) Jesus' resurrection introduced a new movement and a new community of believers called to tell the world about God. This new community is the church, given the name "body of Christ" by Paul when he writes, "Now you are the body of Christ, and each one of you is a part of it" (1 Corinthians 12:27 NIV). After Christ's ascension to heaven, His people became His hands and feet here on the planet. As believers exercise their many gifts, the body of Christ serves and reaches a needy world (Romans 12:4–8).

Few social institutions have been so important to people, and so criticized for failures, as the Christian church. But the Bible's report on the church raises it above mere social institution and, by the way, fully admits to its shortcomings. The church is the creation of God's Word and God's Spirit. The church holds God's Word, the Bible, as its authoritative message to the world and depends on God's presence and power, through the Spirit, to fulfill its mandate to the world. Without Word and Spirit, the church is a mere agency, in some nations a tax-exempt agency,

> **Biblically** the Church is an organism not an organization—a movement, not a monument. It is not a part of the community; it is a whole new community. It is not an orderly gathering; it is a new order with new values, often in sharp conflict with the values of the surrounding society. —*Charles W. Colson*

and in some nations an outlaw agency. But with Word and Spirit, the church fulfills God's purpose of community, creation, and worldwide witness to the gospel.

The church has often been described in two parts, "militant" and "triumphant." The church militant, all living believers, fights against evil in obedience to the divine call. The church triumphant, all deceased believers, lives with God in heaven and is pictured in the book of Revelation as enjoying continuous fellowship with God. The church is a life-giving, life-enabling community, a sanctuary in a wounded world. The church, at its best, models God's love, peace, and joy as real alternatives to greed, fear, and hurt. Membership in the church is by confession of faith in Jesus Christ.

Additional scriptures

- Acts 2
- Romans 7:4
- 1 Corinthians 12:12–13
- Ephesians 4:12
- Colossians 3:15

Born Again

By placing faith in Jesus Christ, the believer receives new life.

In reply Jesus declared, "I tell you the truth, no one can see the kingdom of God unless he is born again." —John 3:3

B

Baptism
Blessed
Body of Christ
Born Again
Bread of Life
Bridegroom

The verb "to be born again" appears in the Gospel of John (3:3, 7), and could as well be translated "to be born from above." Nicodemus clearly took Jesus to mean "again." So that has been the preferred meaning in most Bible editions.

What does "born again" mean? To Nicodemus, the late-night visitor, and thus to all persons, "born again" signals new life in the family of God. Jesus urged Nicodemus to experience a radical change in orientation and identity—from a person natural born to one given new (eternal, purposeful) life through the Spirit of God. Nicodemus's question is everyone's: How can this happen?

Jesus replied that one must be "born of water and the Spirit" (3:5). This puzzling double imperative is not easily explained by reference to other Bible passages. Yet scholars have surmised three possibilities: (1) *water* means baptism and *Spirit* means the work of God, who transforms people from lives of futility to a future of eternal fellowship in God's kingdom; (2) *water* means natural birth and *Spirit* means supernatural; (3) *water* and *Spirit* are two ways of describing the same cleansing work of God, who transforms life from old to new.

Whichever meaning is taken, "born again" is another term for a long tradition of Bible teaching that disqualifies mere observance of ritual and insists that genuine faith is deeply transforming. The prophet Ezekiel quotes God as promising, "I will sprinkle clean water on you. . . . I will give you a new heart and put a new spirit in you" (Ezekiel

36:25–26 NIV). To be born again, then, is to have one's heart changed from "stone" to "flesh." In the Bible, "born again" has no connotation of a social or political movement but of a mysterious, real change of moral and spiritual orientation enacted by God's Spirit.

A light from above entered and permeated my heart, now cleansed from its defilement. The Spirit came from heaven, and changed me into a new man by the second birth. Almost at once in a marvelous way doubt gave way to assurance, and what I had thought impossible could be done.
—*Cyprian*

Yet here is an important public dimension that cannot be missed. *Born again* is associated with a common Bible theme, the new birth. Associated terms—"the renewal of all things" and "the new world"—are used in the four Gospels to identify the kingdom of God. Jesus preached "the kingdom" as part of His mission; all the Bible looks toward "the kingdom" as history approaches its fulfillment. The Bible's forward look to restoration and renewal is Isaiah's great hope (Isaiah 65:17; 66:22) when all nations will recognize the supremacy of God, and Israel will find rest from its troubles. The age to come, Matthew

wrote, will be preceded by rumors of war, famines, and earthquakes (Matthew 24:6–7), but these traumas will lead to the new heaven and new earth, a splendid and joyous place of life with God (2 Peter 3:13; Revelation 21:1, 5). These futures are to be regarded as close at hand (Jesus has come); in the meantime, however, positive, good deeds and faithful living should occupy those given "new birth."

Born again is more gift than reward, more a call to service than a moral designation, and more a sign of hope than of social conservatism. Since a handful of recent United States presidents identified themselves as "born again," and former President Nixon aide Charles Colson has used the term as the title of his famous conversion story (in his book titled *Born Again*), the term has taken on popular meanings remote from the biblical phrase, and in some places is considered synonymous with arrogance and narrowness. Nothing could be less biblical. All Christians are born again, according to the Bible, since without that positive change, one is not admitted to the kingdom of God.

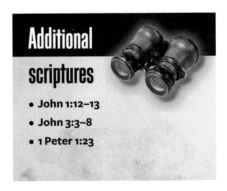

Additional scriptures

- **John 1:12–13**
- **John 3:3–8**
- **1 Peter 1:23**

Bread of Life

Bread is the meal which satisfies the quest for a full and enduring life. It is a symbol for Jesus Himself, who alone meets the deepest human needs.

*Jesus replied, "I am the bread of life. Whoever comes to me will never be hungry again. Whoever believes in me will never be thirsty." —*John 6:35 NLT

Bread as a symbol of sustenance and satisfaction occurs throughout the Bible. In the wilderness wandering after the Hebrews escaped from Egypt, bread played a major part. In barren land unable to support them, the people ate manna, called the "bread from heaven" by Jesus (John 6:31), in the Psalms (Psalm 78:24), and elsewhere (see Nehemiah 9:15). The wilderness manna was provided daily by God, on the ground as the Israelites awoke each morning. And for these wandering Hebrews, it was daily nourishment. The exodus experience so marked the history of Israel that unleavened bread (made and eaten in haste) became the center of a seven-day feast commemorating the event. Passover became the first day of that feast, and the Passover meal eaten by Jesus and His disciples during Holy Week became the bread and wine of the Lord's Supper (communion) celebrated in nearly all Christian churches. During the period of temple worship in Jerusalem, twelve loaves of unleavened bread would be placed every Sabbath in two rows on the table in the holy place. Each week priests would consume the bread as new loaves were set out.

Bread as a symbol for life appears early in the Gospel accounts of Jesus' life. After His baptism by John, Jesus went into the wilderness to be tempted for forty days. The first temptation—"if you are the Son of God, tell this stone to become bread" (Luke 4:3)—allowed Jesus to make the crucial distinction between the "manna" of Moses' time and the true, enduring, and fulfilling life that the Messiah gives. Barley bread provides daily needs for calories and carbohydrates. The bread of life

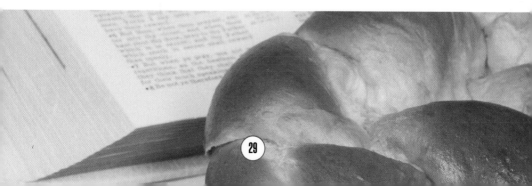

meets the needs of the heart and soul.

Bread appears in the Lord's Prayer as the first request, before forgiveness, escapefromtemptation, or deliverance from evil (Matthew 6:11), emphasizing the reality of daily physical needs in God's world. People are not mere souls but bodies, too. Nonetheless, Jesus' answer to Satan that "people do not live by bread alone" (Luke 4:4 NLT signals an intention to meet a deeper, more spiritual need than those the body craves.

Bread appears in the feast to come, on the day when the kingdom of God appears fully formed—Jesus' teaching in a story within a story (Luke 14). Jesus was dining with a prominent Pharisee (Jewish religious leader) when He performed a healing and posed to dinner guests the dilemma between mercy and law-keeping. Jesus solved the dilemma by recommending that the poor and disabled should be served energetically. Those who did so would be rewarded at the feast in the kingdom of God. In another story, Jesus mentioned a banquet where the needy were given the seats of folks too busy to attend. Eating, feasting, and celebrating at the table are common teaching moments in the Gospels.

"Bread of life" has become one of

God Himself becomes our bread and our truth, both together, unconfused and inseparable. The seed of eternal life lies within them, and once we receive them sincerely, that life not only enters into and grows within us: we also enter and grow into it.

—*Peter Magee*

the most evocative and popular metaphors in the Bible, used in contemporary song lyrics and liturgies. The Bible plainly points beyond the simple nutrition of wheat or barley to the soul food that the metaphor is meant to suggest. To partake of the bread of life is to live in fellowship with God. Obedient trust in God's care and eager reception of the message of Jesus are staples of a Christian diet. The Communion feast (the Lord's Supper) reminds the believer of the intimacy of union with Christ and rehearses the great salvation accomplished on Good Friday and Easter. Of all nutrients needed to maintain health, the bread of life—following Jesus and living by faith in Him—is the one essential. No other meal offers such long-term and enduring satisfaction, "for the bread of God is he who comes down from heaven and gives life to the world" (John 6:33 NIV).

Additional scriptures

- **John 6:48–51**
- **1 Corinthians 10:16–17**
- **1 Corinthians 11:23–26**

Bridegroom

B

Baptism
Blessed
Body of Christ
Born Again
Bread of Life
Bridegroom

A symbol of Jesus, who is said to be like a bridegroom courting and loving His bride, the church. This symbol is intended to show the intimate relationship of care and loyalty between Christ and Christian believers.

He who has the bride is the bridegroom. The friend of the bridegroom, who stands and hears him, rejoices greatly at the bridegroom's voice. For this reason my joy has been fulfilled. —John 3:29 NRSV

Of all ceremonies, a wedding is perhaps the most joyous and hopeful. A man and a woman pledge mutual allegiance in a unique relationship of love and sharing. From that moment on, they are "one flesh," the first Bible book claims (Genesis 2:24). Certainly the joy of the married couple includes the wonders of sexual union, a companionship of sturdy loyalty, and the possibility of children. Weddings, for all the right reasons, are beautiful and celebratory.

The same sense of closeness, joy, and loyalty attends to the person who declares faith in Jesus Christ as Lord, Savior, and friend. The Bible speaks of the believer being "in Christ," that is, loved by Christ, protected and cherished as a bridegroom would feel for his bride. Admittedly, in the modern era, brides and grooms tend toward equal roles and nurture, obscuring dimensions of marriage that would have been obvious in days gone by when a groom was thought to receive his bride, to cherish, and protect her.

Nonetheless, this symbol of intimacy and union speaks to dimensions of faith that make discipleship much more than ritualistic obedience. The Bible in fact pictures the last day—the fulfillment of all God wants to do in the world—as a wedding in which believers (the church) meet the bridegroom, Jesus. Revelation 19 is a joyous song anticipating that "wedding," and Revelation 20 speaks of the end of sorrow as a new era begins—new place, new creation, new terms of existence. A church beaten up by troubles, divisions, evil, and duress now appears as beautifully prepared to meet the waiting bridegroom, who, like bridegrooms everywhere, is ready for long-awaited happiness.

The symbol points to a future of joy and blessedness in God's presence, even though the present may be a time of preparation through service, learning, sacrifice, and sorrow. The symbol also carries this warning, explicitly in the Old Testament's book of Hosea. God intends love and loyalty with His people. To follow other gods is to be, in ancient language, a harlot, and in modern terms, a whore (Hosea 1:2; 2:5).

> **When Jesus says,** "I go to prepare a place for you," he reminds us of the diligent and loving bridegroom making his preparations for the shared home during the time of happy anticipation, that delicious time before the connubial bliss. —*The Dictionary of Biblical Imagery*

The Bible's most endearing appeal for people everywhere to come to faith is this metaphor of a bridegroom urging His beloved to approach. On our part, choices must be made, as the claims of marriage are exclusive. One cannot be married to many, only to one.

Additional scriptures

- **Matthew 9:15**
- **Matthew 25:1–13**
- **Luke 5:34–35**
- **Revelation 18:23**

Calling

God asks that all who follow His will do so by using their callings in ways that help others and witness to God's love for humanity. Each person will have a "gift of the Spirit" to use in his or her calling.

I press on toward the goal for the prize of the upward call of God in Christ Jesus. —Philippians 3:14 ESV

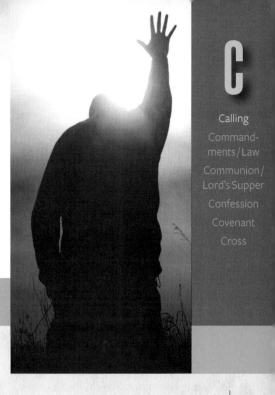

The Bible offers two kinds of "calling." The first is to worship God alone and to believe the gospel, namely that salvation has been won by the death and resurrection of Jesus Christ. God calls people to faith. The second is to live for God through active use of gifts and talents, serving others and renewing creation.

Throughout the Bible, God *calls* people to faithful worship and right belief. Merely acknowledging the existence of God is not enough, as if belief in deity itself were somehow a sign of achievement. Throughout history, all cultures and most people have believed in a creator who also holds people morally accountable. Faith and worship must be directed to the God who is, in fact, the true God. Speaking from the burning bush, God called Himself, "I AM WHO I AM" (Exodus 3:14 ESV). After that, the Hebrews called God "Yahweh," or YHWH. Not just any

deity, but YHWH is God. YHWH alone is to be worshiped (Exodus 20:2–3).

God calls specific individuals to faith: Noah, Moses, Abraham, Samuel. God also calls particular peoples, namely the offspring of Abraham who became Israel (Genesis 17:7). Finally, God calls all people to be faithful followers (1 Thessalonians 2:12). This call of God is to repent of sins and believe the Good News that salvation has come through Jesus Christ.

The second type of "calling" presents believers with a lifelong responsibility to direct energy and ambition to God's purposes for renewing the world. From the beginning (Genesis 1:28), God called people to be stewards of the kingdom. God's creation is good, but now flawed (Genesis 2:17). God's purpose is to redeem it, to restore its original luster, and at the end of time, to renew it beyond our imagination. The calling of stewards is to show mercy and to work for justice (Micah 6:8) as God—mysteriously but surely—guides life toward His purposes (Philippians 2:13). All work should be a response to "vocation" (from Latin, to call), whether medicine or business, construction or the arts. Vocationally motivated believers are to show mercy and justice primarily for God's interests, which, the Bible notes, are often directed to the poor, the orphans, and the widows.

Allied to this second sense of calling are Bible mandates to show, by one's other-centered focus, the reality of God's indiscriminate love. Believers are called to live honestly, openly demonstrating the virtues of love, joy, peace, self-control, and other "fruit of the Spirit" as listed in Galatians 5:22–23. In Paul's well known autobiographical review of his own calling, he disconnected from all reward systems offered by the culture of his day and chose instead "the surpassing worth of knowing Christ Jesus my Lord"; the rewards of the world are "rubbish" in comparison (Philippians 3:8 ESV). The sole aim of a vocationally faithful life is to know the power and love of God in daily experience. For this Paul pressed toward his calling, a prize to be discovered as he lived and died in the service of Christ (Philippians 3:14).

> **The responsible person** seeks to make his or her whole life a response to the question and call of God.
> —*Dietrich Bonhoeffer*

The letter to the Hebrews states that a believer's calling involves perseverance under duress and mutual encouragement to hope in God, no matter how bleak the circumstances (Hebrews 10:23–24). In the end, success in one's calling is a matter of total trust in Jesus Christ as Lord and leader, who has "marked out" the race each person is called to run, and "authored" by His own life and death the proper running of it (Hebrews 12:1–2). Bible people who ignore God's call are often grasping for power or money. In the end, they will hide from God in fear, much as Adam and Eve hid from God in the garden (Genesis 3; Revelation 6:15–17).

The rich biblical theme of calling is beautifully expressed in the Bible's final chapter. There the Spirit of God and the bride (the church, the people of God) call others to "come. . .take the free gift of the water of life" (Revelation 22:17 NIV). All who do will be blessed.

Additional scriptures

- **Romans 8:28**
- **Romans 12:6–8**
- **1 Corinthians 12:28–31**
- **Ephesians 1:19–21**

Commandments / Law

God instructs all people to follow His divine will, revealed primarily in the Ten Commandments. In the New Testament, God's law is summarized: love God and others.

I am the Lord your God. . . . You shall have no other gods before me.
—Exodus 20:2–3

C

Calling

Command-
ments/Law

Communion/
Lord's Supper

Confession

Covenant

Cross

> ...where...
> ...bath day,...
> 12 ¶ Honour... thy...
> mother: that thy...
> upon the land which the...
> God giveth thee.
> 13 Thou shalt not kill.
> 14 Thou shalt not commit adultery
> 15 Thou shalt not steal.
> 16 Thou shalt not bear false witn...
> against thy neighbour
> 17 Thou shalt not c...
> ...our's house, thou s...
> ...hbour's wife, n...
> ...maidserva...

The world invents its own good works and persuades itself that they are good. But Paul declares that good and right according to the world are to be judged by the commandments of God.—*John Calvin*

The Bible has numerous instructions on how to live well. Many stories plainly describe those who did not. Yet these stories never become an excuse for casual disregard of divine law. The Bible's sternest warnings are to people who know the law and fail to obey.

Old Testament law is often associated with the Ten Commandments (Exodus 20:1–17). Actually, the law given to Israel included ceremonial instructions, social and property law, as well as the two tablets received by Moses on Mount Sinai. "Law" today sounds arbitrary, non-negotiable, and well beyond the skill of any person to obey flawlessly. The Hebrew word torah (instructions) engages a more educational way of thinking about divine expectations. A better way of conceiving of Old Testament law is to imagine a gift so wonderful that it deserves one's full respect, awe, and effort. The best response to divine law is to pray that the wisdom of the law—its truth and clarity, guidance and majesty—might be clearer and more precious the closer one examines it (Psalm 119:18, 72). Certainly the law is understood to open God's wisdom to hapless people, as a light on a dark trail (Psalm 119:105). The ones who eagerly submit to divine law are compared to a well-rooted tree (Psalm 1:1–3), prosperous and amply supplied with the necessities of life. Hardship follows people who ignore God's law.

Law plays a critical role in the New Testament. Jesus is often challenged by scholars and interpreters of the law (scribes and Pharisees), who wondered whether this Nazarene rabbi was a lawbreaker or a loyal law-keeper. For example, Jesus healed on the Sabbath (John 9:1–36). To Jewish leaders this was an obvious violation. Yet Jesus insisted that He had not come to abolish the law, but to fulfill its point and purpose. No part of the law may be disregarded or considered obsolete, He taught (Matthew 5:17–18).

Jesus' interpretation of the law reached further into the heart and motivation of people than the scribes and Pharisees imagined. Was the law against adultery a prohibition of intercourse or, more clearly, God's warning against imaginative desire? Was the law prohibiting murder a mandate against killing or, more clearly, against regarding another as so worthless that the act of killing would be morally insignificant (Matthew 5:21–22, 28)? Jesus taught against mere ritual law-keeping, passionless and rote. Indeed, Jesus was finally condemned as a lawbreaker by religious authorities and the Roman empire for implying His own kingship and identity with God (Mark 15:1–5).

Paul, the New Testament's most prolific writer, pressed law on its limits and boundaries. The law cannot save, he preached (Romans 3:20). The law condemns, because no one (except Jesus, the perfect sacrifice) can claim to have kept it (Romans 3:23). A person is made a child of God, brought into God's family and cleansed of sin by faith alone (Romans 5:1–2). Faith in what? Faith that all sin is forgiven by God in the death of God's Son, Jesus Christ, who carried the penalty for humanity's lawbreaking to the cross. Jesus was raised from the dead to show that the dreadful losses due to sin are now forgiven and gone. New life has come as a gift from God for Jesus' obedience (Romans 8:32). Now the old economy of sin and death is replaced with sustaining love strong enough to withstand the most strenuous challenge. The love of God is described as eternally stronger than the power of law to condemn (Romans 8:1–2). "Inseparable" describes the believer's kinship to God; in Christ the law's holy judgment is satisfied forever (Romans 8:38–39).

Additional scriptures

- **Exodus 20:2–17**
- **Joshua 22:5**
- **Matthew 22:36–40**
- **Romans 7:9–12**

Communion / Lord's Supper

Nearly all Christian churches celebrate the death and resurrection of Jesus Christ and its meaning—forgiveness of sin and eternal life—by sharing wine (or juice) and bread, as Jesus did with His disciples on Thursday of Holy Week.

And he took bread, gave thanks and broke it, and gave it to them, saying, "This is my body given for you; do this in remembrance of me." —Luke 22:19

The passing of bread and wine has been a sacrament (or a remembrance) since the first Lord's Supper in Jerusalem during Holy Week. There Jesus washed the feet of His twelve disciples, shared a Passover meal, and spoke in guarded terms of His pending prosecution. "Do this in remembrance of me" was Jesus' instruction to His disciples.

The Christian church from earliest times has celebrated this meal with varying regularity and meaning. In all cases, however, Communion is to remember Jesus' sacrifice on the cross for humankind. In Roman Catholic worship, it is called the Eucharist or Holy Communion.

The Gospels of Matthew, Mark, and Luke include the story of Jesus passing the elements and declaring that each, the bread and wine, carried special reference to His body. The Gospel of John does not retell this event, though John recalls Jesus' teaching that He is the bread of life (John 6:35). Luke further describes the sharing of bread between the risen Christ and two hikers on the road to Emmaus (Luke 24:28–35), a possible reference to the Lord's Supper.

The Bible's most important section on the Lord's Supper occurs in Paul's first letter to the Corinthians. There Paul urged the church in Corinth to discipline itself. Communion had become excessively focused on food and drink, obscuring its meaning. Paul had previously taught the church how to conduct Communion, and he insisted that his model be followed. He then prescribed the familiar liturgy of the Lord's Supper, adding that the meal was a proclamation, a witness, of the significance of Christ's death "until he comes" (1 Corinthians 11:26 NIV). The church should continue to practice the Lord's Supper until Jesus' second coming.

The Bible offers few details on the conduct or actual meaning of the Lord's Supper, though theologians have attempted to fill the gaps. For instance, the Bible says nothing concerning why the food was bread and wine, except that Jesus used both and indicated that each was to be a remembrance. Does the wine, by a miracle, become the blood of Christ, as Thomas Aquinas insisted and as the Roman Catholic Church teaches today? Does the wine participate in the essence of blood without becoming actual blood, as Martin Luther taught and as Lutherans worldwide believe? On these matters the Bible does not speak. How often should the Lord's Supper be eaten? Who should eat it, and who should serve it? Are age or faith requirements important? Is God's blessing actually consumed in the Communion, or is the Supper a memorial to the death of Jesus which secured salvation for all? The history of churches grappling with these issues is long and complex. Churches have tried to answer these questions by reference to other Bible themes and with indirect help from Bible sources, but without an operating manual—the Bible does not provide it.

When did Christians realize that the Lord's Supper was special and should be practiced? Again the Bible provides only hints. The Emmaus Road encounter suggests a very early beginning, and Paul's extensive teaching was written in the early AD 50s. Common meals were widely practiced by many religious movements, and from Paul we learn that first-century Christians enjoyed them, too, sometimes too much. Paul's disgust at gluttony and preferential treatment at Corinth's common meals implies that early in the Christian movement the Jewish Passover meal took on distinctively Christian meanings. Since then the Lord's Supper has become one of the most important ways Christians remember Jesus and witness to His continuing presence among them.

Additional scriptures

- **Matthew 26:26–29**
- **Mark 14:22–24**
- **Luke 22:19–20**
- **1 Corinthians 11:23–28**

Confession

The verbal act of admitting to wrongdoing, with the implicit promise of a better relationship with the offended party. The practice of confession is both for wrongdoing and as a personal statement of faith in Jesus Christ.

Therefore, confess your sins to one another, and pray for one another so that you may be healed. —James 5:16 NASB

C

Calling

Command-
ments/Law

Communion/
Lord's Supper

Confession

Covenant

Cross

Where two or more people gather, relationships will eventually tear over misunderstandings, self-interest, or dishonesty. The Bible is a series of lessons in repairing relationships; its stories include several in which relationships were never repaired, to the great loss of everyone involved.

Confession is the first step in repair and often the most difficult. Without confession, forgiveness is impossible since aggrieved parties, to regain trust and mutuality, must achieve transparency. Wrongs must be set aside and friendship restored.

Sometimes the Bible's accounts of confession sound like excuse-making, as in the first instance of wrongdoing when Adam and Eve ate from the forbidden tree (Genesis 3:1–13). Sometimes, to preserve a relationship, one party must forgive without genuine confession from the other (Hosea). Most frequently, however, confession is the contrite acknowledgment of offense against another, often against God. The psalms (especially Psalm 51) set the Bible's pattern for genuine confession with a wholehearted admission of sin and appeal to God for mercy as the supplicant's life is renewed and repaired. Frequently, the prophets called Israel to confess as a first step in national defense, as did Moses when the wandering Hebrews built an idol, the golden calf (Exodus 32:30–35). Public confession among the Israelites was required for specific wrongdoings (Leviticus 5). Major projects undertaken by the Israelites began with ceremonial confession to create a clean slate. Only after

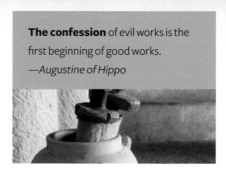

the relationship was restored could they appeal to God for help and success (Nehemiah 1:5–11).

In the New Testament, confession is one of the most important practices of faith (Romans 10:9). Coming to God requires submission, not arrogance; and confession is, if anything, an act of submission. It is also a deeply personal act emerging from one's emotional and intellectual core (Romans 10:10). Words of spoken confession engage a person's identity and create unprecedented vulnerability as the aggrieved party contemplates his or her response.

When history concludes, Paul wrote, all people will confess that Jesus is Lord (Romans 14:11, quoting from the prophet Isaiah), even those who had refused beforehand. In that sense, the Bible portrays all of creation as directed toward confession and praise of God. To do otherwise would be to act contrary to the image of God given to humankind at the beginning and contrary to the purposes of nature.

Christian churches have practiced various modes of confession. In the Roman tradition, confession is given to a priest who stands in God's place with authority to forgive. Among Protestants, public confession is often part of worship. The public recital of creeds in church has formalized the practice of confession. Creeds and confessional documents do not appear in the Bible, but elements of early church confessions and creeds likely were used as background for certain texts (Philippians 2:6, 9–11, for example). Early Christians also used the familiar fish symbol as a confessional tool. The Greek word for fish, ICHTHUS, is an acronym for the rendering of "Jesus Christ, Son of God, Savior." That symbol still appears in jewelry and bumper stickers, signifying that the wearer (or driver) confesses Jesus Christ to be Lord and Savior. For all who confess, John writes, God forgives their sins (1 John 1:9).

To refuse confession carries the offense of regarding sin as unimportant and the repair of one's relationship to God as inconsequential. This offense challenges the Bible's presentation of God's character (1 John 1:10) in relation to morally fallen humanity. To fail to confess is effectively to say about Jesus Christ: He need not have come, should not have died, and has nothing substantial to offer.

Additional scriptures

- **Leviticus 26:40–42**
- **Psalm 32:5**
- **Psalm 38:18**   • **Romans 10:9**
- **Psalm 51**   • **1 John 1:9**

Covenant

A covenant is God's binding arrangement to make creation whole again, to restore people lost to sin, and to move history to its fulfillment. Covenant is a biblical term which describes all that God wants to do, and will do. In the Old Testament, covenants were conditional—do this for God, and God will do this for you. The New Testament covenant is unconditional, signaling a way of life.

For this reason Christ is the mediator of a new covenant, that those who are called may receive the promised eternal inheritance—now that he has died as a ransom to set them free from the sins committed under the first covenant. —Hebrews 9:15

How is the Bible organized? What is God up to? Can people have a relationship with God? These key questions all find an answer around the term *covenant*, found frequently in both Testaments.

At the Creation, God granted the divine image to humans (Genesis 1:26). It was a covenant action, initiated by God on terms set by God. That grant of "image" meant close fellowship: Humans walked together with God in the garden. But the terms of the covenant were broken, and that close relationship was spoiled. After the garden closed, people seemed hell-bent to forget and ignore God (Genesis 3–11).

Surprisingly, God announced renewal through a new covenant with Abraham (Genesis 12:1–3). Abraham was to follow God's direction to a new land and there receive a son, an heir. Then followed another covenant with the Hebrew people through Moses, where the terms became more explicit (Exodus 20): Obey the commandments and receive the promised land of Canaan. Still, human failure drove the covenant into a ditch. Jerusalem was crushed and all the covenant ritual was lost to Babylon's pagan power (as recorded in 2 Kings 25). This crisis appeared to be the end of the road for people relating to God.

> **The bond of** the covenant is able to bear the weight of the believer's heaviest burden. —*William S. Plummer*

But not so. The Old Testament prophets focused on yet another covenant, set in place from the beginning but only dimly known, unlike all which had preceded. This new covenant would involve inner human transformation (a new heart, Ezekiel 36:26). It would fulfill all the shattered hopes and dreams of God's people (Jeremiah 29:11–14). It would succeed. When Jesus was born to Mary in Bethlehem, the new covenant arrived in human form. Angels celebrated (Luke 2:13–14). Wise men gathered (Matthew 2:1). Rulers fretted (Matthew 2:3). The new covenant had come in the flesh. His name was *Immanuel* (Jesus), God with us.

Jesus used the term "kingdom of God" to describe what He had come to show and do, a term synonymous with the new covenant. In the book of Hebrews, covenant describes the patient, persistent, and loving purpose of God to bring His people home. That home, in Hebrews, is called a better country, a city prepared by God (Hebrews 11:16). It is God's kingdom, heaven, the place of rest and fellowship which no adversary can spoil (Hebrews 12:28).

Seven Bible covenants have been identified, from Adam to Christ. In each case, the covenant tells how God will enter history for the blessing and benefit of humankind. The last covenant, which is so crucial to the Bible's story, is written on people's hearts (not on stone tablets like the commandments). Through this covenant, all that was lost by human failure will be restored (Jeremiah 31:31–34). This covenant certifies God's remarkable intention to fulfill the point and purpose of creation in an eternal fellowship of love and joy.

Bible readers may ask—why all these trials and failures? Why didn't God just skip ahead to Jesus from the start? The Bible does not entertain such questions but patiently describes God's successive promises, pointing to Jesus as the final answer.

Additional scriptures

- **Genesis 6:18**
- **Genesis 9:9–17**
- **Genesis 15:18–21**
- **Genesis 17:2**
- **Deuteronomy 9:9**
- **Deuteronomy 29:1**
- **1 Corinthians 11:25**

Cross

The cross is an instrument of death made of wooden beams. Jesus and many others throughout history were executed by Romans and Greeks in this way. The Bible takes as its central symbol this ancient means of shameful death and transforms it into a sign of God's love for humankind. The crucifix (in Catholic worship) and the empty cross (among Protestants) have become the most visible symbols of faith and an obvious reminder of Jesus' death and resurrection.

Let us fix our eyes on Jesus, the author and perfecter of our faith, who for the joy set before him endured the cross, scorned its shame, and sat down at the right hand of the throne of God. —Hebrews 12:2

The cross, so closely associated with death, carries two other important meanings in the Bible: as the symbol for salvation, and as a metaphor for living as a faithful believer. The Bible speaks frequently about all three meanings of the cross: death, salvation, and life.

> **God gives** the cross, and the cross gives us God. —*Madame Jeanne Marie Guyon*

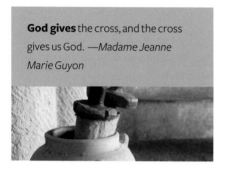

From ancient time, a wooden stake and crossbeam was a slow, humiliating, and painful way to execute criminals and deter political and religious dissent. Pilate (the Roman governor who sentenced Jesus) was surprised that Jesus had died so quickly (Mark 15:44), since most victims would hang on the cross for days or until legs were broken. Criminals who died in this way were fully exposed during their hours of horrendous public agony.

The cross is also a symbol for all that Jesus accomplished by His death. The Bible's core story is God's intention to restore humankind to fellowship and peace with Him. Jesus' mission accomplished that restoration through a final, sufficient sacrifice for sin (Colossians 1:19–20). All who believe in Jesus are forgiven their sins and promised eternal life (John 3:16).

Salvation and restoration are accomplished at the cross. A terrorizing symbol of death has become a memorial to new life.

Faithful discipleship is the third meaning of the cross. Jesus tells His followers to "take up" the cross and "follow me" (Mark 8:34). Cross-bearing means service to God and humanity in ways that reflect other-centered love and mercy, as Jesus lived. Those unwilling to "bear the cross" seek creature comforts while forfeiting the deeper, eternal fulfillment of life with God. Those who "bear the cross" may appear to be losing their lives, but as God counts success, those are the very ones who are finding genuine life (Matthew 10:39).

Additional scriptures

- **Matthew 10:38**
- **Matthew 27:32–56**
- **1 Corinthians 1:18**
- **Galatians 6:12**
- **Galatians 6:14**
- **Colossians 1:20**

Day of the Lord

When God shows up to make His kingdom public, everyone will pay attention. It has happened before. It will happen again, when history is fulfilled.

Now, brothers, about times and dates we do not need to write to you, for you know very well that the day of the Lord will come like a thief in the night. . . . But you, brothers, are not in darkness so that this day should surprise you like a thief. —1 Thessalonians 5:1–2, 4

The Bible constantly points forward. Its story anticipates a glorious and spectacular appearance of God, who then saves His people and judges His enemies. All of God's promises will be made good on that day. All the hopes of God's people will be realized and their fears relieved. A universal renewal will occur. God will be recognized and worshiped everywhere, exactly as it should have been all along.

What really happens on the Day of the Lord? The Bible provides broad-stroke descriptions meant to fulfill human longing for peace and wholeness. For those who revere God, healing and joy are the prophet Malachi's message (Malachi 4:1–3), but the arrogant and self-willed will be carried away by the furnace-heat of God's judgment. The prophet Micah used the well-known metaphor of turning swords into plowshares to illustrate a decisive change in the world's normal politics. By Micah's accounting, the world's least capable and most heavily burdened people will feel like princes on that day (Micah 4:1–7).

Isaiah imagines a fearful darkness at that time (Isaiah 13:9–10), perhaps to cover the terror of judgment falling on the arrogant, the proud, and the wicked. Joel also speaks of darkness (Joel 2:31–32) but adds a mercy: All who call upon the Lord will be saved. Obadiah 15 notes that God's judgment on that day will be no more or less severe than other judgment days, for instance, during the plagues of Egypt (recorded in Exodus 5–10). All the world's desperate cries of "why?" and "how bad can it get?" will then be made right.

> **Truly, when the** day of judgment comes, we shall not be examined as to what we have read, but what we have done, not how well we have spoken but how we have lived. —*Thomas à Kempis*

New Testament writers echo the Old Testament's images of an increase in natural and human-made chaos just before that Day. But the New Testament adds one dramatic element that the Old Testament knew nothing about: *parousia*, the Bible's word for the second coming of Jesus Christ.

Followers of Jesus are assured that He will come again (Acts 1:11). The second coming will be filled with glory and power (Matthew 24:30). Jesus will enter our time-space world once more to defeat evil (2 Thessalonians 2:8) and gather His people. He will judge the world with holy justice (James 5:9). All the glory of deity which Jesus now enjoys in heaven will be evident to all people (Hebrews 2:9). This will bring terror and grief to the wicked, but restoration and relief to all who, by faith, have received eternal life (Romans 6:23).

When will the Day of the Lord occur? The Bible's complex map of history's end has led scholars to three possible scenarios identified by reference to a thousand-year period mentioned in Revelation 20, the Millennium. Pre-millennialists interpret the parousia as "possibly any day" and *before* the thousand-year period of God's reign. Amillennialists find in the Bible evidence that the thousand-year period is history itself, now ongoing, and when that is done, Jesus will return. Post-millennialists believe that God's reign spreads more and more on earth as the gospel is preached and believed. When God's word has been spread nearly everywhere, Jesus will return.

Most Bible scholars agree that the Day of the Lord is future, not past. (Paul warns not to think the day has already occurred, in 2 Thessalonians 2.) Trouble will escalate prior to the *parousia*, but the event itself will be the end of history, a day of new and joyous life, but also a day of reckoning.

Additional scriptures

- **Joel 1:15**
- **Joel 2:1–2**
- **Joel 2:31**
- **Amos 5:20**
- **Obadiah 15**

Death

The end of life. Not what God intended. God's creation is good and should never expire or disappear. But sin has affected the world with this terrible consequence: God's good creation dies. People die. Yet worse than the death of physical bodies is the death of a person's spirit and soul.

For the wages of sin is death, but the gift of God is eternal life in Christ Jesus our Lord. —Romans 6:23

D

Day of the Lord

Death

Decree

Deliverance/ Healing

Demons

Disciple

Doctrine

Doubt

Life and death play important parts in the Bible's account of creation, the fall into sin, and redemption. Only one—either life or death—can be creation's final state. Only one can be our final state. Yet all humans—and all living things—die. Is death the end, then?

Life is God's plan, the Bible teaches. God made life, declared it good, and provides all things necessary to sustain it. But life is more than food and shelter. Life is to know who we are, to whom we belong. Death is to lose our way, forget our identity, be separated from the source of life. And finally, as the Bible grimly puts it, death is to exist in "blackest darkness" (Jude 13), totally apart from hope, goodness, and light, all of which come from God (1 John 1:5).

Death, Bible writers affirm, is the end-point that sin leads to, the negation of all God wants and intends. Death showed up to mar the beauty of

God's world when sin brought violence and judgment. God did not include death in His blueprints for the world. Death owes its origin to disobedience and distrust. Death violates these blueprints, taking from the world the very gift of life which God breathed into Adam (Genesis 2:7).

Human Death is the result of sin and the triumph of Satan. But it is also the means of redemption from sin, God's medicine for Man and His weapon against Satan. —*C. S. Lewis*

The Old Testament does not have a developed story of the afterlife. What happens after life ends is vaguely unattractive there. No Old Testament person wanted to go to the place of the dead. Life and death in the New Testament are more focused as two experiences through which all people pass. To have life in the New Testament is to receive the gift of fellowship with God that survives physical death. This eternal life cannot be threatened by evil, as God Himself gives it and protects it. The apostle Paul in 1 Corinthians 15 provides the core of Christian teaching on the triumph over death by Jesus Christ. Then in Romans 5–8, Paul explains the role sin plays in death and its remedy: Jesus Christ on the cross

has paid the penalty for all sin. Death no longer is the inevitable darkness, the end of all life. Fellowship with God is the gift that overcomes death forever (Romans 8:38).

In an odd reversal of normal usage, the verb "to die" is used occasionally in the New Testament to describe salvation. God calls all people to die to sin. "Count yourselves dead to sin" (Romans 6:11) means to resist what short-term pleasures may come from violation of God's law. When passions flare, when appetites crave forbidden fruit, when the heart wants what the heart wants (Woody Allen's famous excuse), "death to sin" is one way the New Testament describes the need to stay faithful to God's pattern for abundant living. In view of God's gift of life, all people are urged to reckon life as "alive to God," animated by gratitude to God, focused on pleasing God. In this way, the new life in Christ given to all who believe becomes the power to live well, honestly, and gladly.

Additional scriptures

- **Genesis 2:17**
- **1 Corinthians 15:26**
- **1 Corinthians 15:55**
- **1 John 3:14**
- **Revelation 20:14–15**
- **Revelation 21:4**

Decree

An authoritative statement, often in writing, that certifies an order and requires an obedient response. God's decrees set the bounds of nature and the conditions of salvation. Government decrees were supported by armies and guided by the volatile temperaments of the ancient tyrants who issued them.

> *The decrees of the Lord are sure, making wise the simple.* —Psalm 19:7 NRSV

Several national rulers in the Bible issued orders and expected prompt obedience. Decrees are the form in which such orders are packaged; decrees became the day's headlines, for they defined life. One had to adjust to them or suffer the sorry consequences. One of the most famous decrees in the Bible sent Joseph and Mary to Bethlehem to register for a census (Luke 2:1). Caesar's (ruler of Rome) decrees apparently had no escape clause, since Mary's advanced pregnancy would seem a good medical reason to postpone a trip. But Luke 2:3 summarizes public response: "Everyone went. . .to register."

Luke records another Roman decree (Acts 17:7) which carried such weight, even in distant parts of the empire, that leaders quickly incarcerated alleged offenders. No frontier leader wanted

Rome to believe its decrees were lightly regarded.

Ezra 5:13 credits Cyrus with writing a decree that authorized the rebuilding of

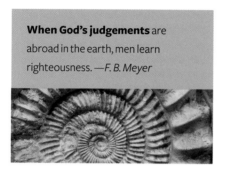

> **When God's judgements** are abroad in the earth, men learn righteousness. —*F. B. Meyer*

the temple in Jerusalem. Darius, King of Persia, respected that decree enough to write one of his own for the same project (Ezra 6:3). Nebuchadnezzar's court astrologers shuddered, no doubt, when the irascible Babylonian king called their bluff and issued a decree that forced them to read his mind (Daniel 2:9). The strength of ancient decrees became the crux of Daniel's encounter with lions in one of the Bible's most famous stories (Daniel 6). In that case, even the decree's author, the king, was without authority to amend it.

After Jesus' ascension, the Jerusalem council—leaders of the early church—assumed authority to reach decisions and distribute orders. These orders functioned much like decrees (Acts 16:4). Though these orders had no army to assure compliance, the authority of God was presumed and obedience expected.

The Bible is clear on this point: Behind all human decrees stands the final authority, God Himself. God directs creation by His decree (Psalm 148:1–6) and human affairs according to His decrees, even when He remains in the deep background (Daniel 4:24). God's decrees set boundaries for nature (Job 28:26), and more importantly, they guide the process of redeeming humankind from sin. God set the conditions of salvation and decreed the means of meeting those conditions (Psalm 2:7–8). Surely, then, the way of salvation cannot be redefined to fit a changing milieu or amended as culture changes. What God has said, holds. The wise person learns God's decrees and obeys them (Psalm 19:7).

Additional scriptures

- **Exodus 15:25**
- **Ezra 5:13**
- **Ezra 6:3**
- **Esther 1:19**
- **Psalm 105:10**
- **Jeremiah 51:12**
- **Romans 1:32**

Deliverance / Healing

D

Day of
the Lord

Death

Decree

Deliverance/
Healing

Demons

Disciple

Doctrine

Doubt

Deliverance is the Bible's offer of restored health for an ill body or mind, or both. Deliverance from disease in the Bible always has theological meaning—it validates a claim about God, namely that God is good and that prayer for healing is heard by God. Healing shows God's power. Never is biblical healing simply a medical issue.

"As long as it is day, we must do the work of him who sent me. Night is coming, when no one can work. While I am in the world, I am the light of the world." Having said this, he spit on the ground, made some mud with the saliva, and put in on the man's eyes. —John 9:4–6

The Bible includes the stories of many people suffering from a variety of diseases. Leprosy is frequently mentioned, as it was incurable, slow, and required the added grim deficit of lifetime quarantine. Deafness, blindness, boils, inflammations, and paralysis are also presented. Of medical cures during Bible times, natural healing was most common, since medical knowledge was little more than what could be seen or felt. Medical cures were largely extensions of natural means.

When Jesus healed, the point was never merely medical but aimed to teach an important truth about God. Mass healings were infrequent, and single-case healings were always attached to understanding sin and spiritual deliverance (John 9:35–38).

Mental illness presents in the Bible in the case of Saul (1 Samuel 16:14–23), Nebuchadnezzar (Daniel 4:29–34), and possibly Daniel himself (who reported illness as if under extreme stress, Daniel 8:27). The Bible's thin line between mental disorder and spiritual oppression (demon possession) must be noted but carefully maintained. Jesus emphatically recognized the difference and

> **There is nothing** irrational about believing that God who made the world can still intrude creatively into it. Christians should recognize that it is not faith in the biblical miracles, and in God's ability to work miracles today should he so wish, but to doubt about these things, that is unreasonable.
> —J. I. Packer

healed accordingly. Demonic oppression also presented physical symptoms (Matthew 9:32; 12:22; Luke 9:37–43).

Healing in the Bible occurs when an illness is suddenly eliminated and the sufferer restored to wholeness; also, when a terminal patient's outlook improves, even if physical healing does not occur.

Throughout the Bible, God is the one who heals (Psalm 103:3), even if medical services are engaged. That is true in every era, biblical days and today. The prayer for healing (James 5:13–16) is not time-bound. Like all healing in the Bible, it includes deliverance from powers of sin, and restoration (wholeness) of spirit, mind, and body. Physical healing is never perpetual, as all persons eventually die. Eternal healing—the end of physical suffering—is God's will for all (2 Peter 3:9), but it comes only in the resurrection at the last day (2 Peter 3:13).

Jesus refutes the connection between disease and punishment in His healing of the blind man in John 9. The old cause-and-effect model is unfair and wrong, He told His disciples. Instead, Jesus focused on compassion and demonstration of God's power. When the blind man was healed, He suffered socially at the hands of suspicious religious leaders, but came to spiritual restoration in His confession of Jesus as Lord (John 9:38).

Additional scriptures

- Mark 9:14–29
- Luke 17:11–19
- Romans 8:19–25
- 2 Corinthians 12:1–10
- Hebrews 9:27

Demons

Spiritual beings opposed to the kingdom of God. Demons inhabit people for purposes of harm, and they challenge the authority and glory of God. Yet even demons are aware of the futility of their efforts.

You believe that there is one God. You do well. Even the demons believe— and tremble! —James 2:19 NKJV

The great conundrum is the problem of evil. We are baffled by it. If God is good and all-powerful, why does evil happen? The Bible never deals with that age-old problem in the abstract, as philosophers might prefer. Instead, Bible writers vividly portray history as the great stage of God's victorious battle against evil. Demons are the spiritual agents who foment evil. They flee from the Word of God, which terrorizes them.

The Bible names the arch-demon Satan, Devil, the Evil One, or Beelzebub (a variant on Baal, the fertility god of ancient Canaan). Demons torment people in the Old Testament (Job 1–2) and operate in pagan cultures as the powers behind magical deeds (Exodus 7:11–12). God promises protection from demons (Psalm 91) for all who ask in faith.

In the New Testament, demons cause chaotic, unpredictable behaviors, screaming, and indifference to pain. They sometimes form an evil team, as in the case of the Gadarene demoniac (Mark 5:1–9; Luke 8:26–30), where their name is "Legion" (many). On four occasions, Jesus "cast out" the demons tormenting people; and on several other occasions, Jesus confronted demons as He healed the sick (Mark 3:10–12). These demons had special insight into Jesus' identity as the Messiah but were commanded to keep silent about it (Mark 1:24–25).

In his letters to churches, Paul warned against compromise with pagan religions. People must not join pagan ceremonies or rituals, he told the Corinthians, for that would compromise the integrity of the Christian community (1 Corinthians 10). Even though pagan gods are false figments and impotent imposters, they represent a spirit of deceit and betrayal that will sway many people (1 Timothy 4:1). Timothy was warned against extremists who misrepresented God through the influence of evil spirits.

In his brief letters, John urged Christians to "test the spirits" (1 John 4:1–3). John identified evil spirits as "antichrists" (2 John 7) or "false prophets" who distort and subvert the gospel. Even to listen to them is to open oneself to subtle perversion. These warnings imply that demons know the truth

> **It is no more** difficult to believe in demons than to believe in God, Christ, the Holy Spirit, angels or the devil.
> —J. W. Roberts

about God and are clever at presenting alternatives that resemble, but finally undermine, that truth. In the book of Revelation, "unclean" demonic spirits deceive world rulers, leading them into conflict with God (Revelation 16:13–14).

The Bible portrays spiritual warfare as backdrop to history and to personal oppressions; yet there must be a way out. The prophet Zechariah knew it, and wrote: "'Not by might nor by power, but by my Spirit,' says the LORD Almighty" (Zechariah 4:6). Christ has triumphed over demons and all evil (Ephesians 2:1–2). On the Last Day, God will make that victory complete forever (Romans 16:20). Until then, Christians are assured that no power of spirit, Satan, or demons can separate them from God's love, protection, and care (Romans 8:38–39).

Additional scriptures

- Matthew 7:22
- Matthew 9:32–34
- Matthew 25:41
- Mark 16:17
- Revelation 12:9

Disciple

D

Day of
the Lord

Death

Decree

Deliverance/
Healing

Demons

Disciple

Doctrine

Doubt

One who follows Jesus, learning from Him and telling others about Him. A disciple walks with the Master Teacher.

Jesus said, "If you hold to my teaching, you are really my disciples. Then you will know the truth, and the truth will set you free." —John 8:31–32

The Bible's story of disciples begins with the prophets. Elisha was a disciple of Elijah, probably the most famous such disciple in the Old Testament. But the term is most importantly associated with the followers of Jesus, especially the Twelve, and among them, the closest three: Peter, James, and John (Mark 14:33).

The ancient world passed knowledge to students not through standard texts and national exams, but by means of eager novices attaching themselves to learned men. The New Testament word for disciples is *mathetes*, meaning learner, adherent, or enrolled pupil.

For Jesus' disciples, "adherent" speaks to the closeness Jesus established with them. The Twelve not only learned from Jesus but traveled with Him and became coworkers in His healings,

feeding of crowds, and other events. The Twelve were especially called to leave behind their former occupations in order to join Jesus in preaching that the kingdom of God was at hand.

Did the Twelve get it? Their record up to the Day of Pentecost (Acts 2) was not stellar. One was Jesus' betrayer, the infamous Judas. Others could not stay awake during Jesus' hour of crisis (Mark 14:37). They misinterpreted the significance of key events in Jesus' life (Matthew 26:8). They seemed distracted with their own future status (Matthew 18:1). Although given power to cast out demons, at times they could not (Mark 9:14–18). When children approached Jesus for a blessing, the disciples tried to prevent them (Mark 10:13). After Jesus' arrest, the leader of the Twelve, Peter, denied that he even knew Jesus (Luke 22:55–62).

The eleven disciples plus Matthias (who replaced Judas, Acts 1:21–26) were slow learners and sometimes timid followers, but they became, after Pentecost, the most effective team of evangelists ever assembled. Made bold by the Holy Spirit, they spread the gospel message to the world. Joining their number as the Christian movement grew was Saul of Tarsus (Paul). His influence was decisive for the development of the church (Acts 9).

Does God want disciples today? The Bible says yes and paints a textured portrait of what discipleship requires. First, a disciple of Jesus must believe that He was the Messiah sent by God to redeem humankind by His death on the cross. Like the original disciples, followers today are called to grow in the Lord, that is, to exercise

> **The disciple** is one who, intent upon becoming Christ-like and so dwelling in his "faith and practice," systematically and progressively arranges his affairs to that end. —*Dallas Willard*

"gifts" granted by God to help everyone come to faith in Jesus. These gifts vary but are generally teaching, preaching, showing mercy, organizing and leading, serving, and encouraging (Romans 12:6–8). Today's disciples witness to God's truth by word and deed, gather together weekly for worship, and trust fully in Jesus for forgiveness of sins and life eternal.

Additional scriptures

- Matthew 10:2–4
- Mark 2:14
- Luke 14:25–27
- Acts 9:10, 26, 36
- Acts 16:1

Doctrine

Instructions and teachings that interpret Bible sections, harmonize their visions, and present a unified framework for understanding.

Do your best to present yourself to God as one approved, a workman who does not need to be ashamed and who correctly handles the word of truth. —2 Timothy 2:15

D

Day of the Lord

Death

Decree

Deliverance/ Healing

Demons

Disciple

Doctrine

Doubt

When God's instructions were being presented by just one messenger, as for example, in the days of Moses or the prophet Elijah, the "truth of God" was what that messenger said. The person had no other source. Opponents of these singular messengers were simply wrong, misguided, and not to be taken as authorities.

When messengers began to multiply, however, as when four writers present their story of Jesus in the four Gospels or multiple prophets commented on the Exile, would the core message survive? The answer to a unified message, as any student of the Bible knows, was doctrine.

In the King James Bible, "doctrine" appears forty-six times. Modern translations use "teaching" or "instruction." Bible texts urging sound doctrine are most frequently found in Paul's pastoral letters to Timothy. The path of wisdom was to follow the precepts and teachings that Paul himself taught, avoid innovation, and stay clear of contrariness or contradiction. Timothy's success as a pastor depended on his adhering to sound doctrine.

Clearly the Christian church needed doctrinal weight to remain a unified movement. In the first centuries of the Christian era, for example, questions arose concerning the nature and identity of Jesus Christ. Bible writers described Him as Son of Man and Messiah, while some texts also strongly implied divinity, notably John 3:16. In

Paul's writings, Jesus is presented as the incarnate Son of God who carried the sins of the world at the cross. But various churches asked, was Jesus the pinnacle of God's creation (but subordinate to God), or was Jesus God in the flesh?

> **It is an undoubted** truth that every doctrine that comes from God, leads to God; and that which doth not tend to promote holiness is not of God. —*George Whitefield*

Likewise, questions arose concerning the status of humankind before God. Was sin a moral lapse in need of better teaching or modeling? Or was sin a barrier to God that only God Himself could erase? The Bible speaks directly to these queries but not as a textbook or manual. The Bible's doctrines on Christology (who was/is Jesus?) and soteriology (how are sins forgiven?) are typically spread among many writers and passages. The church needed to establish a coherent body of teaching, a core message.

Creeds, written by early church scholars and leaders, organized the core message so that churches everywhere would teach alike. The Apostles' Creed is the most famous example; the Nicene Creed is another still used today. These early creeds spell out who Jesus is, what the apostles taught, and what all Christians affirm. This core message is called (in Greek) the *Kerygma*—the truth of God that Jesus commissioned disciples to tell others, so all people everywhere might believe.

Bible doctrine is remarkably cohesive and clear (given the long span of Bible authors and the difficulty of no first editions surviving), while church practices vary. Worldwide, forms of worship and sacraments are practiced differently. Visions of the end of history follow a variety of scenarios. The Bible's elasticity allows for interpretations and teachings conditioned by culture and tradition. But the Bible makes the audacious claim, foundational to doctrine, that God Himself guards core truth, and that faithful spokespersons need only to learn that core, cherish and obey it, and leave the results to God, whose sovereign power maintains the "solid foundation" of divine revelation, generation to generation and culture to culture.

Additional scriptures

- **Matthew 16:12**
- **1 Timothy 4:16**
- **2 Timothy 4:3**
- **Titus 1:9**

Doubt

The common human response to the call to believe and trust God. Of wonderful things, people question their durability or purity. Of promises, people question their integrity and breadth. Self-protection from disappointment and deception are common reasons to doubt, not to mention stubbornness and defiance.

But ask in faith, never doubting, for the one who doubts is like a wave of the sea, driven and tossed by the wind. —James 1:6 NRSV

The Bible everywhere urges people to put doubt behind them and believe the word of God. Yet nearly all Bible characters exhibit doubt, including the famous doubter who was part of Jesus' inner circle.

Doubting God's word, the Bible says, is the ultimate human mistake, often born of rebellion and pride. After all, does God have reason to lie? None at all. The word of God is true (Hebrews 4:12). The Bible never entertains the possibility that God's word might be deceptive, except as a tactic of the devil to lure people away from belief. Doubting God's word was the original sin (Genesis 3).

But honest people have reasons to doubt, the Bible acknowledges. Phony religious claims are common; one must avoid them (Titus 1:10). Be prudent, not gullible, the wisdom of the Proverbs advises (Proverbs 13:16). In the Bible's call to belief, intelligence is never forgotten nor is human reason. Rather, intelligence and reason, coupled with the full panoply of human emotions,

are the means by which God's word enters a life and grows, as it were, from a mustard seed (nearly too small to see) into a tree of sturdy trust (Matthew 13:31–32).

Phony religious claims may deter the gullible, but more likely (and

everywhere in the Bible) doubt arises from disappointment, pain, loss, or the seeming failure of a religious claim. The book of Hebrews was written to doubters of this kind. When life turns harsh, we humans wonder where God went. That bewilderment leads some into doubt, then unbelief. Don't go there, Hebrews urges. "Take care, brothers and sisters, that none of you may have an evil, unbelieving heart that turns away from the living God" (Hebrews 3:12 NRSV). Hold on to hope. God's word is rock solid. Today's trials and hardships are not the end of the story. Instead of doubt, know that God is active, God's word is strong, and persevering faith leads to vindication, even to joy (Hebrews 4:12; 10:22). People's proper response to doubt is mutual encouragement and deeds of love. The evidence that faith begs for will show up (Hebrews 10:35–39).

The Bible's most celebrated doubter was Thomas, one of Jesus' twelve disciples. Presented with reports of Jesus' resurrection, Thomas famously declined to believe until he touched Jesus' wounds and scars. Thomas was not ejected for his skepticism; rather, Jesus allowed the very examination that "Doubting Thomas" needed to make his declaration of trust and allegiance (John 20:24–28).

The Bible admits to reasons for doubt but never surrenders to unbelief. The book of James begins with a call to wisdom and perseverance in the face of life's hardships (James 1:2–8).

A man was meant to be doubtful about himself but undoubting about the truth. This has been exactly reversed. —*G. K. Chesterton*

The "beloved disciple" John, writing late in his life, said plainly: We have seen, heard, and touched (the evidence all humans treasure) this word of life (the truth all humans seek). Doubt has its answer in believing the gospel and letting God fill in the normal, natural blanks.

Additional
scriptures

- **Matthew 21:21–22**
- **Luke 24:38**
- **John 20:27**
- **Jude 22**

Elect / Election

God has a point and purpose in creating the world and redeeming it from the curse of sin. Election is the Bible's strong affirmation that God's purpose will be done.

Even before he made the world, God loved us and chose us in Christ to be holy and without fault in his eyes. God decided in advance to adopt us into his own family by bringing us to himself through Jesus Christ. This is what he wanted to do, and it gave him great pleasure. —Ephesians 1:4–5 NLT

Election means that God has chosen how to remedy the world's sin problem. Always the Bible shows that the motive behind election is God's love and mercy. The Bible cites three "elected" entities: angels, Israel, and all followers of Jesus Christ.

Chosen or elect angels are mentioned only once, in 1 Timothy 5:21. What Paul meant in this singular reference is not easily determined. Perhaps these angels were protected from a primeval rebellion that produced the devil. In any case, the Bible does not develop this theme.

Much more important is God's choice of Israel as carrier of God's word and recipient of God's mercy and saving power. Abraham (Genesis 12) did not receive God's mercy by qualifying for it, nor did Isaac meet divine requirements, nor Jacob, nor the nation that emerged from them. God's election of Israel was His choice, not based on Israel's merit as a people. In fact, Israel is more often described in the Bible as faulty and failing. In Romans 9–11, Paul pondered the nation's long and struggling journey, concluding that the true Israel (the elect of God) are all who follow God's will, including Gentiles who believe in Jesus Christ. Nonetheless, because God's choice of Israel is embedded in God's good will and faithfulness, Paul claimed that all Israel would be saved (Romans 11:26).

God's most important choice is the Bible's core message: Salvation—forgiveness of sin and eternal life—is chosen for all who believe in and follow Jesus Christ. But wait. Isn't belief a matter of human choice? Are not all people urged to believe? The Bible affirms this, but tells a back-story that eliminates pride from the choice to believe and grounds all such decision in God's own love and power. The Bible's back-story is this: Sin takes spiritual vitality from all people. Spiritually dead people face a hopeless dilemma, captured by evil and destined therefore for judgment. Because God has "great love for us," God enables and calls people to faith (Ephesians 2:1–7). Now a wonderful future is open, secured by a bond of God's protection and care (Romans 8:38–39). Who finally gets credit for the decision to follow Jesus? God does, in a way the Bible describes as "grace" (Ephesians 2:8–9) or unmerited love.

Churches have struggled over the strong initiative of God described in Ephesians and Romans, and the imperative to believe (2 Peter 3:9). Paul answers these questions by affirming

> **There are two** great truths which from this platform I have proclaimed for many years. The first is that salvation is free to every man who will have it; the second is that God gives salvation to a people whom He has chosen; and these truths are not in conflict with each other in the least degree.
> —*C. H. Spurgeon*

that God is fair (Romans 2:11), that people are responsible and accountable for their decisions (Romans 9:16–17), and that God's Good News, the gospel, is for everyone.

The Bible does not try to answer the paradox of divine grace and human responsibility but to place the paradox in context. That context is a world created and loved by God and redeemed by God's own powerful plan. That plan reached its key moment in the death and resurrection of Jesus Christ (Ephesians 1:10). The proper response of all people is gratitude, belief, and obedience. Whenever that response is enacted, the credit is God's alone (Ephesians 1:11).

Additional scriptures

- **Matthew 24:22**
- **Matthew 24:31**
- **Titus 1:1**

Eternal Life

E

Elect/
Election

Eternal Life

Evil/
Wicked

Only God is immortal. Since sin spoiled creation, all other living things die. But God has sent His Son, Jesus Christ, to bring eternal life to all who believe in Him. Now, no one needs to fear death.

Very truly, I tell you, anyone who hears my word and believes him who sent me has eternal life, and does not come under judgment, but has passed from death to life. —John 5:24 NRSV

The Bible speaks about life with several terms. But life as an enduring experience is usually the Greek word *zoe*, from which our term zoology comes (the study of living animals). In the Bible, God's life is *zoe* of a special kind: eternal, never-ending, not subject to death or to the limitations that lead to death. This enduring life was God's intention for all living things at creation. The seventh day in Genesis 2:3 has no ending.

Eternal life for all was spoiled by sin. That loss would have meant the end of everything had not God intervened with a way to restore life. The way was Jesus Christ, who paid the penalty for sin, the ransom (to use a Bible metaphor). Indeed, Jesus' message was the good news that eternal life is God's gift to all who confess their sin and accept God's grace in their lives. In the New Testament Gospels, this core message is often called the coming of the kingdom of God. "Eternal life" and the "kingdom of God" are used interchangeably to mean the restoration of God's good life—enduring, peaceful, growing, and relational—for all who believe.

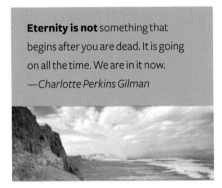

> **Eternity is not** something that begins after you are dead. It is going on all the time. We are in it now.
> —*Charlotte Perkins Gilman*

If eternal life is offered, how does a person obtain it? Throughout its pages, the Bible teaches that the way to life is to follow God's instructions. But that is impossible. Sin prevents perfect obedience, and God cannot live in the presence of sin. Jesus' message, explained by Paul as justification by faith (Romans 3:23–24), is that God gives His life (eternal and good) to all who come to Jesus in faith. Jesus explained this process as coming to "know. . .the only true God" (John 17:3 NRSV). The way to know God is to align with Jesus, to walk with Him, to call Him Lord. Jesus is the sent One whose obedience wins eternal life, restoring God's original plan.

When does eternal life begin? The quick answer is, when earthly life ends at physical death. But that answer is too hasty. Eternal life is part of the present experience of every follower of Jesus, the Bible claims. Scholars have called this "realized eschatology"—a term

that means the future is indeed already here, in the sense that physical death is not the final word and the power of sin is not supreme. God's reign is established but not complete.

A new quality of life is part of *zoe* eternal. God's life is warmly relational: God and others in loving fellowship, in an environment that is peaceful and good. The Bible describes it as beyond expectations (1 Corinthians 2:9). Eternal life has begun, and its here-and-now experience is in sharp contrast to life inclined toward sin and self (1 John 2:15–17). The difference is as crisp as light and darkness (1 John 2:9–11), love and hate, freedom and bondage (Romans 8:2). Eternal life, as the Bible outlines it, is life abundant (John 10:10), able to overcome current troubles (John 14:1) while anticipating a future of joy and peace.

Additional scriptures

- **Matthew 19:16, 29**
- **John 3:16, 36**
- **John 4:14**
- **John 10:28**
- **Galatians 6:8**
- **Revelation 22:1–6**

Evil / Wicked

All that is opposed to God, morally wrong, and hurtful to human happiness. Evil is often personified in the Bible and always to be avoided.

Guard your heart above all else, for it determines the course of your life. Avoid all perverse talk; stay away from corrupt speech. . . . Don't get sidetracked; keep your feet from following evil. —**Proverbs 4:23–24, 27** NLT

Evil in the Bible is described as disobedience to God and God's law. It is often associated with persons who are ignorant of God or despise God (especially in the Old Testament). Satan, or the devil, is named as the personification of evil, its chief purveyor, the one who tempts and turns people from God. At a deeper level—and admittedly an abstract and mysterious level—the Bible speaks of evil as "principalities and powers" (Colossians 2:15 NKJV), warning Christians to avoid their lure, assuring Christians that Christ has defeated them.

If God is good and all-powerful, why is evil part of our world? This question—known technically as "theodicy"—has occupied some of the world's best minds. The Bible never debates this question but consistently describes evil as the penchant to disregard or dismiss God's law and will. The first evil was disobedience to God's decree concerning the one tree in Eden whose fruit was forbidden (Genesis 3). Failing that test, Adam became both the pinnacle of creation (Genesis 1:26–27) and the one who introduced evil into creation—and with evil, death (Romans 5:12). Everything was affected: the environment, work, childbirth, the human conscience, and the power of evil. By the time of Noah (Genesis 6), wickedness had grown such that "every inclination of the thoughts of [humankind's] heart was only evil all the time" (Genesis 6:5). Clearly, this was not the way things should be.

The Bible may well be seen as the record of God restoring creation to its original state of goodness (Genesis 1:31). Opposed to this intense and sacrificial effort is the devil, the powers, and the propensity of humankind toward evil (a condition theologians have called "original sin").

The devil, or Satan, is the biblical name of God's chief adversary, but not His equal. The devil's primary tactic is deception (John 8:44), and the result of his success is death and disruption of God's will. Jesus Christ has defeated Satan's power (Luke 10:18–19), but that power still disrupts life until the truth of God is adopted and trusted (Acts 26:18). At the end of time, evil will be finally and forever defeated (Revelation 20:6).

> **Good has** but one enemy, the evil; but the evil has two enemies, the good and itself. —*Johannes von Muller*

The New Testament describes evil as "rulers of the darkness of this age . . .spiritual hosts of wickedness in the heavenly places" (Ephesians 6:12 NKJV). These terms carry broad meanings. The Bible certainly admits to a spiritual reality beyond the material world in conflict with God. Sometimes these powers are simply a reference and reminder that our world and our questions, troubles, problems, and losses involve more than meets the eye. However they may present themselves, these powers are finally subject to God, whose love cannot be broken by them (Romans 8:37–39).

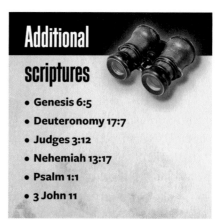

Additional scriptures

- **Genesis 6:5**
- **Deuteronomy 17:7**
- **Judges 3:12**
- **Nehemiah 13:17**
- **Psalm 1:1**
- **3 John 11**

Faith

Faith is what God wants for each person and from each person. Faith believes that God loves all people and that Jesus is Lord and Savior. Faith leads to action characterized by love for God and humankind.

For this is the will of my Father, that everyone who looks on the Son and believes in him should have eternal life, and I will raise him up on the last day. —John 6:40 ESV

God created people with will, reason, and passion—the complex assets of human life—in order to hear God's word and respond faithfully to it.

Abraham was the first Bible character described as one having faith (Genesis 15:6). For Abraham, like Noah before him, faith meant trust that God's word was true and, then, taking action based on that trust. For both Noah and Abraham, acting in faith meant living and behaving against the grain of their culture. Noah built a boat, trusting that God's warning of a flood would come true (Genesis 6:13–14). Abraham left his home, then, in his second great act of faith, stood ready to sacrifice his son, Isaac (Genesis 22:2). These and other Bible characters are models of faith—never perfect but grasping the hope that

Faith is reason at rest with God.
—*Charles Haddon Spurgeon*

reaches beyond sight (Hebrews 11).

The Bible describes faith in the Old Testament as loyalty to God and assent to the Torah, the teaching about God. God is faithful, the Bible says, and faithful people will follow God to Egypt (Genesis 47:27), out of Egypt (Exodus 12), through exile, and into God's kingdom (Malachi 4). Many Bible passages describe the journey of faith. Micah 6:8 is one excellent example: "He has told you, O man, what is good; and what does the LORD require of you but to do justice, and to love kindness, and to walk humbly with your God?" (ESV). Faith points people toward God's good future (Jeremiah 29:11).

In the New Testament, faith (*pistis* in Greek) is often translated as belief or believing. Faith brings life (Romans 3:22) and expressing faith is a sign of eternal life (1 Timothy 6:12). Faith is not simply a human decision to believe but a gift from God exercised when people do, in fact, believe (Ephesians 2:8–9), despite the obstacles. Faith is not contrary to human reason but a reasonable response to God's word expressed in creation (nature) and made personal in Jesus Christ (Hebrews 11:3; 12:2). The early church father Augustine and others reflecting on faith taught that belief and reason work in tandem to increase our understanding of the divine. Faith which is never expressed in action is unreal (James 2:14). Faith expressed in works of love is genuine (James 2:18). Biblical faith goes beyond mental assent toward close relationship with God (Hebrews 10:19–22). Prayer then becomes an expression and privilege of faith, available to all who seek God's help (James 5:14–15). Faith opens new horizons as God's purposes become clearer and God's promises pass the "reality checks" of lived experience (Hebrews 10:35–38). Faith is "a firm and certain knowledge of God's benevolence toward us," said John Calvin, summing up the Bible's record. Faith is the key to life said the prophet Habakkuk (Habakkuk 2:4).

Faith is so central to the Bible's message that in the middle of faith's "hall of fame," the Bible states with emphasis: "Without faith it is impossible to please God, for whoever would approach him must believe that he exists and that he rewards those who seek him" (Hebrews 11:6 NRSV). Few Bible statements are clearer than that.

Additional scriptures

- **Romans 3:22**
- **Romans 4:5**
- **Romans 10:17**
- **Hebrews 11**

Fellowship

Everywhere the Bible describes people of faith bonded to one another in relationships of loyalty, mutual help, and love. No Bible people grow in faith as loners; none celebrate loneliness. All find delight in sharing food, goods, and time.

We declare to you what we have seen and heard so that you also may have fellowship with us; and truly our fellowship is with the Father and with his Son Jesus Christ. —1 John 1:3–4 NRSV

If anyone imagines that people of faith live in monkish isolation, a survey of the Bible's vision of fellowship puts that lonely picture to rest. Bonds of love and loyalty are common themes in both Testaments.

In the Old Testament, bonds of love unite people called by God for special tasks and purposes. Abraham, Isaac, and Jacob created the family that settles in Egypt. When Moses led the Hebrews to freedom, the people created a nation, Israel. The prophets reminded Israel that its mission extended far beyond clan, tribe, and language group. The mission given to Israel was to witness to all the world that God is good, holy, and just—and, remarkably, that God wants fellowship with all people. No other Old Testament deity was ever described as desiring friendship or companionship with their worshipers. Fellowship is precisely the point of the first biblical encounter between God and humankind: They walked together in a garden (Genesis 3:8).

In the New Testament, a new community took shape around the extraordinary claim that Jesus Christ, crucified by the Romans, had been raised to life by the power of God. The disciples (with Matthias replacing Judas, Acts 1:21–26) formed the nucleus of a movement that was called "Christian" first in Antioch, then throughout the world. Early in this movement, a rare sense of fellowship formed around meals, mutual needs, learning the apostles' teaching, and worship (Acts 2:42). These early Christians shared property and witnessed miracles and wonders. Their care and concern for each other was like a magnet for others eager to know the reasons for such friendship. The community was, the Bible insists, a work of God (Acts 2:47), and believers should get together regularly (Hebrews 10:25).

The Bible offers practical suggestions to sustain and deepen fellowship among Christians and with all people. Paul describes the power of partnership in sharing the gospel (Philippians 1:5), mutual help during troubles (2 Corinthians 1:7), and sharing resources (2 Corinthians 8:4).

The Book of James includes insight on listening well, forgiving, avoiding status conflicts, and suppressing ill-tempered words that disrupt friendships. Hospitality is a social gift that builds community and sometimes holds unusual surprises (Hebrews 13:1–3). When old traditions work against fellowship, they need to be changed. Philemon, for instance, was to welcome back his runaway slave Onesimus as a brother (Philemon 15–16).

Despite the problems that show up in any group (churches included), the faithful disciple of Jesus is to work toward peace and unity. When that requires personal sacrifice, the Christian should follow through, trusting God that fellowship is a happier, more fulfilling lifestyle than isolation. This is the Bible's consistent report.

Additional scriptures

- **Exodus 20:24**
- **Galatians 2:9**
- **2 Corinthians 13:14**
- **1 John 1:6–7**

Filled with the Spirit

The filling of the Spirit is God's desire for every believer. The term refers to a dimension of life that overcomes the hurts, disappointments, and evil that permeate the fallen world.

Don't be drunk with wine, because that will ruin your life. Instead, be filled with the Holy Spirit. — **Ephesians 5:18** NLT

The Holy Spirit (third "person" of the Triune God) has a strong role in the biblical record from the beginning (Genesis 1:2). References to the Spirit pepper the Old Testament, but in the New, the Spirit is unleashed in a special way fifty days after Passover, as Jesus had promised (Acts 1:8) and as the prophet Joel had predicted (Joel 2:28).

This unleashing at Pentecost (celebrated today seven weeks after Easter) begins a period in which God's Spirit fills believers with boldness, persuasiveness, and power to successfully contend with evil. The book of Acts is a commentary on this new authority and power that believers use to confront evil and disease. In some cases, the filling of the Spirit does not lead to escape and relief but, rather, sustains believers in their most painful experiences (Acts 7:54–60).

The filling of the Spirit enables people to contend with all the evil that Satan can muster. This encounter is often called "spiritual warfare." Clearly the Spirit's presence in one's life is essential to a faithful outcome

(Ephesians 6:17–18). This "warfare" intensifies as the Last Day approaches, so the Spirit's filling is all the more important as Jesus' coming draws near (Romans 8:19).

Churches have taught about the filling of the Spirit with various points of emphasis. In Pentecostal and other churches engaged with charismatic renewal, fillings are special occasions when the Holy Spirit enables healings, the use of languages not known by the speaker, and moments of ecstasy. Paul refers to such occasions in 1 Corinthians. Holiness churches teach a two-step approach to Christian faith in which a believer is "saved" by believing the gospel, but then "sanctified" through the filling or baptism of the Spirit.

At the center of the Bible's teaching is the Holy Spirit active throughout history, evident especially in the life, death, and resurrection of Jesus (Hebrews 9:14), and poured out to the church at Pentecost for the task of preaching the gospel to all peoples. To be filled with the Spirit is to confess that Jesus is truly Lord, a confession which is enabled by the Spirit. Special moments of spiritual power may follow, especially during crisis encounters with evil. The Bible discourages ranking believers (as if an elite corps with certain gifts of the Spirit hold higher status, see 1 Corinthians 12; Ephesians 1:13). Nonetheless, on occasions Jesus' followers need more spiritual power or insight than they possess (John 9:1–6). These occasions point to a learning curve in which the Spirit plays the key role.

Difficulty understanding the work of the Holy Spirit should be no surprise. The Corinthian church was abusing gifts of the Spirit. Paul wrote to them: Focus on love, not charismata (1 Corinthians 13).

> **The Spirit of God** is given to the true saints to dwell in them, as his proper lasting abode; and to influence their hearts, as a principle of new nature or as a divine supernatural spring of life and action. —*Jonathan Edwards*

As at the beginning (Genesis 1), the Spirit of God moved where it willed. Everywhere, the Spirit teaches believers to do God's will and work (Acts 1:8) in trust and great faith. Clearly, no one who seeks the Spirit's filling and power is denied (Psalm 139:7).

Additional scriptures

- Luke 1:15
- Acts 2:4
- Acts 4:8
- Acts 4:31
- Acts 13:52

Forgiveness

A holy judge faced with disobedient subjects (who have no credible defense) would rightly declare their guilt and apply a just sentence. God, however, chooses a different way: to forgive, renew, and begin again.

If we confess our sins, He is faithful and just to forgive us our sins and to cleanse us from all unrighteousness.
—1 John 1:9 NKJV

F

Faith
Fellowship
Filled with the Spirit
Forgiveness

Without forgiveness, human relationships would be unbearable and impossible to maintain. Everyone makes mistakes. Does that mean God *must* forgive? This seems unlikely. No pagan deity in Bible times was obliged to forgive anything. The gods were above such a show of weakness or contrition.

To the surprise of nearly everyone in the Bible, the Lord God Almighty, Creator of heaven and earth, forgives as an expression of His character. God loves people (another surprise, compared to pagan gods) and wants fellowship with people (2 Chronicles 7:14). One of the earliest descriptions of God's character (actually a self-description) says God is "keeping mercy for thousands, forgiving iniquity and transgression and sin, by no means clearing the guilty" (Exodus 34:7 NKJV). God forgives, but that forgiveness is not automatic or universal, since God cannot deny His essential holiness. Forgiveness and punishment are the two most frequent responses of God to acts and attitudes of people in the Bible. Both responses intend to establish God's holy character, and embrace and renew the creation that has fallen into disobedience and sin.

Forgiveness begins with God (1 John 2:12) but includes, even requires, a movement of the heart by people who need it. In Peter's first sermon (Acts 2:38), he urged his listeners to repent, be baptized, and be forgiven. In the model prayer (called the Lord's Prayer), Jesus instructs people to ask for forgiveness (Luke 11:4). Sinners approaching the holy God must not presume upon God's favor, but in humility, sorry for disobedience, ask God for what God longs to give (2 Kings 5:18). In the book of James, forgiveness sought and received is the environment in which healing can occur and life can prosper (5:15–16).

Are all sins forgivable? The Bible assures that God does not withhold forgiveness from any who seek it (Luke 7:36–50). But the book of Hebrews warns that God's patience may be exhausted (10:18). Writing to Christians who are suffering persecution, the writer to the Hebrews pleads with the readers not to disown the Lord or deny their allegiance to Christ. If they do, would they ask Jesus to be crucified again in order to save them again (Hebrews 6:4–6)? Keep faith, Hebrews urges. The "unforgivable sin," mentioned in the Bible with just enough ambiguity to keep everyone alert, is likely the offense of attributing Jesus' power to the devil (Mark 3:28–30). That sin subverts the very effort of God to offer forgiveness, and forecloses the repentance that forgiveness requires.

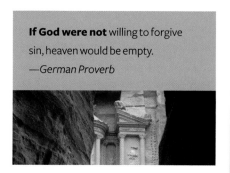

If God were not willing to forgive sin, heaven would be empty.
—*German Proverb*

The Bible's consistent teaching is to seek forgiveness and place faith in the sacrifice of Jesus Christ as the remedy and reason for God's forgiving people of all sin.

Additional scriptures

- **Psalm 130:4**
- **Matthew 26:28**
- **Ephesians 1:7**
- **Hebrews 9:22**

Glory

Denotes the immeasurable power and brilliance of God, and also the proper response of all people to God ("give glory"). The term points to the fulfillment of history, when all the world will know and see God.

For the earth will be filled with the knowledge of the glory of the LORD, as the waters cover the sea. —Habakkuk 2:14 NKJV

***Glory* carries the** biblical story of God and the world from beginning to end. God as Creator and Protector of the world is glorious (Psalm 24:7–10). God will lead the world and His people to glory, to complete fulfillment and joy in His presence (Isaiah 40:5). In the Last Days, Old Testament prophets said, all the world's people will acknowledge God's glory, vindicating the faith of Israel (Ezekiel 39:21–23). In that light, the old priest Simeon declared that he had seen the glory of God even in the infant Jesus, who would be the Savior of the world (Luke 2:29–32).

Simeon's declaration, while a sidebar to Jesus' birth narratives, is actually a major turning point in the Bible's story of God (and glory!). Simeon was the signal to Israel that the Messiah

(God's glory) had come.

The Old Testament term for glory, *kabod*, belongs exclusively to God. To YHWH (the Old Testament name for God) all glory is given; God is glory, wisdom, and honor. These Bible themes carry to the New Testament. God is the Father of glory (Ephesians 1:17); God lovingly shares His glory with the world and humankind (Romans 9:23); God demonstrated power in creating the world (Romans 1:20) and in calling people, then enabling them, to believe His word (Ephesians 4:1–6). Yet with Simeon's declaration, the Bible's focus on glory moves from YHWH to Jesus Christ.

The synoptic Gospels (Matthew, Mark, Luke) apply glory to Jesus as He dies on the cross (Luke 24:26), a stark contrast to what the Roman empire must have thought of Him: a rural rabbi, troublemaker, out of sorts with the religious establishment. (The Bible's vision is nearly always at polar opposites from secular perspectives.) Jesus on the cross is God's glory revealed (Hebrews 1:1–4). John's Gospel finds glory throughout Jesus' life, and even beforehand. Jesus was the glory of God prior to birth (John 12:41), during His earthly ministry (John 8:54), and on the Cross (John 12:16). John's vision of Jesus overflows with glory from before the beginning to

> **Our great honor** lies in being just what Jesus was and is. To be accepted by those who accept him, rejected by all who reject him, loved by those who love him and hated by everyone who hates him. What greater glory could come to any man? —A. W. Tozer

past the end.

Paul understood the work of Jesus as a new chapter in the glory of God. God's plan for saving humanity runs deep with glory (Ephesians 4:1–6). Glory is expressed in creation (Romans 1:20) and shared with humankind (Romans 9:23). But the glory of the Old Covenant is given new brilliance in the resurrection of Jesus (1 Corinthians 15:42–43). Jesus' glory brings people into fellowship with God in ways unprecedented, mediated by the Holy Spirit (2 Corinthians 3:6). This new paradigm of glory points toward a future and a hope (Jeremiah 29:11) that Paul, in exuberance and gratitude, struggles to adequately describe (Philippians 3:20–21). At the end of time, when the glory of God is public and visible, the new creation shimmers with energy, life, and beauty (Revelation 21:11, 22–26).

Additional scriptures

- **Exodus 16:7–10**
- **Exodus 40:34–35**
- **1 Kings 8:11**
- **1 Chronicles 16:29**
- **Psalm 8:5**

God

God, the only one, and the holy one, created the world, and it was good. When evil arose, God saved the world from the barriers and separations that sin caused. All the world will one day know God as its loving Creator and Redeemer.

And God said to Moses, "I AM WHO I AM." And He said, "Thus you shall say to the children of Israel, 'I AM has sent me to you.'" —Exodus 3:14 NKJV

The Bible is the story of God, told as a story, not as a catechism. Yet few Bible topics generate so many questions. Who is God? If God is good, how can evil happen? Why does God forgive? Can God feel emotion? Does God speak? What does God want? To the many questions people have about God, the Bible invites readers to the story of God. From Genesis to Revelation, the Bible tells parts and pieces of this story until finally, history (the story) is complete, God's purposes are realized, and new beginnings unfold.

God is one, not many. The most important confession in the Old Testament is Deuteronomy 6:4. The ancient Jewish *Shema* identifies God as singular, true, and the right focus of all human worship. Everything depends on God: our very existence (Genesis 1), our heritage of promise and blessing (Genesis 12), our liberty to live and worship (Exodus), moral boundaries (Leviticus), songs (Psalms), hurts and deep questions (Job), strength under duress (the Prophets). Even our wisdom comes from God (Proverbs), our sense of dignity (Esther), and the core belief that God knows our future and it is good (Jeremiah, Isaiah). When Moses asked, "God, who are you?", the answer came back: I am mercy and holiness you cannot directly see (Exodus 33:19). Though unseen and unable to be seen, God speaks throughout the Bible revealing His nature and purposes.

> **God does not** belong to the class of existing things...not that he has no existence, but that he is above all existing things, nay even above existence himself. —*St. John of Damascus*

The New Testament confronts Jewish monotheism with a paradigm shift. The one, holy God is actually three persons in unity: Father, Son, and Holy Spirit (Matthew 28:18–20). Jesus carries the message of the Triune God in bodily form. At the same time, Jesus is the *Logos* (the "Word") of God, God indeed, Creator and Redeemer (John 1:1–12). The New Testament never attempts to lay out a scheme explaining the Trinity (God, Son, Spirit), but its stories and teachings tell of God's once-for-all self-sacrifice in Jesus Christ to create an inseparable bond (Romans 8:38–39), a bond maintained by the power of the Holy Spirit.

God makes a major difference to every other Bible theme. Without a good God at the heart of the universe, we couldn't conceive a Bible (God's Word) or a triune Being who loves and acts on that love. While bad gods have been invented in the past, current world thinking dismisses "bad gods" as irrelevant to life in any way. If God is not good, civilizations will not sustain their belief in God.

As important as the story of God is to human life and nature, the Bible is not a book of quick recipes or easy answers. Rather, the Bible invites thoughtful reading, meditation, and prayer, as its words reveal God to us. The right reader response is belief in the Bible's portrait of God and obedience to its guidance as the living Word of God (Hebrews 4:12).

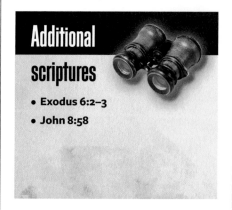

Additional scriptures

- **Exodus 6:2–3**
- **John 8:58**

Good News / Gospel

The gospel, or good news, is the powerful message from God told throughout the Bible that God restores sinful humans to fellowship with Himself through faith in Jesus Christ.

I am not ashamed of the gospel, because it is the power of God for the salvation of everyone who believes: first for the Jew, then for the Gentile. For in the gospel a righteousness from God is revealed, a righteousness that is by faith from first to last, just as it is written: "The righteous will live by faith." —Romans 1:16–17

The gospel was not good advice but good news. —*William Ralph Inge*

The Bible describes history in three broad terms—creation, fall, and redemption. God created a good world with one rule to guide humankind, "You must not eat from the tree" (Genesis 2:17). That rule was violated, and humankind "fell" out of fellowship with God; but God did not give up. Through many interventions (Hebrews 1:1), God communicated the Good News that forgiveness, restoration, and eternal fellowship with God are still intact. We are not lost in the cosmos, adrift in the universe, cut off from our Maker. Rather, we belong, body and soul, in life and in death, to our precious Savior, Jesus Christ (Heidelberg Catechism—published in 1563, this document, based on the scriptures, is used in many churches). This is the gospel that Old

Testament believers looked forward to, that Jesus' disciples saw and witnessed, and that Christians today confess: God saves lost humanity through a sacrifice of Jesus, which eliminates the barrier caused by sin and restores the fellowship that we need and God wants.

The beginning of the Old Testament only hints at the gospel (Genesis 3:15). The prophets anticipated a Messiah (Isaiah 53) but even so, Jewish leaders were still caught by surprise when the Messiah turned out to be a suffering servant rather than a political freedom fighter. Jesus' message was not liberation from Rome but the arrival of the kingdom of God, the victory of God over evil, and the love of God for all people. This was the gospel message: God so loved (John 3:16). As spectacular as that message was, Jesus ran into trouble with religious authorities when the gospel's universal reach became apparent (Luke 4:24–28).

Paul's writings make clear that a tragedy (Jesus' crucifixion) was precisely the divine victory that constitutes the gospel. Jesus' death and resurrection was the turning point in God's economy of salvation for all the world. A new era had begun. It was the last era, leading to the final judgment and new heavens and earth.

The right response to the gospel is faith. Clearly people are unable to achieve eternal life by their own will or goodness. The gospel is God's gift of eternal life, the penalty for sin paid in full by Jesus Christ. It is received by faith as people surrender their lives and futures to God.

What about add-ons to the gospel, given its two thousand-year history? Paul warned against anyone who would add, subtract, or alter the message (Galatians 1:6–12).

What about showing cordial and non-judgmental attitudes to people of other faiths? Dignity is to characterize all human relations, but with respect to the gospel, God has spoken. God's Word is not subject to multiple variations, storylines, or lead characters (John 14:6).

How can a person find the gospel today, with so many religious choices available? The gospel is the message of Jesus (John 3:18; Hebrews 1:2) taught in the Bible and confirmed to everyone who seeks truth (Romans 8:15–16). Alternatives may show some fascinating features, but all hope, faith, and trust belong finally to Jesus Christ alone. God in mercy has "made us alive together with Christ" (Ephesians 2:5 NKJV). He alone is Savior and Lord.

Additional scriptures

- **Matthew 24:14**
- **Mark 1:1**
- **Mark 16:15**
- **Romans 15:20**

Grace

In the New Testament, grace is equivalent to all that God has done to eliminate the penalty of sin and restore humanity to its proper relationship to God.

For it is by grace you have been saved, through faith—and this not from yourselves, it is the gift of God—not by works, so that no one can boast.
—Ephesians 2:8–9

Grace translates to the Greek word *charis*, which is similar to the common greeting among ancient Greeks. But in Paul's letters to churches, *charis* is both greeting and goodbye, and between them, the very content of the gospel Paul teaches.

Grace is God's unmerited favor directed to all people and centered on the work of Jesus Christ. Through Christ's death, the penalty for sin has been paid. Now salvation is the free gift of God to all who trust in Christ. God's grace is directed in the Bible to creation, to the needy, to sinners, and to all who believe. Grace blooms, as it were, as people respond to God's Word in faith. Grace guides one's entire life so that God is pleased and life is full (1 Corinthians 15:10). Paul knew from hard personal experience that grace did not mean a free ride. Trouble and an undefined ailment were Paul's constant reminders that the flesh is weak, but grace is strong and grows stronger, in the face of human weakness (2 Corinthians 12:9).

Grace, a common word and name (even the name for prayer before meals), denotes a most amazing reality. While scientists may look at a nature void of purpose and politicians may clash swords over abstract rights and traditional legal rules, the Bible tells of a universe made, loved, and redeemed by God. John the apostle, even in old

Grace is the love that cares and stoops and rescues. —*John Stott*

age, did not forget the startling difference graces makes. He urged readers: Look. . .see . . .(where did this come from? Who would have guessed? Isn't this amazing?). . .that God loves (1 John 3:1). Grace means that the vast expanse of space is not a universe of mere gas and mass, that the tragedies of human existence are not mere bad luck. By grace God created, and by grace God redeemed and will restore all that has been lost.

The most startling moment of grace, however, is God taking human form in Jesus Christ, dying to save humanity from the consequences of sin and rising from the dead in demonstration of supreme goodness and power. Then, by grace, God invites all to join His family (2 Corinthians 4:15).

The Bible uses several terms related to grace. Mercy is often coupled with it. Loving-kindness is a common Old Testament equivalent. Kindness and love are used as descriptions of grace in Titus 3:4, which leads to the simple declaration, "He saved us" (Titus 3:5). God's act of "saving" is the life transformation that grace desires and achieves.

The Bible's emphasis on grace as undeserved favor, freely given, led some new Christians early on to imagine that following God's law had become passé. They thought, since grace trumps obedience (or disobedience), let the party begin! But Paul countered this notion

by indicating that grace is transformative. Receiving grace changes a person's inner life and motivations (Romans 6:1–2). The grace-filled believer is not a prude who paints the world gray but, instead, is a person raised, as it were, from death to a new life (Romans 6:4). Thus grace is descriptive of both God's character and the transformative power God provides for people who ask for it. Grace enables healthy relationships, human good will, and gratitude.

It is appropriate then, to welcome one another as Paul does: "Grace and peace to you" (Romans 1:7). Defining oneself as called, set apart, and belonging to God by grace is right. The first and right response to grace is always "I thank my God" (Romans 1:8). This astonishing grace, a gift given "before the beginning of time" (2 Timothy 1:9), turns every darkness and fear into power, love, and capability (2 Timothy 1:7).

Additional scriptures

- **John 1:17**
- **Romans 3:22–24**
- **Romans 6:15**
- **Ephesians 1:7–8**
- **Ephesians 2:4–5**

Heaven

The abode of God. Details of heaven's geography and architecture are revealed in the Bible only symbolically. But relationships are more clearly defined, and the moral texture of heaven is fully described.

But our citizenship is in heaven. And we eagerly await a Savior from there, the Lord Jesus Christ, who, by the power that enables him to bring everything under his control, will transform our lowly bodies so that they will be like his glorious body. —**Philippians 3:20–21**

A popular campfire song tries to fill in the misty blanks: "Heaven is a wonderful place, filled with glory and grace." But such generic descriptions miss all the important questions: Where is it, who's there, what's going on? In popular entertainment, heaven isn't always desirable. "I'll see you in hell" is the movie tough guy's way of saying that sissies and softies have their place, but real men will continue the contest in their non-heavenish place. Against the dreamy songs and cloudy stereotypes, the Bible makes this clear about heaven: It is there; it is good; it is both God's place and part of the created world that will one day be renewed.

Where is heaven? In the Bible, "paradise" is a park or garden, pleasant, and fruitful. When Jesus promised one of the thieves on the cross beside Him that they would meet in paradise (Luke 23:43), the prospect was a sweet reunion in a good place. Paul "boasts" of entering paradise at one point, but his reserve at so fantastic a claim—and so wondrous a place!—is evident in his use of the third person to describe it (2 Corinthians 12:1–4).

"Paradise" is another biblical name for heaven, where God and angels live (Genesis 28:12; 1 Kings 8:30). It is also the dwelling of the pre-incarnate Christ (before He took on flesh, as a man), the place He ascended to, and the place from which He will return (Ephesians

4:9–10; Philippians 3:20). But where? Is heaven skyward, outside the known universe, somewhere far away? The Bible only suggests that heaven in dimensionally other, not spatially remote. Heaven may best be understood as

in heaven is (or will be), it involves praise, festivity, and community par excellence (1 John 3:2). Full of hope and life (Colossians 1:5), heaven is a "better place" than any other (Hebrews 10:34), a homeland (Hebrews 11:13) especially prepared

a spiritual sphere coexisting with the time-space world. The curtain separating heaven and earth may sometimes be crossed, as Paul experienced. Rulers, authorities, angels, and agents of evil pass through the curtain in an ongoing drama of God's goodness and Satan's wickedness (Ephesians 6:12).

The Bible uses "heaven" to describe another part of creation, too. Above the earth, the sky, the stars—that, too, is "heaven" and will be renewed on the Last Day (Hebrews 1:10–12; 12:26–28).

Who is there? God dwells in heaven (Matthew 5:16), and all the deceased who are saved by grace. Paul describes them as "fallen asleep" in Christ (1 Corinthians 15:20). Life in heaven after death, even during the long wait for the resurrection of the body, is described as active and good (Matthew 25:21).

What's going on? Images of harpists riding clouds may discourage the robust from longing for such a passive existence. But the Bible never permits such images. Whatever the schedule

for all who believe (John 14:3), where flawed humans saved by grace are made like Jesus Himself (Romans 8:29). In heaven, we are turned away from all that hurts toward all that amazes and glorifies (Romans 8:30). The prophet Ezekiel describes heaven as the place where all God's promises will be fulfilled (Ezekiel 37:26–27). The book of Revelation uses beautiful images (river of life, water clear as crystal) to describe heaven, then issues the welcome, " 'Come!' Whoever is thirsty. . . take the free gift of the water of life" (Revelation 22:1, 17).

Indeed, the Bible's heaven is a wonderful place, filled with glory and grace.

Additional scriptures

- **Psalm 20:6**
- **Luke 23:43**
- **2 Corinthians 12:4**

Hell / Damnation

A place of darkness where God is absent, hope is lost, and recovery is impossible. Medieval art offers pictorial images of hell, but the Bible offers very few. Hell in the Bible is more a quality of existence in which all good human aspirations are totally frustrated and forever out of reach.

He will reply, "I tell you the truth, whatever you did not do for one of the least of these, you did not do for me." Then they will go away to eternal punishment, but the righteous to eternal life. —**Matthew 25:45–46**

God punishes evil, including the evil of disregarding or disbelieving God's message, whether it was sent through prophets of old or by Jesus, the Son of God (Hebrews 1:1–2). To disregard or ignore God is to cut oneself off from life and light. The alternative, in effect the punishment, is darkness and eternal death (2 Peter 2:1–10).

In the Old Testament, "Sheol" (Numbers 16:30 NRSV) is the place of death. All the dead go there, good and bad, righteous

and evil. Concerning what happens next, the Old Testament is not explicit. Daniel 12:2–3 speaks of resurrection and judgment. Some in Sheol receive divine favor, others punishment. Most references to Sheol, or Hades, describe a place of no return, sleep, and silence. Gehenna, the third Bible term for hell, is a valley south of Jerusalem where the kings Ahaz and Manasseh offered sacrifices, including sons, to the god Molech. The prophets condemned the practice and the place.

> **There are only** two kinds of people in the end: those who say to God, "Thy will be done," and those to whom God says, in the end, "*Thy* will be done." All that are in Hell, choose it. —*C. S. Lewis*

In the New Testament, hell, called the destiny of Satan, is variously described as blackest darkness (Jude 13), a place of destruction (2 Peter 3:16), and a fiery lake of burning sulfur (Revelation 19:20). Clearly hell is where all things unfit to reside in God's presence are sent. Jesus urged people to avoid hell at all points and at any cost (Matthew 5:29). Jesus' mission was explicitly to save people from such a curse (2 Timothy 1:10).

Most Bible scholars have taken references to eternal judgment in hell as a sentence to unstoppable suffering. The Bible offers no detailed landscape or regimen, but this is clear: Hell is punishment for evil and unbelief; hell is absent love and compassion, absent God, absent kindness and mercy, absent hope and human companionship.

How long? Most Bible timelines suggest that hell has no end point. Some fewer references to hell allow for the idea that hell is annihilation, the cessation of conscious life.

Hell (Sheol, Hades, Gehenna) is where the devil will be consigned at the final judgment. In the same company are all who spurned God's truth or stubbornly violated God's laws. Here's the good news: Jesus saves us from this destiny. His obedient death fully paid God's holy judgment on sin. No one who trusts in Jesus suffers the penalty of hell. The forgiven instead live in peace and, ultimately, in heaven.

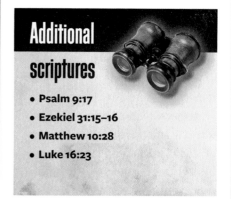

Additional scriptures

- **Psalm 9:17**
- **Ezekiel 31:15–16**
- **Matthew 10:28**
- **Luke 16:23**

Holiness

Holiness is what God is and wants. God seeks this quality in all He has made, and pays the high cost for it in the death of Jesus Christ.

Great and marvelous are your deeds, Lord God Almighty. Just and true are your ways, King of the Ages. Who will not fear you, O Lord, and bring glory to your name? For you alone are holy. —**Revelation 15:3–4**

The common questions—who is God? where is God?—are both answered and not answered, in the Bible's discussion of holiness. Central to the Bible's core teaching is that God is holy, without impurity, no blemish of badness, perfect goodness. Holiness defines God, and God defines holiness in the Bible's laws for living. But the clearest expression of all is the life, death, and resurrection of Jesus Christ. Because God is holy, God is said to dwell in a holy place—heaven.

Knowing this about God, how, then, do mortals find Him? How can we know Him? Moses reached such a crisis several times in his eventful life. Three months after their exodus from Egypt, the Hebrew people, led by God through Moses, camped at the base of Mount Sinai. Thereafter, Moses ascended the mountain seven times while God descended to meet him. The meeting was mostly aural.

A visible face-to-face would present an impossible approach between God's holiness and Moses's lack of it. Exodus 19–40 recounts the difficulty of knowing God—who He is and where He is. What Moses learned about God was no more and no less than what God allowed him to learn. The initiative was all God's. That's the pattern throughout the Bible: God enables; humans cautiously encounter.

> **He called them** that they might be holy, and holiness is the beauty produced by His workmanship in them.
> —*Thomas Watson*

Primarily, God is known in the Old Testament by the law, often called the Pentateuch (the first five books, Genesis through Deuteronomy). This law was summarized in the Ten Commandments (Exodus 20) and elaborated in many rules and procedures that implemented the law and fixed violations of it. Humankind knew of God's holiness, it would seem, by the rules, regulations, commandments, and rituals outlined by Moses and practiced imperfectly by the people of Israel.

Jesus clearly had no intention of becoming a conventional teacher of this law. In the Gospel of Mark, we find Jesus overriding the law and thus projecting a new holiness centered on God's mercy and justice. In Matthew's Gospel, we see him reinterpreting the law (Matthew 5:21–48). John describes Jesus' first miracle (changing water to wine at Cana, John 2:1–11) as symbolic of the change from Old Covenant to New. Clearly holiness was taking on a new paradigm in Jesus' teaching.

Paul taught holiness to early churches under the twin ideas of justification and sanctification. The former is the once-for-all pardon for sin achieved by Jesus on the cross. The latter is the responsibility of all Christians to allow the "life of the Spirit" to free them from sin's allure and draw them obediently closer to God, the holy One (1 Thessalonians 3:13). Paul used slavery as one of his favorite metaphors. Formerly slaves to sin, believers are freed by Christ to be "slaves of righteousness" (Romans 6:16–18). Thus holiness, so shrouded in mystery at the beginning, becomes by the end a way of life for God's people, no longer rule based, but Spirit based. The promise of Ezekiel has come: hearts of stone turned to hearts of flesh, with holiness the goal and prize (Ezekiel 36:26).

Additional scriptures

- **Exodus 15:11**
- **Psalm 29:2**
- **Isaiah 6:3**
- **Romans 6:19**

Holy Spirit / Comforter

The Bible describes God as three "persons" in unity, or Trinity. The Holy Spirit is God present in the world to comfort, protect, and instruct.

But the Counselor, the Holy Spirit, whom the Father will send in my name, will teach you all things and will remind you of everything I have said to you. —John 14:26

Each era of history and each civilization present opposition to the truth of God, the Bible affirms. The reason for such opposition is human pride, which universally resists submission to a higher power. How does truth survive?

The Bible points to a grace (known as a "chrism," a sheer gift of God) that enables the truth of God not only to survive, but to thrive. This gift is the Holy Spirit, the "third person" of the Trinity. All believers are given this chrism, the presence of the Holy Spirit, who then mediates and confirms the truth of God (1 John 2:20–23). The Holy Spirit works to extend the reign of God and establish the truth of God. On points where the Bible is silent or when leaders cannot agree on the meaning or proper application of the Bible, the Holy Spirit leads truthfully forward (Acts 15:8).

Before His ascension, Jesus promised that the Holy Spirit would be among the disciples, enabling their mission (Acts 1:8). Indeed, the Spirit arrived among them dramatically on the day called Pentecost (Acts 2:1–2). Descending on them like fire, the Holy Spirit gave them unusual courage and confidence in their message. That same "coming of the Spirit" was promised to all who believe (Acts 2:38–39).

We would be mistaken, however, to think that the Holy Spirit is absent from the Bible before Pentecost. Indeed, from beginning to end, the Spirit works to implement and confirm God's will. At creation, the Spirit hovers over primeval waters (Genesis 1:2). On history's last day, the Spirit invites all to come to the new heavens and the new earth (Revelation 22:17). The prophet Joel tells of the Spirit's important mission (Joel 2:28), and Ezekiel refers to the breath of God, the Spirit, as life-giver amid "dry bones" (Ezekiel 37).

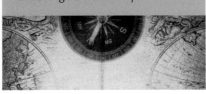

Every time we say, "I believe in the Holy Spirit," we mean that we believe that there is a living God able and willing to enter human personality and change it. —*J. B. Phillips*

Another mistake would be to assume that the Spirit's work in the world is simple, straightforward, and universally understood. Paul wrote to the Corinthians to correct, indeed to admonish, leaders whose understanding of the Spirit was causing hurt, confusion, and discord. Paul urged the Corinthian Christians to consider that the Spirit always leads toward love and unity, not disintegration of the church into elites and under-class (1 Corinthians 13). In Romans 8, Paul presents a remarkable vision of the Holy Spirit as chief agent in transforming life (v. 2), in setting proper behaviors (v. 5), in defeating perverse appetites (vv. 6–8), in promising resurrection (v. 11), in confirming salvation (v. 16), in serving as helper and prayer partner (vv. 26–27), and in performing as agent in the work of God, beginning to end (vv. 29–30). This long roster is meant to assure Christians that the power that created the universe is the same that carries them through life and beyond, to God's presence in eternity (vv. 35–39).

John's Gospel and letters calls the Holy Spirit our Counselor (John 14:16, 26; other versions of the Bible use the terms Advocate or Helper). The "breath of God" in John is the breath of Jesus, who gives the Spirit to His disciples (John 20:22).

The Holy Spirit communicates God's wisdom and will to believers (1 Corinthians 2:10–16), bridging the gap between timeless mystery and human history. The Spirit's wisdom focuses on the crucified Savior, Jesus Christ, whose death and resurrection form the core of the Bible's message.

Additional scriptures

- **Mark 3:29**
- **John 14:16–17**
- **Acts 1:8**
- **Acts 2:1–4, 17**

Hope / Blessed Hope / Second Coming

The salvation God has Himself secured in Jesus Christ has a future tense: Christ will come again. This is the blessed hope of all who are part of God's family.

For the grace of God that brings salvation has appeared to all men. It teaches us to say "No" to ungodliness and worldly passions, and to live self-controlled, upright and godly lives in this present age, while we wait for the blessed hope—the glorious appearing of our great God and Savior, Jesus Christ.
—Titus 2:11–13

Critics are heard to lay this charge against followers of Jesus Christ: otherworldly, indifferent to the problems of here and now, "eyes on the skies" while neighbors suffer. The charge is not without some merit. The Bible clearly teaches that Christ will return (Acts 1:11), and some Christians have assumed that investing in earthbound improvements are a waste of effort. Momentarily, they say, the environment, the infrastructure, the delicate economies of nations and neighborhoods—all will be presumptively overhauled (or dismantled and burned) by Christ's return.

The Bible does not direct followers of Jesus to lax indifference but teaches, instead, a two-fold orientation: Do the work of God while there is time, because one day (known to God alone) time will be finished (John 9:4). This final day will be (to use a common biblical phrase) "Sabbath-rest" for God's weary workers (Hebrews 4:9).

When is this "blessed hope"

scheduled to happen? This was the question on the lips of the disciples in the last conversation with the risen Christ—albeit with their understanding still a bit fuzzy (Acts 1:6). It is every person's question: What will tomorrow bring? The Bible's consistent answer is: God knows (Psalm 139).

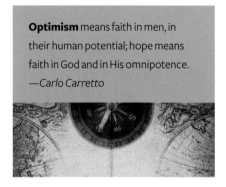

Optimism means faith in men, in their human potential; hope means faith in God and in His omnipotence.
—*Carlo Carretto*

Nonetheless, Bible scholars have designed three frameworks for understanding the blessed hope. The first, called the *Preterist* view, assumes that Jesus could return at any time, especially in view of the Roman persecutions that threatened to extinguish the new movement. The blessed hope would see Roman tyranny overthrown and the kingdom of God established.

The *Historicist* view prefers to believe that "great tribulation" has been the story of the entire Christian movement, and that the blessed hope is the culmination of history in the worldwide victory of God.

A third view, called *Futurist*, considers the blessed hope to be an event yet to come, along with most of the other signs associated with Christ's second coming. This view, like the other two, must deal with a complex set of biblical data, often in the form of dreams and visions (the books of Daniel and Revelation). Many theories try to weave this data into a coherent picture, even timetable, of future events. Futurists find many possible scenarios, some of which have enjoyed sporadic popularity. The *Left Behind* book series, for example, was a market success.

While scholars contend and theories rise and fall, on some matters all agree: The Bible's history begins with Creation and ends with God's kingdom fully formed in the new heaven and new earth. On the Last Day, Jesus Christ will return as Savior and Judge. All who have died and believers who are then living will be gathered and transformed with bodies like Jesus' resurrection body, thereafter to live joyfully with God. Whatever trouble we frail humans face today, the Bible presents this hopeful future, calls it blessed, and surrounds it with assurances of everlasting wonder and happiness in the presence of God.

Additional scriptures

- **Matthew 24:30**
- **Mark 14:62**
- **2 Thessalonians 2:1–3**

Idol / Idolatry

Throughout the Bible, people seeking some measure of control over nature, illness, the economy, childbirth, or harvests did so by appeasing divine beings, represented by idols. God commands believers to stay clear of any such practice.

Idol / Idolatry

Image of God

Incarnation

Inspiration / Scriptures

You shall not make for yourself an idol, or any likeness of what is in heaven above or on the earth beneath or in the water under the earth. You shall not worship them or serve them; for I, the LORD your God, am a jealous God, visiting the iniquity of the fathers on the children, on the third and the fourth generations of those who hate Me, but showing lovingkindness to thousands, to those who love Me and keep My commandments. —Exodus 20:4–6 NASB

Are little statues that big a deal? Herman Melville, in his great American novel Moby Dick, has the Calvinist Ishmael befriend the noble cannibal Queequeg. In a gesture of solidarity, Ishmael joins Queequeg in idol worship. The result: nothing. That "insignificant bit of black wood" could not possibly offend "the magnanimous God of heaven and earth," Melville notes. But every Bible writer emphatically disagrees.

Israel was to have no idols in its worship of the one true God (Deuteronomy

6:4). By refusing to imagine that a rock could have divine power, Israel would resist surrounding cultures which constructed idols for essential life business, from live births to wheat sales. Israel's God was never to be reduced to material form. When the nation faltered in this area, the prophets thundered warnings (Isaiah 10:10–11).

The New Testament world was thick with idols of various sorts. The Roman emperor himself was considered to be a god and was worshiped as one. And the Greeks were given to idols that advertised sex and sorcery. What were Christian converts to do?

Church leaders in Jerusalem (AD 49) decided that Gentile converts must abstain from secondary connection to idolatry by refusing meat dedicated in pagan temples (Acts 15:19–20). Later, Paul elaborated on this rule in response to queries from the church at Corinth where idols and pagan rituals were so imbedded in the culture that buying meat or attending social functions—commonplace events—involved compromise. In 1 Corinthians 8, Paul agreed that idols are of no account, so a person of strong faith may eat meat associated with idols without harm. But the person of weaker faith should not eat (the conscience deserves careful guarding). That observation then became the reason for the person of strong faith to also abstain, if his or her eating would create negative examples for the weak. Paul noted that the issue is bigger than "bits of wood," to use Melville's dismissive phrase. In many early cultures, idols were associated with spiritual evil (1 Corinthians 10:20). Because of that, Paul's best advice was to flee idolatry (1 Corinthians 10:14)—advice also echoed as the last note in John's first letter (1 John 5:21).

Idols are speechless (1 Corinthians 12:2), senseless (1 Thessalonians 1:9), and useless (Acts 14:15). Nonetheless, association is dangerous. The alliance between Idols and evil creates a dividing line: Idols have no place in God's kingdom (Galatians 5:16–21).

Additional scriptures

- **Exodus 32**
- **2 Kings 17:15**
- **Acts 7:41–43**
- **1 Corinthians 8:4–6**
- **Colossians 3:5–6**
- **Revelation 21:27**

Image of God

God created the heavens and the earth; but when God focused creative action on humankind, something unique was given: God's own image.

Then God said, "Let us make man in our image, in our likeness, and let them rule over the fish of the sea and the birds of the air, over the livestock, over all the earth, and over all the creatures that move along the ground."
—Genesis 1:26

Few elements of Bible exposition are as limited as this one—the image of God—and yet so important in our overall understanding of what it means to be human. Unlike many other themes, this one receives only occasional mention and no extended treatment. What the "image of God" means, then, and what difference it makes to life experience, has been left to theologians who must apply brief Bible teachings to sort out what humanity is all about. How are humans different from beasts? What obligations or opportunities does the difference present?

The image of God is mentioned in the Old Testament in Genesis 1:26–27, 5:1–3, and 9:6. That is it. In Genesis 5:3, the image appears also in Seth, son of Adam, indicating that it was a grant for all time, not merely to the original "parents." The image of God makes all humans distinctively human.

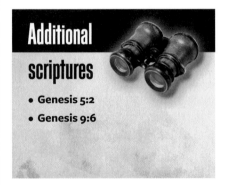

Man still stands in the image of God—twisted, broken, abnormal, but still the image-bearer of God.
—*Francis August Schaeffer*

Some say that God's image is human reason, the capacity for problem solving, for logical thinking, deduction, for abstract calculation and self-awareness. Minimal versions of these skills have been observed in some non-human species, but clearly humans are well ahead of beasts in mental activity.

The great church father Augustine suggested that the image was a capacity for memory (hence history and self-understanding), along with will, love, and justice. Again, some species exhibit limited capacity for all of these, though such discoveries happened well after Augustine's time.

The renowned theologian Karl Barth did as much as anyone to locate the image of God in a distinctive biblical frame. In the New Testament, Jesus bears the image (2 Corinthians 4:4; Philippians 2:6; Colossians 1:15). Jesus does so as the fullest expression, the complete manifestation, of God's unfailing love for humankind. Jesus establishes a new covenant or promise with humanity, and humans know (beasts do not) that a purposeful life means growth in this covenant relationship with God. We understand ourselves as we know God. Motivation to live well, do good, and regard others' welfare arises from gratitude for God's promise of eternal covenant with us.

A scientific or physiological explanation shows that humans have much larger frontal cortexes than animals. In that part of the brain, we solve problems, engage in critical thinking, feel compassion, and so forth. Could the mysterious grant of God's image be connected to brain size and function?

Despite its ambiguity, the Bible's teaching that we bear God's image has been monumentally important, informing issues from childbirth to international rights. Contemporary arguments concerning the right to life depend largely on the belief that all humans are "made in God's image." Calls for justice for refugees, ethnic minorities, and women and children are similarly grounded in the uniqueness and majesty of human life.

Additional scriptures

- **Genesis 5:2**
- **Genesis 9:6**

Incarnation

Jesus Christ is the Son of God. He came to earth as human but at the same time, fully divine. He is uniquely the image of God. Jesus is God incarnate, in the flesh.

For God so loved the world that He gave His only begotten Son, that whoever believes in Him should not perish but have everlasting life.
—John 3:16 NKJV

Idol/
Idolatry

Image of
God

Incarnation

Inspiration/
Scriptures

The doctrine of the incarnation separates Christian belief from all other versions of the meaning and purpose of Jesus' life. Muslims revere Jesus as one of the prophets. Humanists respect Jesus as a (sometimes) wise teacher. Even skeptics offer moments of admiration for Jesus' historical importance. But these all regard Jesus as on par with humanity. The Bible's teaching on incarnation means Jesus is human indeed, but uniquely God indeed, both together, in fact both united. No other birth was like His, no other person like Him.

Two Bible passages have led Christians to the conviction that Jesus was one person with two natures, human and divine. In Philippians 2:5–8, Paul asks believers to live humbly as Jesus did. Jesus was in very nature God, or in "the form of God" (RSV). Yet Jesus humbled Himself and took human form to save people from the separation caused by sin.

> **The Word** became flesh that he might become enfleshed in all men, thus crowning the created universe in the redemption of new-created souls.
> —F. F. Shannon

The second element of this exceptional claim is described in the first part of the Gospel of John. There John interprets Genesis 1 by explaining that Jesus is the eternal Word (logos) responsible for Creation itself. In other words, Jesus did not become God at the resurrection, or Transfiguration, or baptism—but He always was and is God.

The mind staggers at the paradox of divine and human together in one person. Early Christians did have their difficulties understanding and explaining it. Not until AD 451 did the church adopt confessional language that settled the many theological efforts to describe Jesus. The Nicene Creed, still used today, refers to Jesus as "the only begotten Son of God, begotten of his Father before all worlds, God of God, Light of Light, very God of very God, begotten, not made, being of one substance with the Father." All these claims were deduced as the true meaning of the Bible's teaching that Jesus was the Christ (anointed savior), Son of Man (Jesus' preferred title), Son of God (124 times in the New Testament), Messiah (anointed), Lord and Savior.

Thus did the emphatically monotheistic account of God in the Old Testament (Deuteronomy 6:4) turn toward a monotheism in three Persons (Father, Son, and Spirit). And thus did the birth of Jesus of Nazareth to a virgin named Mary in obscure Bethlehem become the occasion when the omnipotent God took human form. Never should the quick recitation of a creed or reading of a Bible verse diminish the magnitude of this shocking claim. It speaks magnificently to the dignity of humanity (that God would do it) and to the possibility of humanity (God did it that we might know Him). More than anything, it speaks to the heart of God, who loves us to such extent and depth.

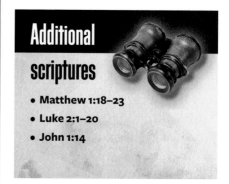

Additional scriptures

- **Matthew 1:18–23**
- **Luke 2:1–20**
- **John 1:14**

Inspiration / Scriptures

From Genesis to Revelation, the Bible is God's self-revelation, intended to communicate to all people who God is, what God wants, and how life is be related to God. Because God inspired the Bible, it carries authority beyond other literature. That authority enables people at all times and places to know God, love and serve God, and be clear about practical priorities of life.

All scripture is God-breathed and is useful for teaching, rebuking, correcting and training in righteousness, so that the man of God may be thoroughly equipped for every good work. —2 Timothy 3:16–17

Where did the writers of the Bible get their ideas? How are the words of the Bible any more illuminating than lines of other great literature? Why does the Christian church set the Bible apart as a special text? All these questions are addressed in the word translated "inspired" or "God-breathed" in 2 Timothy 3:16. The Bible is unique, authoritative, and clear on the major matters because God, who wants to reveal Himself, did so to prophets, poets, disciples (apostles), and others.

God inspired the Bible. The content of the Bible is God's Word to all people.

SANTA BIBLIA
—
HOLY BIBLE

It orients life, it explains life's purposes and possibilities, and it leads people everywhere to a knowledge of God that is relational and comprehensive. The Bible is relational because it does not intend to be a textbook on every subject, but rather a guidebook to personal knowledge and love for God. The Bible is comprehensive, not because it contains answers to every historical or scientific question, but because it opens readers to the character and acts of God in a way that human intelligence alone could never do. Its message leads to eternal life, for it binds people (created in God's image) to the source of life (God Himself) in love, faith, and joy.

God "inspired" the scriptures from beginning to end, in the choice of words to the compilation of the canon (the process of assembling the writings into the Bible). Thus the Bible is inerrant (without error) in the original manuscripts. God continues to inspire when the Bible is read, preached, and taught. God does this through the Holy Spirit working in the church, the community of people called by God to bear witness (word and action) to the truth of His Word.

Since the Enlightenment, the inspiration of the Bible has been attacked as patriarchal, imperialist, ridiculous (no book is "inspired by deity"), or self-serving (its readers claim a special glimpse on truth). These important claims have been argued by scholars who examine the history of texts and their interpretations. Throughout this long and complex process of exploring the Bible's origins, culture, earliest copies, and social uses, the God-breathed Word has continued to speak to people

> **Divine inspiration** makes the Bible uniquely the Word of God and not merely a book containing the Word of God, and as such is different from any other book sacred or secular.
> —M. F. Unger

everywhere, calling them to faith in God, to eternal life in Jesus Christ, and to new life through the indwelling Holy Spirit. In that sense, the Bible's "inspiration" is a matter of faith, supported by scholarship, and proven in practice by those who treasure its message.

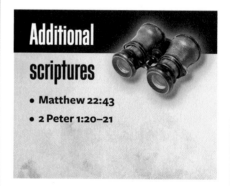

Additional scriptures

- Matthew 22:43
- 2 Peter 1:20–21

Joy

In sharp contrast to many stereotypes of grim Puritans trudging into a dark church, the Bible is a book filled with references to joy as one of the many outcomes of God's saving love for us.

I pray that God, the source of hope, will fill you completely with joy and peace because you trust in him. Then you will overflow with confident hope through the power of the Holy Spirit. —**Romans 15:13** NLT

What is this joy? One way to discover its meaning is to trace the occasions when joy is the dominant feeling. They are many, but notice how joyful was the birth of Jesus. First, Jesus' cousin John brought "great joy and gladness" to his elderly parents (Luke 1:14 NLT). The angel told shepherds "good news of great joy for all the people" at Jesus' birth (Luke 2:10 NRSV). Jesus Himself was a joy-filled person (John 15:11). So were His close followers (Luke 10:17). Paul often referred to his joy (Romans 16:19) though he had many reasons for opposite emotions (2 Corinthians 7:4). The old disciple John, though imprisoned, wrote often of his joy (2 John 4). Followers of Jesus are promised "fruit of the Spirit," one of which is joy (Galatians 5:22). The psalms are as full of joy as any other feeling (such as Psalm 92:4). Apparently, joy—a sense of delight and well-being—is a common feeling for people who spend time around God.

Why does joy so often seem as though it is here today but gone tomorrow? Even in the Bible, angels are not always singing. But neither is the Bible's description of joy quite so fleeting as up-tick markets. Instead, the Bible's joy endures grief (John 16:22–24), very bad situations (Philippians 1:12–26), and very tough conditions (1 Peter 1:6). One of the amazing reversals in the Bible is the declaration that joy replaces hurt, disgust, disappointment, and loss at just the point when those negative feels ought naturally to dominate (James 1:2–4). How does that happen?

> **Happiness** depends on what happens; joy does not. —*Oswald Chambers*

It is heaven's gift (John 3:27) for all who trust and obey. For people with eyes to see, God does "mighty things" (Psalm 118:15). Naturally, then, in the light of God's love, the human heart shouts joy. In the deeply personal parts of the New Testament, Jesus points to joy that cannot be taken away (John 16:22), reflected in Jude 24 as the great sense that comes from a life open to God, united to Christ, and kept from falling (into despair or temptation) until the day of eternal happiness. This joy animates descriptions of the new heaven (Revelation 21:1–5) when tears are wiped away and God makes all things new.

Psalm 34 is a song of joy. The singer has been delivered from trouble. Happy are those who take refuge in God. Be radiant, he urges. Taste and see that God is good. Apart from the goodness and love of God, joy would have flimsy foundations. But everywhere and through all troubles, God points to a joy that will not fade.

Additional scriptures

- **Psalm 126:3**
- **Jeremiah 15:16**
- **2 Corinthians 2:3**
- **Philippians 4:4**

Judgment / Wrath

God's response to disobedience and indifference is always mercy and patience, but finally holy anger. Judgment (and the older, more weighty word for anger, "wrath") is the other side of mercy, for in the end, God turns away from and repudiates sin. At the same time, God's judgment is the good news of forgiveness to all who trust and obey.

It is appointed for mortals to die once, and after that the judgment.
—Hebrews 9:27 NRSV

Here is Hollywood's stereotype of God—the potentate who brooks no transgression of His every whim, who devastates all opposition, who bellows His anger like an exploding volcano. If that were the Bible's portrait of God—full of bluster and intolerant of every small thing—then nothing else would matter. Hope, life, and love would be doomed. We cannot pacify an angry tyrant.

Fortunately, Hollywood's version of God is informed by too little study of the Bible and perhaps too much attention to preachers with an attitude.

Yet the Bible's God is no patsy. Judgment is a major Bible theme from beginning to end. When sin spoils Eden, God judges the sinners (Genesis 3:23–24). At the last day, God will judge sin and the devil (Revelation 20:7–10). Judgment cannot be avoided. The Bible claims for itself the high status of God's Word and warns that disregard and disobedience, all known to God, will result in divine anger (Romans 1:18) and expulsion from God's presence (Matthew 25:41).

God hath appointed a day, wherein he will judge the world by Jesus Christ, when every man shall receive according to his deed; the wicked shall go into everlasting punishment; the righteous, into everlasting life.
—*James Boyce*

Many questions of fairness surround these visions of judgment, but all such questions are subsumed under the Bible's assertion that God is right to judge. Humankind cannot blame God for lack of fairness (Romans 2:1–11). About the many "what ifs," the Bible affirms that divine love, mercy, and justice will sort out all the details (Psalm 96:10).

The common-sense version of divine judgment has God counting acts of greed, obsession, dishonesty, lust, etc. God appears like a moral accountant, adding up the bad and, with lines drawn by permanent markers, issuing judgment. When the Bible speaks of judgment, its focus is much more on relationships. Judgment is not the result of bad acts but a lost relationship. To the sinner, the Bible says: Do you believe God's Word and trust Jesus Christ as your Savior? Apart from that relationship, judgment awaits (2 Thessalonians 1:9). Is your claim to believe mere verbal posturing, without any hint of desire to live in faith? Mere words are not free tickets (Hebrews 10:26–27). But people who believe are, in biblical terms, "in Christ Jesus" (protected by His saving power); no condemnation faces them (Romans 8:1).

Always, mercy accompanies the warnings. Even the most severe warnings (such as those that describe God judging even the thoughts and attitudes of the heart, Hebrews 4:12) are followed immediately by assurance of help and sympathy (Hebrews 4:14–16).

An important side note: People are not to presume to step into God's prerogative and judge people themselves (Matthew 7:1). That common mistake is another Hollywood stereotype altogether, painfully real but not the Bible's way.

Additional scriptures

- **Exodus 12:12**
- **Deuteronomy 32:22**
- **2 Chronicles 12:7**
- **Psalm 38:1**
- **Psalm 76:8**   • **Isaiah 9:19**

Justice

J

Joy

Judgment/
Wrath

Justice

Justification

God is just. Justice is God's character. In the Bible, justice (the consequence fits the action) is wrapped and entangled in two other characteristics of God—righteousness (perfectly holy) and love (mercy is always greater than the action deserves).

For all have sinned and fall short of the glory of God, and are justified freely by his grace through the redemption that came by Christ Jesus. God presented him as a sacrifice of atonement, through faith in his blood. He did this to demonstrate his justice, because in his forbearance he had left the sins committed beforehand unpunished—he did it to demonstrate his justice at the present time, so as to be just and the one who justifies those who have faith in Jesus. —**Romans 3:23–26**

In liberal democratic governance, justice is accountability to clearly defined law. To convict a criminal, a just legal system must prove action and malevolence (that the criminal knew his or her actions to be wrong). In a perfect system, all people who violate the law are given equal treatment and consequence. Most people who have experience in courts of law know it to be a rule-driven, impersonal process. Biblical justice is much different.

In the Bible, justice emanates from God, who is total love and righteousness, stupendously generous, and without a hint of character flaw. God's justice permeates creation and motivates the redemption of all that God loves, especially humans, the pinnacle of God's creation. In the New Testament, Paul describes justice as identical to righteousness and permeated by love. God's justice is always alongside of and embedded in God's love.

The just God expects His beloved to be just. God commands that people live rightly and justly (Genesis 18:19), which is to say, obediently, following God's will as expressed in God's law. To accomplish that with perfection is impossible, for two reasons. First, moral perfection is found nowhere on earth; and second, since Adam's sin in Eden, the fallen world is incapable of righteousness. Following the fall (the first sin), the rest of history is set for a just judgment that must be condemnation: no chance for parole.

Now the Bible announces a dimension of justice nearly unthinkable: the just outcome of sin will be replaced by a gift. Those who cannot survive the just judgment (that's everyone, unless you are perfect) are offered a righteousness they could never earn. It is earned by God Himself, in Jesus Christ (Romans 8:10). That gift is accepted by faith (the forgiven believe the gospel). Then the gift of righteousness—lovingly granted—will motivate expressions of justice and righteousness in the lives of the faith-full.

> **There is no virtue** so truly great and godlike as justice. —*Joseph Addison*

The Bible's account is stunning. Justice is required in God's world. The offense of sin brings death (Romans 6:23). But God intervenes, at immense cost. Christ carries God's judgment to the Cross, obedient to the Father's will. Then love grants justice anew to all who will receive it. The inescapable condemnation is negated through a gift. Life is renewed (Romans 8:1). Justice is served.

Additional scriptures

- **Leviticus 19:15**
- **Psalm 11:7**
- **Psalm 89:14**
- **Psalm 140:12**
- **Proverbs 29:4**
- **Micah 6:8**

Justification

One of the most important themes of the Bible, justification is nearly self-explanatory. It means "being put right" and refers to the work of God, who "puts right" sinful humanity. This happens because God's holy justice is satisfied by the sacrifice of Jesus Christ.

Yet we know that a person is justified not by the works of the law but through faith in Jesus Christ. And we have come to believe in Christ Jesus, so that we might be justified by faith in Christ, and not by doing the works of the law, because no one will be justified by the works of the law. —Galatians 2:16 NRSV

Justification is a term of the courthouse as well as the synagogue and church. A case brought against an accused criminal must be proven with solid evidence and reasoned arguments—justified to the satisfaction of the jury, or in biblical terms, the elders or judge. In the Bible's presentation of humankind's dilemma, the accusation is sin, and the solution is judgment. The accused (all who sin, that's everyone so far, minus one) have no credible excuse or defense. No argument or evidence can lift the verdict. The accused stand guilty as charged.

Then, just as the gavel is about to go down, an advocate steps forward, answers the charges completely, and demands that the accused go free. This is the gospel, and justification lifts the penalty. The accused is acquitted, given new life.

The prophet Zechariah (in Zechariah 3:1–5) illustrates justification with a courtroom scene where Satan is the prosecuting attorney who has all the evidence on his side. The man in the hot seat is high priest Joshua, and Satan has every reason to bring a solid case against him. About Joshua's failure and folly there can be no doubt. His shabby, dirty clothing illustrate his guilt. Then suddenly something amazing happens. The offended party shows up. "Get him out of those rags," he orders. "Dress him with clean clothes. Drop his charges, set him free." The prosecutor Satan, evidence at the ready, is left holding a loaded briefcase and empty handcuffs, so to speak.

Zechariah's vision is described with forensic precision in the New Testament. The accused are sinful humanity. The advocate who appears to counter the court's charges is Jesus Christ. He

The means by which we are justified is faith. Faith is like a channel through which the benefits of Christ flow to us. We are not justified on account of faith; we are justified through faith. It is the work of Christ, not our faith, which is the foundation of justification. Faith itself is a gift of God. —*Alister McGrath*

alone has authority to "put right" the accused, nullify the sentence, and close the case. We are "put right" with God through Jesus, who bears our sins Himself. We accept our reprieve by faith in Him.

Justification is like a heaven's court declaration, with a standing order to do something about it. Justification has a purpose: new life committed to God (James 2:24). We are saved by Jesus' wounds but are obliged to live for righteousness—to make good on life's new lease. Justification is all gift, God's gift (Romans 3:24)—but like Joshua, those newly dressed and forgiven are called to service, word and deed, telling and serving (Romans 6:1–4).

Additional scriptures

- **Romans 3:24–26**
- **Romans 4:25**
- **Romans 5:1**
- **Romans 8:30**
- **Galatians 3:11, 24**
- **Titus 3:4–7**

Kingdom of God

God reigns, but where is that reign manifest? God rules, but how is that rule enforced? Not through armies or legislations, but spiritually, through the victory of love over hate, good over evil, life over death. God's kingdom is the sphere in which God's rule and reign is recognized and properly respected.

After John was put in prison, Jesus went into Galilee, proclaiming the good news of God. "The time has come," he said. "The kingdom of God is near. Repent and believe the good news!" —Mark 1:14–15

The Lord's Prayer, known worldwide, begins with this petition (following the address): "Thy Kingdom come" (Luke 11:2 KJV). Jesus, who taught the prayer, announced as His major theme that God's kingdom was near, indeed, that it had come in His own person. This kingdom was not a temporal power or anything similar to secular politics; instead, it is the rule and reign of God over all other claimants to sovereignty, and most especially over evil, represented as Satan, death, or the arrogant claims of some to divine status (for example, the Roman emperors).

This was a development few expected. Old Testament references

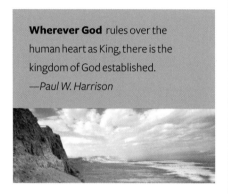

> **Wherever God** rules over the human heart as King, there is the kingdom of God established.
> —Paul W. Harrison

to the kingdom of God anticipate the establishment of Zion as the center of worship, a great assembling of people coming to God's throne (see Obadiah). Jesus taught that the kingdom (reign and rule, not place or bounded territory) had come in His person, and that a radical response of faith was needed to see it and experience it, to know its mystery. The faith Jesus asked His followers to adopt is explained in the Sermon on the Mount (Matthew 5–7) which begins with nine statements of "blessedness," called Beatitudes. Who are the blessed of this kingdom? Not the powerful or rich, but those whose "spirits" (sense of self, personal power) are weak and whose emotions are frayed and fragile; not warriors but peacemakers; not champions but the ones who feel tramped in every sense— yet who cling to the vision and hope of God's mercy and justice. This is a kingdom that may not look like one, except to people with eyes to see.

The kingdom is both now and not yet, present and future, much as Jesus taught in the parables. A mustard seed is so small that most eyes will not see it, but the tree it produces is big enough to give shade (Mark 4:30–32). A pinch of yeast penetrates the entire lump of dough (Matthew 13:33)—something so small affects everything. God has established His kingdom in the coming of Jesus. Yet God's reign must work itself out through the life and death of Jesus, the disciples, and the church— until the Last Day. All who align with this kingdom, despite its appearance of economic and political weakness, will discover that it is like a "pearl of great price," worth everything, totally joyful to find, totally available to be possessed (Matthew 13:45–46 NKJV).

At the end of time, the book of Revelation pictures an angel and voices from heaven shouting that the kingdom of God has indeed come, in splendid fulfillment of all God's promises to preserve, save, and renew (Revelation 11:15).

Additional scriptures

- Mark 4:26–29
- Mark 10:14–15
- Luke 6:20
- Luke 8:1

Lamb of God

As a reference to Jesus, Lamb of God connotes the sacrifice for human sin accomplished in Jesus' death. The phrase links Jesus to Isaiah's description of the Suffering Servant, suggesting that the Messiah who will save His people not through political leadership but through something closer to the Old Testament's use of lambs for sacrifice.

The next day John saw Jesus coming toward him and said, "Look, the Lamb of God, who takes away the sin of the world!" —John 1:29

Only from the mouth of John the Baptist is the phrase "Lamb of God" found in the Bible. John identified Jesus as Lamb of God at His baptism and then the day after (John 1:36). What did John the Baptist mean by it?

In the Old Testament, lambs were sacrificed daily in the temple (Leviticus 3:6–7). The animal was to be without defect. The rite illustrated one of the

Bible's deep mysteries: The removal of moral blame and guilt required blood. Someone or something must die in place of the person, the actual sinner—in the Old Testament system, a lamb or other animal died.

Another more probable link to John's declaration is the Passover, celebrated in remembrance of the exodus from Egypt. God had instructed all the Hebrews to "take a lamb" (Exodus 12:3), kill it, and sprinkle its blood on the doorframes of each home to save the family living there from the last plague. For John to identify Jesus as the Lamb of God became, then, a bold, audacious claim that was sure to upset, indeed redefine, the religion of Israel. This rabbi named Jesus, John's cousin, was the equivalent of the Passover lamb, the Savior of Israel.

Other Old Testament sources also provide links between Jesus and the "Lamb of God." In Isaiah 53:7 the prophet describes a character who has come to be known as the Suffering Servant. Could Isaiah be speaking about Jesus? Only by the faintest threads of prophecy; yet who else fits this description? Jesus alone bore the sins of the world centuries later. Isaiah's "servant" fits Jesus very well. In any case, this chapter in Isaiah is often cited as a glimpse into the nature of the Christ.

In Genesis 22, a lamb is discovered to take Isaac's place on the altar: "God himself will provide the lamb" (v. 8), Abraham explained to his young son in a remarkable act of faith and obedience.

Revelation 5:6 uses a lamb to picture the victorious Christ. About Him the heavenly chorus sings: "Worthy is the Lamb, who was slain" (Revelation 5:12).

Because the Passover was the preeminent Jewish celebration, we are safe

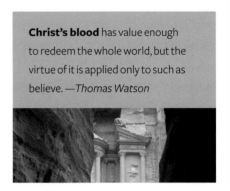

> **Christ's blood** has value enough to redeem the whole world, but the virtue of it is applied only to such as believe. —*Thomas Watson*

to conclude that it was in John the Baptist's mind as he spoke of Jesus. But the full Bible picture of the sacrificial lamb provides a portrait of Jesus as obedient, submissive to the will of the Father, and substitute for the sins of everyone, the last sacrifice. After Jesus, no more blood is required to remove sin. All who believe are covered in His.

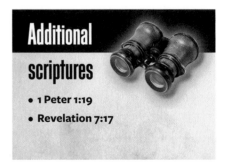

Additional scriptures

- **1 Peter 1:19**
- **Revelation 7:17**

Love

The preeminent attitude of God toward all of creation. The right attitude of all people toward God and others.

And I pray that you, being rooted and established in love, may have power, together with all the saints, to grasp how wide and long and high and deep is the love of Christ, and to know this love that surpasses knowledge—that you may be filled to the measure of all the fullness of God. —**Ephesians 3:17–19**

Love is the center of the Bible's message. "For God so loved" is the well-known start of the Bible's well most well-known verse (John 3:16). Nothing good happens in the Bible without love driving it. All the trouble the Bible reports springs from lack of love.

Love in the Bible is both declaration and obligation, totally transforming the point and purpose of life. The

Bible declares that God is love (1 John 4:16). The heart of the universe is not a cold expanse of gas, of which earth is a speck. Rather, love created the heavens and the earth, and love moves the story of creation toward its climax, when finally love is fully manifest in the glory of God revealed everywhere. The Bible declares this. If you look for love ("Where is God? Why doesn't he love me?"), look at Jesus Christ. In Him, the love of God appeared (Titus 3:4).

The Bible uses two words to express most love references. *Agape* is other-centered concern, the love of a mother for a child, God for sinners. It is sacrificial, the needs of the other before one's own. *Phileo* is brotherly love, kindness, sharing, and affection. *Agape* leans toward love not earned but lavishly given. *Phileo* leans toward the love of close friends. Both convey the key attitude which leads to a happy life.

The Bible urges people to express both *agape* and *phileo*. This urging hardly needs explanation. It's right and natural to love. It's God-given to love. It's pitiable when a person's soul has shriveled to the "bah humbug" level of relationships, or worse, to exploitation and greed. When Jesus was called upon to explain His understanding of the Torah (Old Testament teachings), He summarized all of it—centuries of tradition and complexity—with two commands: love God, and love each other as you do yourself (Matthew 22:37–39). To love God and others fulfills the intentions and purposes of every part of God's law. To love is to obey God and imitate God.

Paul wrote the Bible's great love poem in 1 Corinthians 13. Love is patient and kind. Love is full of hope because it fully trusts the loved one. Love's value exceeds money, martyrdom, even faith. Great words from great minds are hollow without love. Love persists when all else fails. Among all that we treasure, love is supreme.

And love is God's supreme attitude, so much that God sacrificed the Son to achieve love's purpose (John 3:16). All the difficulties of life are overcome in love (Romans 8:28). None of the obstacles to a good life can match love's power (Romans 8:37). Love is our inseparable bond with God and, through that love, to each other for timeless eternity (Romans 8:38–39).

Additional scriptures

- **Psalm 36:5**
- **Luke 11:42**
- **1 John 3:16–18**

Marriage

The union of man and woman in lifelong partnership.

[Jesus] answered, "Have you not read that he who made them from the beginning made them male and female, and said, 'For this reason a man shall leave his father and mother and be joined to his wife, and the two shall become one flesh'? So they are no longer two but one flesh. What therefore God has joined together, let not man put asunder."
—Matthew 19:4–6 RSV

Marriage of man and woman—a faithful, lifelong, sexually monogamous partnership—is woven into the creation (Genesis 1–2) and never questioned thereafter in the Bible. Jesus affirmed the sanctity of marriage, and Paul elaborated on how marriage should work but never doubted that persons, created male and female, should marry. God's plan is that intimate relationships should be the source of comfort, joy, companionship, and lifelong personal growth. So clear was this to Paul that he used marriage as analogy for the relationship of God to His followers, and vice versa (Ephesians 5:23–24). Certain conditions might advise against marriage—for example, incapacity for intercourse (Matthew 19:12), or times of

crisis or distress (1 Corinthians 7:26)—but these should be exceptional circumstances and not rules that govern specific cases. Paul did not advise that church leaders refrain from marrying (1 Timothy 3:2), though he himself was unmarried.

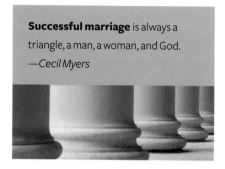

Successful marriage is always a triangle, a man, a woman, and God.
—Cecil Myers

The Bible's treatment of husbands and wives, their roles and responsibilities, their status within marriage, the availability of divorce, and the possibility of same-sex marriages are all modern questions but, remarkably, not so modern after all. The ancient cultures in which the Bible was written knew all of these issues. The Bible's consistent teaching, from Old to New Testament, is that marriage is inviolable and permanent, a partnership of equals before God, identified before God as "one flesh" and intimate to the point that each partner's body belongs to the other (1 Corinthians 7:3–4). While Paul calls the husband the head of his wife (1 Corinthians 11:3), he clearly places that position within the context of mutual submission and care (Ephesians 5:25–33). To be head is to act toward a wife with the same love Christ enacted for us. To submit is to reflect the same obedience that Christ demonstrated to God.

Divorce is barely conceived in the Bible (contrary to its surrounding cultures) because marriage is God bringing two people together in lifelong love. Yet divorce happens; and while it is discouraging, allowances are made (Mark 10:2–5, 1 Corinthians 7:11). Adultery is forbidden, as is incest (Exodus 20:14; 1 Corinthians 5:1). Ancient cultures took a more lax view of all three situations. The Bible calls men and women to faithful, loving, and durable marriages as a pattern for lifetime happiness and as an expression of God's gifts of love, joy, and close relationship.

Great marriages in the Bible were not without their stress and points of humor. Often, Bible marriages do not fit "perfect form"—life takes its odd turns. But Jesus' answer still stands, "What therefore God has joined together, let not man put asunder" (Matthew 19:6 RSV).

Additional scriptures

- **Genesis 2:24**
- **Nehemiah 13:25–26**
- **Jeremiah 29:6**
- **Matthew 22:30**
- **Hebrews 13:4**
- **2 Corinthians 6:14**

Mediator

M

Marriage
Mediator
Mercy
Messiah
Millennium
Mystery

God is holy, humans are sinful. Yet the holy God loves these sinners, whom He does not approach directly. God uses go-betweens to communicate His will. Jesus is the supreme mediator of God's will and purpose for humankind.

For this reason he is the mediator of a new covenant, so that those who are called may receive the promised eternal inheritance, because a death has occurred that redeems them from the transgressions under the first covenant. —**Hebrews 9:15** NRSV

Christ's work as Mediator was unique: it was to restore us to divine favor and to make us sons of God, instead of sons of men; heirs of a heavenly kingdom instead of heirs of hell. —*John Calvin*

Of the many ways Jesus is described in the Bible, Jesus as Mediator comes closer than any to the mystery of His dual nature, human and divine. Three times in the book of Hebrews, Jesus is called the Mediator of the new covenant. As Mediator, Jesus both communicates God's will and character and fulfills God's loving intention to save people from the consequences of their sin. Jesus mediates the gift of eternal life, as High Priest of the New Covenant (of forgiveness of sins as the free gift of God).

The Old Testament is the story of a covenant people, the Hebrews, whom God chose to represent His presence and will to the world. At several key points, God made a covenant (a series of promises) to bless certain persons or people, to make them prosper despite the external difficulties of the natural world, and to show them the truth about their needs and responsibilities. God chose Abraham and made a covenant with him. Later, God gave the Hebrews a covenant through Moses, namely the Ten Commandments and associated laws. As the New Testament era dawned and the Christian church began, Bible writers explained how one promise from God (the older covenant) was replaced by another. That is, how the system of blood sacrifice associated with Old Testament worship was replaced by forgiveness of sin through faith in Jesus Christ, the final sacrifice for all sin.

The New Testament explains this change by comparing and contrasting the mediators who announced the Old and New Covenants. In 2 Corinthians 3:7–18, Moses and Jesus are contrasted. When Moses delivered God's law to the Hebrew people at Sinai, Paul wrote, his face was veiled to prevent the people from seeing the glory of God and its fading luminosity (Exodus 34:29–35). The content of the covenant which

Moses delivered was the Law (Ten Commandments and associated laws). Its central problem was human inability to perfectly obey. Jesus mediates a new covenant based on faith in His sacrificial death. Salvation is revealed as a gift of God freely given to all who believe. The New Testament interprets all previous mediators (prophets, priests, etc.) as affirming this view.

Paul's first letter to Timothy explains further that Jesus alone successfully mediates between God and humankind because He alone is both human and divine (1 Timothy 2:5). None other can mediate the sin problem—not angels (Colossians 2:18) and not Moses, for Moses' mediation was temporary, superseded by Christ (Hebrews 3:3).

All people today are invited, indeed urged, to know and serve God through faith in the great Mediator, Jesus Christ.

Additional scriptures

- **Job 33:23**
- **Galatians 3:20–22**
- **Hebrews 8:6**
- **Hebrews 12:24**

Mercy

This virtue describes God's character as well as any other mentioned in the Bible. Mercy is linked to love, grace, and compassion throughout the Bible as the core and heart of divine character and will. Mercy is the virtue of assessing a just solution, then relieving the loved one of the burden of justice, and taking that burden upon oneself.

But God, who is rich in mercy, out of the great love with which he loved us . . .made us alive together with Christ. —**Ephesians 2:4–5** NRSV

Mercy sounds good, but in a tight economy, or any tight situation, why be merciful? Mercy is one of those attitudes that reduces penalties, shares scarce resources, or simply feels for the plight of another. It rarely accomplishes anything for the Self. It is, by definition, a denial of self-interest and a heightened regard for another.

This should hint at mercy's origin, point, and purpose. Mercy celebrates mutuality. It is beneficent, generous, even sacrificial action directed to another. It must arise as a gesture of Other-care that can only be explained as compassion. The Bible describes God as radiant with these attitudes, abundant in mercy, immensely caring for the other. Who is that other? It is humankind first, the summit of God's good creation.

Bible people show mercy, and are urged to do so. The friendship of David and Jonathan was generous with expressed compassion (1 Samuel 20). The church at Philippi sent help to Paul at one point (Philippians 4:16). Jesus' parables urge the show of mercy, even to the extent that a king might forgive the debt of a slave (Matthew 18:27).

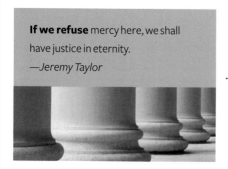

> **If we refuse** mercy here, we shall have justice in eternity.
> —*Jeremy Taylor*

Paul explores God's mercy in several ways. As a backdrop to salvation, mercy is costly and plentiful. As reasons for praise, the mercy and compassion of God rank high (2 Corinthians 1:3). Paul was all too aware of the mercy God showed to him personally, saving him despite his persecution of the Christian church (1 Timothy 1:12–16). Paul was especially intrigued with the situation within Judaism, for the Messiah had been rejected, indeed crucified, and many Jews had not adopted Christian faith as Paul had. Was God's mercy broad and deep enough to cover this widespread Jewish refusal? Romans 9–11 is Paul's definitive answer, indeed yes. Paul explained that mercy will finally lead Jews to salvation (Romans 11:25–32).

Mercy is incentive to service. A person shown mercy by God has motivation to be loyal to the giver (Romans 12:1); mercy makes faith complete by eliminating forever the barrier sin poses to a relationship with God (James 2:13); it will restore all that suffering has taken away (1 Peter 1:3–9).

Bible readers may be amused at a biological footnote associated with mercy. Mercy arises, the Bible says, from the bowels, the entrails, the ancient seat of emotion. Today we would locate mercy in the heart, which would doubtless be just as amusing to first-century people. Considering the dearth of mercy in so many human institutions today, one should follow the Bible's recommendation to show mercy (Micah 6:8) using whatever organ it comes from.

Additional scriptures

- **Exodus 33:19**
- **1 Chronicles 21:13**
- **Matthew 5:7**
- **Luke 1:50**

Messiah

M

Marriage
Mediator
Mercy
Messiah
Millennium
Mystery

The ancient Jewish hope was a leader with the stature of King David and the insight of a prophet who would lead the Jews into an era of freedom and prosperity. Jesus is the Messiah, but His was a messianic career that almost no one expected.

The woman said to him, "I know that Messiah is coming" (who is called Christ). "When he comes, he will proclaim all things to us." Jesus said to her, "I am he, the one who is speaking to you." —John 4:25–26 NRSV

The episode in John 4 points to the difficulty of identifying the Messiah, or even what sort of leader the Messiah should be. Various expectations attend to the Messiah throughout the Old Testament. The Messiah (God's "Anointed One") would be like King David, able to fight for Jewish national interests (Psalm 2:2–8). Or maybe like a prophet bearing a new message from God to the people (Malachi 3:1). The portraits of Messiah were varied; His task was multidimensional. Perhaps because popular expectations were so high, the Messiah came to be seen as the solution to all that troubled Israel: national identity, security, and prosperity.

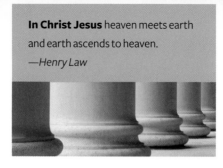

> **In Christ Jesus** heaven meets earth and earth ascends to heaven.
> —*Henry Law*

When Jesus began His public ministry, He would establish His identity as the Messiah, the person to whom the Old Testament pointed. Jesus identified Himself as Messiah to a variety of people, sometimes provoking an intense negative reaction.

The New Testament describes seven occasions when Jesus either accepted someone else's claim—or made the claim Himself—that He was God's Messiah, the Christ. Peter confessed Jesus to be the Christ at Caesarea Philippi, and Jesus affirmed His pronouncement (Matthew 16:13–20). The Pharisees (Jewish leaders) urged Jesus to rebuke His disciples for their messianic claims. Instead, Jesus rebuked the Pharisees, allowing crowds to acclaim Him king (Luke 19:38–40). When Jewish leaders questioned Jesus concerning His identity as the Christ, He agreed with that assessment (Matthew 26:62–64). When Pilate probed Jesus at His trial, Jesus again agreed (Matthew 27:11). In John 4:26, Jesus disclosed His messianic identity to the Samaritan woman and, in John 9:37, to the man born blind, who believed and was promptly excommunicated from the synagogue for his alleged blasphemy. Martha confessed Jesus' messianic identity in John 11:27. John recorded no particular response on the part of Jesus, but their continued dialogue is tacit acceptance.

Early in the book of Acts, Peter preached that Jesus was Lord and Christ (Acts 2:38). Paul's writings are essentially the presentation of a universal Messiah who has brought salvation to all who believe and will return to complete the renewal and transformation of God's creation (Philippians 3:20). In Revelation 1:8, the coming One is the Lord God, the Almighty. Christian faith everywhere confesses that the Messiah is Jesus, the Christ. He is God's anointed one, the Savior of all.

What happened to Old Testament expectations? They are transformed into a new vision of the kingdom of God, not located in and around Jerusalem and not in association with temple worship. The kingdom Jesus brought is the spiritual community of God's family, gathered around the Christ in faith and allegiance, ready for His return at the last day.

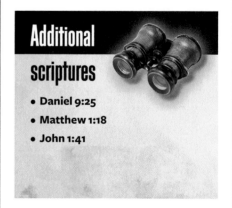

Additional scriptures

- **Daniel 9:25**
- **Matthew 1:18**
- **John 1:41**

Millennium

M

Marriage
Mediator
Mercy
Messiah
Millennium
Mystery

The thousand-year period described in Revelation 20 featuring the binding of Satan and the reign of Jesus.

He seized the dragon, that ancient serpent, who is the Devil and Satan, and bound him for a thousand years, and threw him into the pit, and locked and sealed it over him, so that he would deceive the nations no more, until the thousand years were ended. After that he must be let out for a little while. —**Revelation 20:2–3** NRSV

While the word "Millennium" does not explicitly appear in the Bible, this concept comes directly from Revelation 20. This passage describes a thousand-year period in which Satan is bound and unable to deceive the nations (vv. 2–3) and Jesus rules with the saints (vv. 4–5). This period also features the resurrection of martyrs, with a second resurrection occurring after the thousand years (v. 5). The release of Satan from his prison ends this thousand-year period of peace, as he then leads the nations in a final, unsuccessful rebellion against God. After this defeat, God casts Satan into hell, where he will face everlasting punishment (vv. 7–10), and the final judgment of all people occurs (vv. 11–15).

The apocalyptic genre of the book of Revelation and its abundant use of figurative language make it difficult for theologians to understand the exact meaning of the description of this period. Numbers often have a symbolic value in works like Revelation, so the thousand years might be a symbol of an ideal, extended period of time or an exact number of years. The reference to resurrection might be a physical resurrection or could be the spiritual idea of being born again (John 3:3). The reign of Jesus might refer to His rule from heaven after His ascension or a throne on earth in the future. The binding of Satan could express that he is limited and not able to stop the gospel message from spreading (Luke 10:17–20) or that no evil is occurring on earth. Finally, Revelation 19–20 could describe two different events or could be two descriptions of the same event.

These different possibilities have led to three major views about the Millennium. Some theologians see the Millennium as occurring after Jesus' return to earth (Premillennialism, as Jesus returns *before* the Millennium). This position understands the Millennium as Jesus' rule on earth for a thousand years, with a final rebellion happening at the end of this era. Others see the Millennium happening before

My eyes have seen the glory of the coming of the Lord. He is trampling out the vintage where the grapes of wrath are stored. He has loosed his fateful lightning from his terrible swift sword. Our God is marching on. Glory, Glory, Hallelujah—his truth is marching on! —*The Battle Hymn of the Republic*

Jesus returns (Postmillennialism, Jesus returns *after* the Millennium). This perspective sees the church as ushering in the millennial kingdom and Jesus returning to stop the rebellion at the end of this period. A third view does not see the Millennium as a physical kingdom in the future but the current spiritual kingdom of Jesus (often called Amillennialism, literally "no-Millennium"). According to this position, the description of the Millennium shows that Satan presently cannot deceive the nations because people from all nations will believe the gospel, and evil will rise at the end of time.

Each view has its strengths and weaknesses, and various theologians throughout church history have held to each view. A diversity of opinion on this subject probably will remain until Jesus returns, at which point we will see which view (if any!) is correct.

The concept of the Millennium is not just something for theologians to debate; it should encourage Christians today. It gives Christians hope that Christ will be victorious in the midst of the evil in this world; Satan's work has a limit and an end. In addition, one sees that salvation is not just something that happens to individuals but to the whole world order. Christians can also learn from the diversity of views on this issue, as Christians can have different views on certain issues that are secondary, not central, to the gospel message. Finally, the lack of clarity among theologians reminds Christians that some things will remain a mystery until the very end; only God knows all things. No matter which millennial view we may hold, we look forward to the fact that Jesus will return and will make all things right.

Additional scriptures

- **Psalm 90:4**
- **2 Thessalonians 2:8**
- **Revelation 20:1–8**

Mystery

The plans and purposes of God that were hidden in the past but now revealed to the saints in the gospel of Jesus Christ.

I have become its servant by the commission God gave me to present to you the word of God in its fullness— the mystery that has been kept hidden for ages and generations, but is now disclosed to the saints. —**Colossians 1:25–26**

God is far above human comprehension; the finite, human mind could never ever grasp the infinite God, and by extension, His plans for the world. Therefore, God and His plans are said to be "mysterious." In the New Testament, however, the idea of mystery is not something that humans *do not understand* but something beyond human comprehension that God *has revealed* to His people. The mysteries of God remained hidden in the past but are now revealed, as Jesus spoke of revealing mysteries to His disciples (Matthew 13:11). The apostle Paul often discussed these mysteries, helping us understand why God reveals them and their content.

To the apostles God has revealed truths that humans cannot fully understand so that they would proclaim these mysteries to the world and help people know God. These truths have been secrets in the past because the world could not understand them in its own wisdom. In fact, this lack of understanding of God's ways led the authorities to crucify Jesus, rejecting God's plan (1 Corinthians 2:8). Since the world cannot understand these truths, they had to be revealed by God to humanity. And He was pleased to give them to the apostles and prophets through the Spirit (Ephesians 1:9–11; 3:5). This revelation occurred so that Gentiles might come to faith (Romans 16:25–26); God revealed His mysteries so that He might have a relationship with people of all nations. That's why ministers of the gospel are called "stewards of the mysteries of God" (1 Corinthians 4:1 NASB) and why Paul asked for prayer to help him proclaim the mysteries of the gospel (Ephesians 6:19; Colossians 4:3).

These mysteries feature both present and future ramifications. In

Ephesians, Paul wrote that the full inclusion of the Gentiles into the people of God is the mystery of Christ (Ephesians 3:4–6). In the Old Testament, God worked through the nation of Israel, but now God invites people from all nations and ethnic groups to be His people in Christ (Galatians 3:26–28). In Colossians, Paul added that his proclamation to the Gentiles included the mystery of "Christ in you, the hope of glory" (Colossians 1:27). The indwelling of Christ gives believers assurance of their salvation because they know that just as Jesus rose from the dead, so God will raise also them.

A mystery that still lies in the future is the transformation of the bodies of believers who have died and those alive at the return of Jesus (1 Corinthians 15:51–56); Christians will receive glorified bodies. Another mystery is God's plan with Israel. Though it might seem as though God has rejected the people of Israel, He has not. They have hardened their hearts and rejected Him temporarily so that Gentiles can also come to God through faith. The end of time will feature the inclusion of many Jews back into the people of God (Romans 11:25–36).

The simple, absolute and immutable mysteries of the divine Truth are hidden in secret. For this darkness, though of deepest obscurity, is yet radiantly clear; and, though beyond touch and sight, it more than fills our unseeing minds with splendors of transcendent beauty. And we behold that darkness beyond being, concealed under all natural light.
—*Dionysius the Areopagite*

The understanding of mystery in the New Testament is much different from the way that other religions in the first century used the term "mystery." In other religions, people were supposed to stay quiet about the mysteries their religions revealed; these were to remain secrets to the privileged. In the gospel, however, God calls Christians to share these mysteries with the world; He has revealed them so that our hearts might feel them and our mouths might proclaim them. Christians should ponder the unity of Jew and Gentile in the church and the presence of Christ in them, while looking forward to the transformation of their bodies and the complete gathering of God's people from the Jews and Gentiles. While waiting for that day to arrive, though, Christians pray for boldness to proclaim these truths.

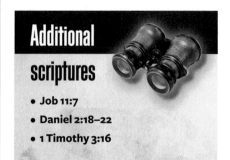

Additional scriptures

- **Job 11:7**
- **Daniel 2:18–22**
- **1 Timothy 3:16**

New Creation / New Heaven and New Earth / New Jerusalem

God's renewal of the cosmos at the end of time so that He might dwell with His people in complete and perfect fellowship.

Then I saw a new heaven and a new earth, for the first heaven and the first earth had passed away, and there was no longer any sea.
—Revelation 21:1

The bookends of the Bible are similar descriptions of God creating heaven and earth and living in relationship with humans in these places. The Garden of Eden in Genesis 1 and 2 and the New Jerusalem in Revelation 21 and 22 both feature rivers and the tree of life (Genesis 2:9–10; Revelation 22:1–2). Humans enjoyed a special relationship with God in the Garden. The fall caused humans to leave Eden, however, with the Bible showing how God restores His relationship with them. But the New Jerusalem of Revelation 21 is not just a restoration of Eden; it surpasses Eden in that God lives with His people (Revelation 21:2–3). Heaven and earth meet in the New Jerusalem as the dwelling place of God (heaven) and the dwelling place of humans (earth) intersect.

Since a new earth will be formed, we might wonder what will happen to the current earth. The statement that the current heavens and earth will pass

away (2 Peter 3:10; Revelation 21:1) does not appear to mean that they will be annihilated. Paul's words in Romans 8:19–21 point to a renewal; the new earth is the old earth "set free." God called the earth "good," He probably would not destroy it. Since believers will live in their resurrection bodies, which will be like Jesus' resurrected body and have similarities and differences with

their earthly bodies, we can view the new earth as a glorification of the old. The current world is not a temporary illusion we should despise, therefore, but a sneak preview of the future earth, knowing that the new earth will be much better than the current.

The picture of life on the new earth is amazing. While the description of precious jewels and a street of gold points to its tremendous beauty, the more incredible truth is that humans will dwell with God and live in worship of Him. The whole city is the temple, and God is the only light needed. It will include the believers of all times, as shown by the names of the 12 tribes of Israel and the 12 apostles being etched on the gates and walls. These saints will come from all nations, and kings will bow down and give their glory to God. This new earth will have no weeping, death, night, or darkness. Instead of the burdensome labor and conflict with nature caused by the fall, the new earth will feature fruitful labor and peace in creation. Sin and sinners, however, will be excluded. Life will be so splendid that no one will even remember the old creation (see Revelation 21–22 along with Isaiah 65–66)!

The promise of the new heaven and new earth should spark faithful and holy living. The purpose of John's description of it in the book of Revelation was to remind the persecuted churches in Asia Minor to remain faithful because God had great promises in store for them—and for us! Peter reminds his readers to live holy lives in light of the fact that a new world will replace the present (2 Peter 3:10–13). This does not mean that Christians should treat this earth with disrespect or disdain. Instead, it compels Christian to seek to bring the character of the new earth to the present earth as they wait for the transformation of the world by God. The Bible does not end with Christians going to heaven but heaven coming to earth. Christians seek to model the heavenly kingdom now as they live on earth since they are already part of the new creation (2 Corinthians 5:17).

Additional scriptures

- **Luke 21:32**
- **1 John 2:17**
- **Revelation 3:12**

Obedience

Joyfully following God's commands out of thankfulness for Christ's obedience to God's law on our behalf.

This is love for God: to obey his commands. And his commands are not burdensome. —1 John 5:3

God created humans to have a relationship with Him; and if Adam and Eve had obeyed God in the Garden of Eden, they would have been righteous and had a perfect relationship with Him forever. Unfortunately, Adam and Eve did not obey God, bringing sin and death into the world, so that no one can truly obey God and be righteous before Him. This righteousness, however, is again possible because of Jesus Christ.

Jesus Christ came to obey God perfectly and bestow this obedience on those who believe. As God Himself, whom the demons and forces of nature obey, Jesus perfectly fulfilled the Father's will (John 4:34), including suffering and dying on the cross. All who place their faith in Christ receive credit for His obedience; Jesus' death pays the punishment for sin and His obedient life brings the righteousness that God demands. Now, the obedience that God requires is to put faith in Jesus Christ (Romans 10:9–10); the ultimate act of disobedience is rejecting the gospel (2

Thessalonians 1:8).

Christians respond to the gift of righteousness with the "obedience that comes from faith" (Romans 1:5). This obedience is a response to God's saving work through faith. Christians obey God from the heart through the power of the Holy Spirit because they love Him. This does not mean that Christians obey God perfectly but that obedience will be a part of their lives.

Part of obeying the commandments of God involves obeying authorities and structures in place in the world. This includes obedience to parents (Ephesians 6:1), employers (Ephesians 6:5), church leaders (Hebrews 13:17), and civic rulers (1 Peter 2:13–17). God views disobedience to these figures as serious offenses (Romans 13:1–2). But when governmental authorities require *disobedience* to God's commands, believers are required to obey God rather than people (Acts 5:29).

Obedience to God has never been able to make a person righteous before God. Since God gave Israel the law *after* He led them out of Egypt, they did not need to keep God's laws in order to be delivered by Him; but God did call them to reflect Him to the pagan world. Their disobedience led to them not enjoying the benefits of their covenantal relationship with God, and they were

Let the ground of all religious actions be obedience; examine not why it is commanded, but observe it because it is commanded. True obedience neither procrastinates nor questions. —*Francis Quarles*

disciplined (just as Christians are) for disobedience (Hebrews 12:7). Christians obey God, therefore, not to earn salvation, but to enjoy the world as God designed it and to reveal the character of God to the world. But just as many Jews in the Old Testament misconstrued obedience as the basis for their salvation, Christians must also be aware of this danger.

At the root of the biblical words for obedience is the word "listen"; obedience is what it truly means to listen to the word of God. This includes hearing the will of God, seeking to understand it, remembering it, and then doing what it says in applicable life situations. Christians do this not to become righteous but *because* they are righteous through Christ; obeying God is something that we do joyfully as an act of worship to the God who saves us by faith through the perfect obedience of Jesus.

Additional scriptures

- **Judges 2:17**
- **John 15:9–11**
- **Romans 5:19**
- **Romans 6:16**

Ordain

The formal setting apart of a person for a specific ministry and service of the church.

While they were worshiping the Lord and fasting, the Holy Spirit said, "Set apart for me Barnabas and Saul for the work to which I have called them." —Acts 13:2

Throughout the Bible, God uses some people in special roles to bring His grace to the world; the people themselves are not special but their ministry. Since the community of faith formally recognizes the roles of the people, they have been ordained for this service.

In the Old Testament, ordination happened for priests. God called priests from the sons of Aaron to serve the people by offering sacrifices and representing them before God. This included a ceremony recognizing this role and service (Exodus 28–29). Since Jesus Christ is our High Priest, and His sacrifice on the cross is the final sacrifice, the New Testament church did not ordain priests. Though prophets received a special call and mission from God, it does not appear that the nation formally set them apart for this role, so they were not ordained.

Although New Testament churches did not ordain priests, they did ordain people to particular ministries of spreading God's Word. For example, the church in Antioch set apart Barnabas and Saul to travel to new places to preach the gospel. On his journeys, Paul appointed elders in each town (Acts 14:23), a task that he also delegated to Titus (Titus 1:5). Timothy was set apart for ministry by Paul and the elders of the church (1 Timothy 4:14). The Jerusalem church appointed seven men to help the apostles by serving the widows (Acts 6:1–6). So the early church seems to have ordained missionaries, pastors, elders, and deacons.

The New Testament describes ordination as a prayerful and public process.

Times of prayer and fasting would precede the ordination of individuals, perhaps imitating Jesus' prayer and fasting before He appointed the apostles (Luke 6:12–16). Furthermore, ordination would happen through a public ceremony where the leaders of the church would lay their hands upon the person being ordained and offer prayer. Those who were ordained seemed to sense a call to this ministry, with the church confirming the legitimacy of this desire by observing the character and capacity of this person over a period of time.

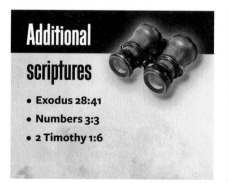

It's far better to have someone ask, "Why isn't he ordained?" than "Why did he ever get ordained?"—Lloyd Perry

The purpose of ordination is about service, not power. Jesus' example shows that Christian leaders are meant to serve others. The charges that Paul and Peter gave to elders emphasize the need to be humble in serving the church and living faithful lives (Acts 20:28–35; 1 Peter 5:1–5). The failure of Nadab and Abihu (Leviticus 10:1–3) and the sons of Eli (1 Samuel 2:12–34) to offer proper priestly service clearly shows that ordination does not make people sinless or more holy. Thus an ordained leader must constantly be challenged to stay faithful to God and his ministry.

The ordination of individuals is an ongoing gift to the church to help fulfill the Great Commission. Churches today differ in their practices concerning ordination. Some churches only ordain pastors while other churches ordain their pastors, elders, and deacons. Several denominations ordain both men and women while other churches believe that only men are called to these offices. While practices differ, the concept of service remains the same, as specific people minister in official, appointed capacities. The ordaining of people does not mean that only they do the ministry with the rest of the church doing nothing. Quite the contrary, as the church first spread through the work of non-ordained people! The purpose of ordained leaders is to preach the gospel to the world and equip the church to do so as well. Ordained servants are those set apart to help lead the church in its work of world evangelization.

Additional scriptures

- **Exodus 28:41**
- **Numbers 3:3**
- **2 Timothy 1:6**

Parable

A story that features imagery from the everyday life of the listeners told to move the audience to respond to the message of the kingdom of God.

With many similar parables Jesus spoke the word to them, as much as they could understand. He did not say anything to them without using a parable. But when he was alone with his own disciples, he explained everything. —Mark 4:33–34

Good communicators utilize figurative language such as metaphors, similes, proverbs, and stories to help people understand and remember their messages. Jesus was no exception, as figurative speech appears throughout His teaching. While figurative sayings such as proverbs (see Luke 4:23) and similes (see Luke 5:36) are sometimes labeled as parables, many scholars delineate a particular figure of speech known as a "parable-story." These stories draw from everyday life experiences to reveal spiritual truths and elicit a response from the listener. A parable differs from an allegory because an allegory has every character or event symbolize some truth, while the point of the parable comes from the story as a whole.

Parables occur throughout scripture but find a heavy concentration in the teachings of Jesus. Examples of Old Testament parables include Nathan's story to David about the rich shepherd who steals the poor man's lamb (2 Samuel 12:1–10) and Ezekiel's example of two eagles (Ezekiel 17). The majority of Jesus' parables occur in Matthew and Luke, with Mark repeating some of them (Mark 4:26–29 is the only parable unique to Mark); John employs figures of speech other than parables. These teaching stories may appear in groups or individually. The parables of Jesus address many different topics, but common themes include the kingdom of God (see Matthew 13:1–50; 25:14–30), the invitation to sinners to enter the kingdom of God (Matthew 20:1–14; Luke 14:16–24; 15:3–32; 16:19–31), and the rejection of religious leaders who refused to believe (Matthew 21:33–46; Luke 18:9–14).

In addition to being memorable illustrations of spiritual truth, the use of parables by the Messiah fulfilled the prophecy of Psalm 78:2 (Matthew 13:34–35). It also fulfilled the words of Isaiah 6:9–10 because, through the parables, people heard the truth but did not understand it (see Matthew 13:11–15). This happened because parables reveal truth to those who seek it, but they also conceal the truth from those who do not want to know it. So blessing comes from seeking to understand and then obeying the point of the parable (Matthew 13:36, 43), though some of the Pharisees understood the truth of the parables and rejected Jesus because of it (see Luke 20:19). Thus, Jesus urged His audience to "listen to the explanation of the parable" (Matthew 13:18 NLT).

> **I sometimes wonder** what hours of prayer and thought lie behind the apparently simple and spontaneous parables of the gospel. —*J. B. Phillips*

Frequently, modern Christians miss the message of these stories. They are often not aware of cultural details that shape the point of a particular parable. Having a Samaritan be a hero, for example, would be shocking to the original audience (Luke 10:29–37) because of the inherent prejudice between Jews and Samaritans. In addition, many of the parables have become so familiar that some Christians think they already know the "point" of the story; for example, people know the parable of the Prodigal Son in Luke 15, but usually miss the point that the story actually focuses on the father seeking to recover *two* sons who are lost.

Christians today can still hear the challenge of parables. Since the imagery of Jesus' parables comes from first-century Palestine, we should consult resources such as study Bibles and commentaries to understand their cultural background. In addition, we should pay particular attention to any contextual indicators about the occasion and audience of the parable, as the context can help show its purpose. Another key to understanding the point of a parable is to focus on the main characters in the story and identifications that the original audience might have with them; a king or father is often identified with God, an obedient person with the Pharisees, and the disobedience or wayward with sinners. We should also pay attention to the ending of the story because the climax is critical. Regularly, the parable will feature a shocking element; discovering the shock value helps unlock the message.

Once we have determined the original meaning of the parable, we can make this same point in today's language, modernizing the parable so that the audience can respond to the message of Jesus.

Additional scriptures

- **Ezekiel 24:3**
- **Matthew 15:15**
- **Luke 19:11**
- **Luke 21:29**

Peace

The proper state or condition of creation that leads to universal flourishing and well-being of people.

For God was pleased to have all his fullness dwell in [Christ], and through him to reconcile to himself all things, whether things on earth or things in heaven, by making peace through his blood, shed on the cross. —Colossians 1:19–20

A brief glance at the news reveals that the world is full of chaos, strife, and war. This world has lacked peace since the fall, but the Bible speaks of the possibility of peace. The biblical idea of peace is not just the absence of war; it is the way that God intended things to be and leads to the well-being and flourishing of human existence. While sin has taken away this peace, Jesus Christ restores this lost peace, allowing Christians to have this peace.

Peace is a key concept of the Bible that begins in the Old Testament and continues into the New Testament. The Hebrew word for peace is *shalom*, and it appears in contexts that point to well-being and health; it has the idea of "wholeness." In fact, translations often render shalom as wellness (see Genesis 29:6; 43:27–28). The name of God that Gideon uses in Judges 6:24, "The Lord is Peace" (*Jehovah-Shalom*), shows that only God can bring this wholeness. This is why the blessing in Numbers 6:22–26 asks God to grant a peaceful life, one that is full of well-being and flourishing. Sin prevents this peace, for it breaks the intentions of God. Instead of peace, Israel experienced calamity, leading up to their captivity outside of the promised land.

Since they did not experience this peace of God, the nation of Israel longed for it. False prophets proclaimed peace, but their counterfeit prophecies ignored the fact that peace could not come while evil and sin remain (Isaiah 48:18); righteousness and peace go together (Isaiah 32:17). So the true prophets of God opposed these false prophets and spoke of a covenant God made to bring peace to the land (Ezekiel 34:20–31). This would happen through a "Prince of Peace" (Isaiah 9:6).

We've got to recognize that we are not working (primarily) for a peaceful world. Peace will be a by-product of something else. We are working for a world of justice and rightness. Peace is a by-product of justice and mercy.
—*Stanley High:* The Evangel

The promise of peace finds its fulfillment in Jesus Christ, as He has made peace and reconciled people and the universe back to God on the cross (Colossians 1:20). Thus the gospel message can be called the "gospel of peace" (Ephesians 6:15), and many of the New Testament letters begin by sending greetings of "grace and peace." The gospel proclaims peace because it brings the spiritual and social world back to the way that God intended. It brings peace with God through the blood of Jesus (Romans 5:1), restoring the fellowship between humans and God that God designed. Jesus also brings peace and

wholeness to the social order by making Jews and Gentiles one body through His death (Ephesians 2:14–18); humans are no longer divided against each other but united under God. This peace is only partially experienced right now but will come in its fullness in the future; Christians still have trials (John 16:33) but know that the God of peace will soon crush Satan, who opposes peace (Romans 16:20).

Christians should experience and extend this peace. Paul commands Christians to let the peace of Christ rule in their hearts (Colossians 3:15) and to live in peaceful relations with one another as much as possible (Ephesians 4:3). In fact, peace is one of the fruits of the Spirit (Galatians 5:22). In addition, Christians should be peace-makers in this world (Matthew 5:9); they should promote justice and care for creation and for people. Christians should recognize the peace that they have and seek to model it in the world; they live in the *shalom* now while they wait for the promise of *shalom* for the whole world.

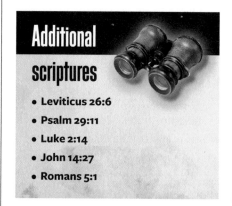

Additional scriptures

- **Leviticus 26:6**
- **Psalm 29:11**
- **Luke 2:14**
- **John 14:27**
- **Romans 5:1**

Perseverance

God giving grace to believers to continue to have faith in Jesus Christ until the end of their lives.

I give them eternal life, and they shall never perish; no one can snatch them out of my hand. My Father, who has given them to me, is greater than all; no one can snatch them out of my Father's hand. —John 10:28–29

While all one must do to be saved is believe the gospel, a true Christian cannot simply believe the message one day and then forget about it or renounce it. On the contrary, one must continue to believe the gospel message and persevere in faith until death. Jesus told His disciples that they must continue in His word and hold to His teaching in order to truly be His disciples (John 8:31–32); He also stated that only those who stand firm to the end will be saved (Matthew 10:22). Paul wrote in Colossians 1:23 about the need to continue in faith to receive the fulfillment of the promises of God. And the book of Hebrews features many warnings to Christians about the peril of losing faith (Hebrews 2:1; 3:6, 13; 6:11; 10:35–39). Christians must stay faithful all of their lives; they must believe and continue to believe.

This does not mean that Christians remain faithful through their own strength or lack assurance of their salvation. The way that a Christian perseveres is by God's grace; Christians *persevere* because God *preserves* them. Perseverance reflects the human perspective, as Christians persevere in their faith despite their circumstances; while *preservation* reveals the divine perspective, as God preserves His saints by giving them the grace to continue to believe throughout their lives. This promise of perseverance can give Christians assurance, as God will not forget about them and will keep them faithful. In fact, Christians are encouraged to know that they have eternal life (see 1 John 5:13).

The New Testament emphasizes God's promise to preserve His saints in faith. Jesus said that He would not lose even one whom the Father had given Him (John 6:38–40) and that no one is able to snatch a believer out of the Father's hands (John 10:27–29). Romans 8 is a rich chapter on perseverance. There, the apostle Paul wrote that everyone whom God justifies, He also glorifies, showing that no one who receives justification loses it. This is because nothing has power to separate a believer from the love of God. In Philippians 1:6, Paul added that God will finish the work that He begins in the life of a Christian. God brings a person to salvation and keeps him or her saved through faith, as Peter echoes (1 Peter 1:5). Thus, a Christian perseveres with the assurance of salvation because of the grace of God.

This does not mean that every person who makes a confession of faith will persevere or that Christians will never sin. The Parable of the Sower describes people who make professions of faith but fall away (Matthew 13:20–22). Not every confession of faith is authentic, because Jesus said that some who call Him "Lord" would be punished at the end of the age (Matthew 7:21–23). It also does not mean that Christians will never fall into sin. King David (2 Samuel 11) and the apostle Peter (Matthew 26:69–75) are examples of followers of God who committed great sins but later repented. Those who make confessions of faith may fail at times, but God will give grace to those who return in repentance. The difference between a true believer and a false believer is whether the person returns in repentance to God.

The idea of perseverance is, therefore, both a challenge and a promise. It is a challenge to Christians to continue in faith and repentance; Christians cannot rely on their faith of yesterday but need to have faith each new day. When Christians sin, they are to run back to God in faith and repentance. The promise of God's continual work in the lives of believers gives them confidence that they can persevere, since just as Christ has saved them, He will keep them until they meet Him. We see God's power and grace in salvation from beginning to end.

> **Perseverance is** not a long race; it is many short races one after another.
> —*Walter Elliott*

Additional scriptures

- **Romans 5:3–4**
- **2 Thessalonians 3:5**
- **Hebrews 12:1**
- **James 1:2–4**
- **2 Peter 1:5–7**

Prayer/Intercession

Speaking to God in the name of Jesus by praising His holy character, confessing our sins, thanking Him for His acts of faithfulness, and asking Him to grant our requests.

Do not be anxious about anything, but in everything, by prayer and petition, with thanksgiving, present your requests to God. —**Philippians 4:6**

Conversation is at the heart of every human relationship, which makes prayer—communicating with God—a vital element of the Christian life. Since God made us to have a relationship with Him, we might assume that prayer should come easily for humans, but sin has affected our ability to communicate and interact with God. So the Bible helps guide us into how we should pray.

The examples of prayer in the Bible show that prayers include praise, confession, thanksgiving, and supplications/intercession. Perhaps the most famous is what is called the "Lord's Prayer" (Matthew 6:9–13; Luke 11:2–4). This prayer shows praise, confession of sin, and supplications (requests) for physical and spiritual needs. The prayers Paul prays in his letters for churches teem with thanksgiving and supplication (see Ephesians 1:15–23; Philippians 1:3–11; Colossians 1:3–14). Significant examples of prayer from the Old Testament are the pleas of Abraham (Genesis 18:16–33) and Moses (Exodus 32:31–33:6) against God's wrath on disobedient people, Solomon's prayer of dedication for the temple (1 Kings 8:22–53), and Ezra's confession of the people's sin (Ezra 9:6–15). The book of Psalms is a collection of prayers

of the people featuring examples of praise, confession, thanksgiving, and supplications. These prayers all provide examples in how to pray to our holy Father.

The goal of prayer should be to deepen one's relationship with God. Since God already knows what we need before we ask Him (Matthew 6:8), prayer is not about informing God of our needs. Instead, the purpose is to declare our dependence upon God and affirm His character as a good Father who gives His children what they need (Luke 11:9–13). Praise, confession, and thanksgiving are vital elements of prayer since they remind us of who God is and what our hearts are like. Our requests should be in faith (James 1:6), believing that God will act for the good of His children. These requests, however, also need to be for His will (Matthew 26:39; 1 John 5:14). At times, our prayers may seem unanswered; in these situations, we must persist in prayer (Luke 18:1–8), as sometimes God's plan seems, to us, slow to develop. We should also examine our hearts, as sometimes our requests are not according to God's will but our selfish desires (James 4:3). We know that God's plan is good for us (Romans 8:28) and that He works at just the right time. Therefore, even unanswered prayers should move us into a deeper dependence and closer relationship to God.

When we pray, we should remember that we are approaching the Triune God who has saved us in Christ. When Jesus taught His disciples to pray, He told them to address God as Father (Matthew 6:9). He also commands us to pray in His name (John 14:13–14; 15:16; 16:23–24). Praying in Jesus' name is not a magical formula so that we automatically receive our requests; instead, praying in Jesus' name means coming to God with the authorization of Jesus and praying in light of his character. The Holy Spirit helps to make our weak prayers effective (Romans 8:26–27); thus, a great way to approach prayer is to pray to the Father in the name of the Son with the help of the Holy Spirit. The overarching principle is to remember with whom we are speaking; we cry out to Him because we are completely dependent upon the God who has invited us back into relationship and conversation with Him through the cross.

Additional scriptures

- **Nehemiah 1:5–6**
- **Isaiah 53:12**
- **John 17**
- **1 Timothy 2:1**
- **Hebrews 4:14–16**

Predestine

God's determination before time of all events in the history of world, including those whom He will save, for His glory.

In him we were also chosen, having been predestined according to the plan of him who works out everything in conformity with the purpose of his will. —Ephesians 1:11

The Bible is the story of God creating humans to be in relationship with Him, humans losing this relationship, and God restoring this relationship in Jesus Christ. This story, however, is not one of improvisation, because God has planned all events before the creation of the world. Not only does God know what will happen, but He decrees what will happen and is in control of these events. This is the theological concept of predestination, which means that God has a plan that no one can thwart (Psalm 33:11) and that the purpose of this plan is His glory (Ephesians 3:11).

While predestination includes the election of particular people to salvation, it also extends to all the events and occurrences of the world. The Bible clearly teaches that Jesus' crucifixion occurred according to the purpose and plan of God from before the creation of the world (Acts 2:23). God has also predestined certain good works for believers to perform (Ephesians 2:10) and has foreordained (determined ahead of time) the days and actions of each person (Job 14:5; Psalm 139:16). As Ephesians 1:11 says, God works out *everything* to be in conformity with His purposes.

God executes this plan through providence: Predestination is the plan and providence is its implementation. "Providence" means divine intervention. Thus, through His providence,

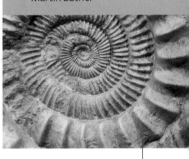

In the wounds of Christ alone is predestination found and understood.
—*Martin Luther*

God sustains and governs His creatures and all their actions. One element of providence is God's upholding and maintaining creation and the laws of creation (Colossians 1:17). If God were to remove Himself from the natural order, then the world would collapse (Job 34:14–15). So even natural events that simply work according to the laws of nature are part of God's providence; God's providence is in the mundane as well as miracles. Providence also includes God's control over nations (Acts 17:26), animals (Psalm 104:21), and the universe as a whole (Psalm 135:6), including events that seems insignificant to us (Matthew 10:29–30).

The concepts of predestination and providence are mysterious. God uses evil events for His good purposes (Genesis 50:20) without being the author of evil or the cause of sin (James 1:13–15). In fact, the biggest injustice of the world—the death of Jesus—was the plan of God (Acts 2:23)! We must remember that God does not force people to make evil choices against their will; for example, Pharaoh hardened his heart against God and, therefore, willingly chose to resist God (Exodus 8:15). How God uses evil without causing evil is difficult to understand. Another mysterious aspect of predestination is how God can plan everything but still have humans make choices and hold them responsible for these actions. The apostle Paul declares that God is completely sovereign but that we are still accountable for our wicked choices, though even he seems puzzled about how these things both can be true (Romans 9:16–21)! Somehow, God ordains our actions without making us robots with no responsibility.

While the doctrines of predestination and providence are difficult to understand, they hold tremendous value for everyday life. Even though the world can seem chaotic, everything that happens is part of God's plan; therefore, Christians can trust that God is in control and that things will ultimately work out for His glory and for the good of believers. This should evoke humility in Christians because *we* do not know what is best. We should also respond with praise and thankfulness to the God who knows what is best and is able to do it. Far from taking away human responsibility and choices, these ideas reveal that our choices are the means through which God works out His plan, and this motivates us to make choices that reflect and extend the glory of God. Our choices are part of the greatest story of them all—God redeeming sinful people!

Additional scriptures

- Isaiah 14:24–27
- Isaiah 46:10
- Romans 8:29–30
- Ephesians 1:5
- 1 Peter 1:20

Priest / Priesthood

A special group of people who served as intermediaries, facilitating the sacrifice system in the Old Testament. In the New Testament era, priests take a completely new profile. All who believe in Jesus Christ are priests, with access to God through prayer.

But you are a chosen people, a royal priesthood, a holy nation, a people belonging to God, that you may declare the praises of him who called you out of darkness into his wonderful light.
—1 Peter 2:9

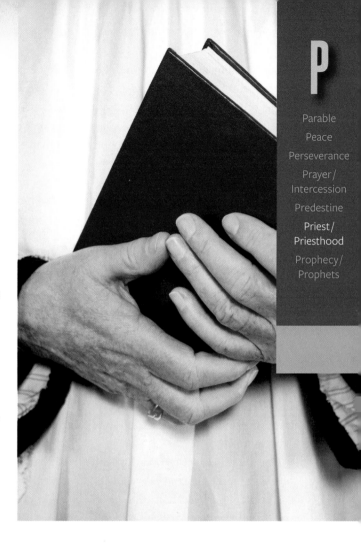

When Peter called new Christian believers a "chosen people, a royal priesthood," he radically redefined all that the Old Testament taught about this special calling, with one exception. New Testament "priests" (meaning everyone who confesses faith in Jesus) are granted the privilege of mediating God to the world. They can (and should) pray, teach and preach, and build the church. New Testament Christians are not all ordained in a church ministry, but all have access to God because all are united to Jesus Christ, who stands in the place of the high priest as an eternal advocate with God the Father (Hebrews 4:14–15).

Where did priests come from? When Moses charged the twelve tribes of Israel with new responsibilities, the tribe of Levi was called to assist in worship. They became assistants to the priests in the preparation and disposal of animal sacrifices. Levites also provided music in and around the wilderness tabernacle and later, the temple of Jerusalem. Priests, however, came from the family of Aaron, who was Moses' lieutenant in the exodus and thereafter. Another line of priests came from Zadok, appointed during the reigns of King David and Solomon. Yet another, rather mysterious line of priests (or maybe only one) dates from the time of the patriarch Abraham. His name was Melchizidek, and he might have been a forgotten footnote in Old Testament history but for the comparison between him and Jesus in the book of Hebrews. There Melchizidek is presented as a preview of Jesus, who was not in the line of Aaron but is nevertheless the eternal high priest whose sacrifice covers all sin (see Genesis 14:18–20; Hebrews 7:11–17).

The Jewish priesthood went through several ups and downs. The high priest held special honor; he alone would offer sacrifice once a year in the inner chamber of the temple, called the Holy of Holies. When Babylon destroyed the temple in 587 BC, the influence of priests declined and prophets ascended. Priests returned during the Second Temple Period under Ezra and Nehemiah and functioned until Rome destroyed that edifice in AD 70.

During Jesus' time, three priests are named and bits of their story told. The old priest Zechariah, father of John the Baptist, went speechless until John's birth (Luke 1:5–22). Annas was high priest from AD 4–15, then his son-in-law Caiaphas took over (AD 18–36). Both examined Jesus after His arrest in Jerusalem. Caiaphas approved Jesus' execution order issued by Pilate, the Roman governor of Judea.

> **A priest ought to** be in no place where his Master would not go, nor employed in anything which his Master would not do.
> —*Henry Edward Manning*

Today, Christians affirm the shared role between the Old Testament's high priest and Jesus (Hebrews 6:19–20). Christians also acknowledge the new priesthood of believers, which signals the coming of God's kingdom in Jesus Christ. When that kingdom takes its final form, all of heaven's citizens will be priests, but without the veil which now separates earth from heaven (Revelation 20:6).

Additional scriptures

- **Exodus 40:15**
- **Numbers 18:7**
- **Psalm 110:4**
- **Hebrews 2:17**

Prophecy / Prophets

P

Parable

Peace

Perseverance

Prayer/
Intercession

Predestine

Priest/
Priesthood

Prophecy/
Prophets

Typically associated with visions that tell the future, biblical prophecy is much broader. The Old Testament prophets were the conscience of the Hebrew nation, calling its people to repent, to abandon pagan deities, and to serve the true God faithfully through deeds of love and justice. They preached justice and love, and occasionally, foretold future events.

But now God has shown us a way to be made right with him without keeping the requirements of the law, as was promised in the writings of Moses and the prophets long ago. —**Romans 3:21** NLT

The Old Testament prophets were neither priests nor necessarily learned scribes or politically powerful people. Rather, they were called by God to speak His word to the people of the day and to future generations. Their message constituted the core beliefs of the Old Testament: the goodness of the one true God; the folly of sin among the people, especially the sin of false worship; the judgment that is certain to come; the ultimate salvation to be enacted by God. This salvation would come with the Messiah, the son of David. For people to receive it, they would need a "new heart," which God Himself would give (Ezekiel 36:26).

The Old Testament has seventeen books of prophecy. All but one bear a prophet's name. The longer books are called Major Prophets: Jeremiah, Isaiah, and Ezekiel. The twelve shorter books are called Minor Prophets: Hosea through Malachi. Also included in the prophetic books, though different from the fifteen, are Daniel and Lamentations. Much of Daniel is a foretelling of

climactic political change, and Lamentations tells of the prophet Jeremiah's lament.

Moses was the first prophet. He heard the Word of God and told the people its truth and meaning. Elijah and Elisha, two familiar Bible names, were constantly causing trouble for corrupt kings and queens of Israel. A prophet's life was often grim. Daniel spoke of needing long periods of recovery to mend from the stress of his prophecies. Ezekiel enacted his prophecies in bizarre dramatic fashion, often after initial resistance to God's order. Hosea married a prostitute to illustrate Israel's unfaithfulness to God.

New Testament writers saw the main point and purpose of the prophets to be telling of the coming of God's kingdom in Jesus Christ. Jesus is the one of whom the prophets foretold, Paul and others insist. The kingdom arriving in Jesus is the "mystery" to which the prophets pointed (Colossians 1:26). Mystery it was, indeed, for even the best-educated Jews in the first century—devoted to the Torah—were suspicious of Jesus' claims and finally failed as a group to believe in Him. When Paul wrote that the mystery had now been revealed (Ephesians 3:3), he was teaching that the Suffering Servant of Isaiah 53 was Jesus and that Joel had predicted the new era of the Spirit begun at Pentecost (Joel 2:28–29; Acts 2:14–21). For Paul, the kingdom that the prophets foretold was not a political solution to Roman rule but a spiritual solution to persistent sin. All the nations converging on Zion to worship God (a common prophetic picture) is, in fact, the worldwide response to the gospel's call to trust in Jesus.

In the New Testament, the only yet-unfulfilled prophecy is the coming in glory of Jesus Christ to resurrect and transform all who are bound inseparably to him through grace and faith (1 Corinthians 15:50–58).

Additional scriptures

- Deuteronomy 18:22
- Daniel 9:24
- Acts 7:52
- 1 Corinthians 13:2
- 1 Corinthians 14:1–6
- 2 Peter 1:20–21

Ransom

In Bible times, this referred to the amount paid to free a slave. That Jesus acts as a ransom means that He paid the price to free us from slavery to sin.

For even the Son of Man did not come to be served, but to serve, and to give his life as a ransom for many. —Mark 10:45

Jesus and twelve disciples were approaching Jerusalem, where Jesus knew His life would end in a bad way. It would involve betrayal, humiliation, and pain (Mark 10:33–34). Oddly, when Jesus spoke about it, he used the honorable title of Son of Man (from Daniel 7:13, where the Son of Man received great honor and an everlasting kingdom).

The seeming mismatch between "Son of Man" and painful, humiliating death apparently led the disciples to hear the "honor" part but ignore the "pain" part. At any rate, Jesus' "ransom saying" was in response to an overture from the two sons of Zebedee, James and John, who had set their sights on the marvelous future of the Son of Man and were not bashful about asking Jesus for a major stake in it (Mark 10:37). This set the stage for Jesus to bring His under-

Of the world's ransom, blessed Mary's Son: this land of such dear souls, this dear, dear land. —*William Shakespeare*

standing of "Son of Man" into line with another important Old Testament archetype, the Suffering Servant of Isaiah 53. Jesus redirected the grandeur of Daniel's vision by indicating that the Son of Man must first be the Suffering Servant. Were these two ambitious disciples ready for that?

Next, the other disciples became agitated that James and John had been negotiating for special privileges. Jesus brought the group together for a strong talk on what lay ahead. Unlike the normal exercise of power, He said, God's way involves a colossal reversal. To be great is to be a servant (Mark 10:43). To be Disciple-in-Chief is to be, in the world's accounting, a person without status at all, a slave. Then followed Jesus' remarkable statement about the meaning of His death, His interpretation of the difficult, terrible, but God-glorifying week just ahead: Jesus would be a ransom for many.

In legal terms (in Jesus' day), a ransom was the price paid to free a slave. The "ransom saying" teaches that Jesus' death would emancipate many people from the hopelessness of life without God and the inevitable judgment of God on sin. Jesus' death would set many free (Hebrews 9:15).

Who are the "many"? All who believe, from every race and place, without distinction or preference as to status or background (1 Timothy 2:6).

Who receives the ransom? The Bible never mentions a recipient. Perhaps this question, reasonable in law, stretches the metaphor beyond Jesus' intentions. It is enough to suggest that the Son of Man and the Suffering Servant are both Jesus' roles, to be played out in grim and glorious reality during the week ahead. For the disciples (then and now), Jesus' dual roles demand attention. Their service to the Lord should be modeled on His service to the many. Their lives should imitate His, their identity conform to His, though Jesus alone is able to serve as ransom.

Additional scriptures

- **Numbers 35:31–32**
- **Psalm 49:7–9**
- **Jeremiah 31:11**
- **Hosea 13:14**
- **Matthew 20:28**

(listing continues on p. 163)

Reconciliation

In Greek literature, reconciliation happens when enemies put down their weapons and resolve their disputes. The result is peace. In the New Testament, Paul uses these Greek terms (peace and reconciliation) to describe the significance of Jesus' death on the cross.

Therefore, if anyone is in Christ, he is a new creation; the old has gone, the new has come! All this is from God, who reconciled us to himself through Christ and gave us the ministry of reconciliation: that God was reconciling the world to himself in Christ, not counting men's sins against them. And he has committed to us the message of reconciliation. —2 Corinthians 5:17–19

The letters of Paul explain the meaning of Jesus' death and resurrection. Paul uses many analogies from Greek culture to show that Jesus' death was not simply Pilate's bad decision or a mob's momentary frenzy; instead, the crucifixion of Jesus was part of God's eternal plan to change the entire direction of His creation. At the heart of the event was the trajectory of His most beloved, the people of the world, who alone bear God's image. Their natural trajectory, after the fall into sin, was death (Romans 6:23). At the death of Christ, that trajectory turns upward to eternal life as people are reconciled to God by faith.

> **Some people think** reconciliation is a soft option, that it means papering over the cracks. But the biblical meaning means looking facts in the face and it can be very costly; it cost God the death of his own Son. —*Bishop Desmond Tutu*

Is God an enemy to whom we must be reconciled, in the manner common to Greek culture? God is not an enemy set against us, but human sin presents a barrier. The holy God does not and will not tolerate sin. God must turn away from it; indeed, God is clear that He will punish it. In the remarkable turn of the story that is the core of the Bible's message, however, God Himself is the agent of reconciliation. In a stunning reversal of Greek cultural norms, Paul describes the offended party (God) as the one who initiates peace. God does this through the death of His own Son, Jesus Christ (Romans 5:10). Sin-stained humanity is, in Christ, made allies and

friends again, so much that the very life of God flows freely to humankind again, full of love, peace, and joy.

In Romans 5:8–11, reconciliation, peace, and justification overlap and build a profile of life that lifts humankind from its disdain for God. The cross of Christ generates, as it were, a peace that speaks of unity, love, and fellowship. All this is by God's design. God wants it. Humans, reeling in the dead zone of sin, do not naturally want it. But God provides the want. Colossians 1:19–23 shows that God makes it happen, and we are to trust the divine action—it is good, and we want it, too.

Being reconciled to God—being friends, no longer enemies—will lead to changes in how we live. Ephesians 2:14–17 indicates that one of the big changes will be peace and friendship between people, between ethnic groups, between all peoples of differing cultures, languages, and traditions. That extended project is to be showcased in the church, the community of God's reconciled people.

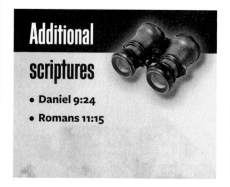

Additional scriptures

- **Daniel 9:24**
- **Romans 11:15**

Redemption

The central problem of human life is the separation of the one holy God from His beloved creation. How will these parties get back together, and why? Redemption is one of the main terms used to answer those preeminent issues.

In him we have redemption through his blood, the forgiveness of sins, in accordance with the riches of God's grace that he lavished on us with all wisdom and understanding. —Ephesians 1:7–8

If human life were simply a process of birthing, growing, re-producing, and dying, a person might live indifferent to whatever God or gods may exist. But humans are not that way. We want to know more, feel more, and achieve a more meaning-filled life than veg-etation or what are called the "higher mammals." The Bible answers that quest: God cre-ated the world good. Humans disobeyed, introducing sin to that good creation (a creation that included the command to obey but also the freedom to rebel). The holy God loved all His creation, and because of love alone (God's character), God Himself initiated the rec-onciling work that will one day be complete and total. The Bible draws on human experience to explain this process, and uses "redemption" as a central analogy. To redeem is to snatch from loss, to emancipate from slavery, or to save from destruction. In whatever venue the term is applied, the picture is of someone saving something valuable that would otherwise be dissipated, lost, or wasted.

> **When Jesus Christ** shed his blood on the cross, it was not the blood of a martyr, or the blood of one man for another; it was the life of God poured out to redeem the world. —*Oswald Chambers*

In the Old Testament and ancient cultures, prisoners of war could be redeemed through payment of a price— higher for kings, lower for foot soldiers. Even through the Middle Ages, enemy captives were executed or kept alive based on their value in the redemption market. In the New Testament, the redemption for slaves could be done through financial arrangements organized around local temples and cults. In any case, people held in bondage are freed. The Old Testament uses "redemption" to describe God delivering the Hebrews from Egypt (Exodus 13:15). Later, the Persian ruler Cyrus set free a group of Israelites to return and rebuild Jerusalem. Cyrus wrote the order, but God was moving history toward His plan, His redemption (Ezra 1:1).

Paul explained the mission of Jesus Christ as a work of redemption. Through His death, Jesus redeemed creation (with special interest in humankind) from the catastrophe of judgment and separation on account of sin. We are to understand life's value and significance as centered in the expansive new life of love, joy, and peace opened to all who believe (1 Corinthians 6:20).

This redemption price was paid in full by Christ, but redemption is not yet a completed process. Paul noted a "day of redemption" yet to come, when Jesus would return (Ephesians 4:30). The book of Hebrews assures us that the redemption bought by Christ is eternal (9:11–14), and Paul underscores that the renewal of friendship between God and humankind is solid despite all challenges (Romans 8:35).

Additional scriptures

- **Leviticus 25:23–55**
- **Deuteronomy 15:15**
- **Revelation 14:3**

Regeneration

The Bible claims that something quite marvelous happens when a person recognizes that its message is true and confesses faith in Jesus Christ. "Born again" or "born from above" are two Bible phrases that describe regeneration, which means, of course, to "generate again."

But when the kindness and the love of God our Savior toward man appeared, not by works of righteousness which we have done, but according to His mercy He saved us, through the washing of regeneration and renewing of the Holy Spirit, whom He poured out on us abundantly through Jesus Christ our Savior. —Titus 3:4–6 NKJV

"Renewal" is used in modern Bible translations for the older term *regeneration*. The clear point of both terms is to signal new life. John 3 reports on one of the most famous late-night interviews in all of history. A distinguished member of the Jewish Sanhedrin (council), Nicodemus, found Jesus and began asking about Him. Perhaps Nicodemus was curious, interested, or ready to believe. Whatever his state of mind, Jesus had no interest in delivering a lecture on religion. Instead, Jesus broke new ground with the learned Nicodemus by a startling assertion: "You must be born again" (John 3:7). When Nicodemus presented further questions, Jesus explained that the Spirit

of God was the agent who accomplished this renewal. Beyond that, Jesus alluded to regeneration with a reference to the uncertainty of the direction of wind. This was to say, "Trust me, this new birth happens. It's important, but don't assume you can figure it out."

> **The manner of** regeneration cannot be fully comprehended by believers in this life. Notwithstanding which, they rest satisfied with knowing and experiencing that by this grace of God they are enabled to believe with the heart, and to love their Savior. —*Canons of the Synod of Dort*

What happens then? The Bible provides no long sections, no elaborate teachings, on regeneration. A person (any person) who is "dead in transgressions" becomes "alive with Christ" solely at God's initiative (Ephesians 2:5). Regeneration signals a change in attitude and purpose—change occurs, from the inside out. A regenerated person seeks, finds, and follows Christ. None of this makes a person perfect. But growth in love, joy, and peace follows as surely as a healthy natural birth also leads to growth. Passions associated with personal comfort recede, and those associated with compassion and generosity take on new meaning and urgency.

The Greek term translated "regeneration" occurs only twice in the Bible. In Matthew 19:28, the reference is to the renewal of creation when God's kingdom fully arrives. Jesus' birth and ministry signal the kingdom's arrival, and His second coming will be its completion. In Titus 3:5, regeneration refers to a more personal "new birth" in which a person, confessing faith that God's word is true, becomes a member of God's family.

To Nicodemus's good question— How is a person born again?—the Bible is clear. It is a gift from God, who never fails to respond to the prayer—Lord, renew me—of a person who wants to know more.

Additional scriptures

- **Psalm 51:2**
- **Romans 12:2**
- **Ephesians 4:23**

Remnant

God promised to lead, guide, and protect the Hebrews who escaped slavery in Egypt—indeed, to give them a land where they could build a temple. But Israel's history was not to be that easy or straightforward. Devastated, the people asked, "Who are God's people now?" And the answer: There is a remnant. God will save the nation through those few who remain faithful.

This is what the LORD, the God of Israel, says to the shepherds who tend my people: "Because you have scattered my flock and driven them away and have not bestowed care on them, I will bestow punishment on you for the evil you have done," declares the LORD. "I myself will gather the remnant of my flock out of all the countries where I have driven them and will bring them back to their pasture, where they will be fruitful and increase in number." —Jeremiah 23:2–3

Canaan was to be Israel's "promised land" forever. Joshua led the people into it, David secured it, Solomon built its grandeur, but then. . .bad leaders, compromised religion, wrong-headed allegiances—and the divided nation was trampled. Assyria conquered the northern kingdom, Israel, in 722 BC. Babylonia crushed the southern kingdom, Judah, in 597 BC. The "chosen people" were prisoners again, their temple a pile of dust and ash. Was this the end?

No, declared the prophets, a faithful minority, the "remnant," will be preserved, continuing the lineage of God's people. Nearly all the prophets direct a new message to Israel: repent, learn, and God will restore the nation. Seventy years after the exile in Babylon, the Persian leader, Cyrus, granted Jews permission to return to Israel and rebuild the temple (Ezra 1:1–4). Only a small band (a remnant, again) took the offer; most stayed behind in Babylon. And none of the ten northern tribes ever returned. Thus the Second Temple Period was born, and a new question arose: Who is the true Israel now?

Paul took up that engaging question in Romans 9–11. He wrote that not every descendant of Abraham was the real Israel; he claimed that the new Israel is a covenant of grace, and its cornerstone is not a temple but a person, Jesus Christ. This was radical news to first-century Jews. Did Paul mean that only a small minority, a remnant, would inherit God's promises, but the remnant was now both Jew *and* Gentile? The inclusion of Gentile and Jew in God's new covenant community is a strong part of Paul's teaching. But he added at the end the intriguing proclamation: "And so all Israel will be saved"

(Romans 11:26). Bible scholars have asked: What does Paul mean by "all"?

> **The fact that** a remnant survives emphasizes both the grace of God and the dawning of a new age and a new community, which inherits the promises of God as it springs from that remnant. —*Walter A. Elwell and Philip W. Comfort*

Throughout the Bible, either the nation or a remnant of the nation (and in the New Testament, the church of Jesus Christ) are described as recipients of God's promises to bless, save, and prosper. But the Bible everywhere notes this tension: Not all who appear to be included really are. Even among the followers of Jesus—those who call him "Lord"—some are not genuine (Luke 6:46). The sincere are the remnant who will inherit the blessing.

Additional scriptures

- Genesis 45:7
- 2 Kings 19:4
- Ezra 9:15
- Isaiah 10:20–22

Renewal

The Bible offers a new approach to God on nearly every page. The new way to God is called a new birth, a new heart, new strength or spirit, or simply renewal. Clearly God is not interested in His people growing rusty, but everywhere calls into being the "new creation," as if to say, creation is going on wherever God is at work.

He saved us, not because of righteous things we had done, but because of his mercy. He saved us through the washing of rebirth and renewal by the Holy Spirit, whom he poured out on us generously through Jesus Christ our Savior. —Titus 3:5–6

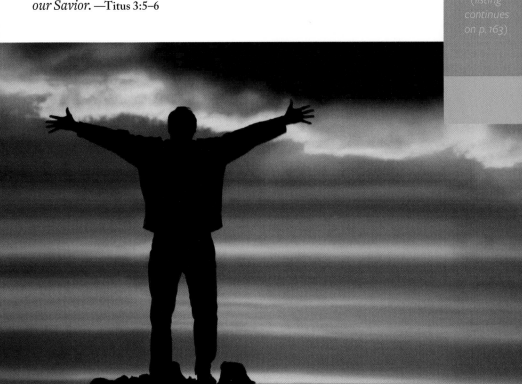

When God promises renewal, what is actually at stake? At the center of the Bible's message is God's action to restore fellowship with humankind and all of creation, separated from God by sin and disobedience. This action the Bible ascribes to a central character trait of God: love. God's love moves to unite, save, and bless. In this process, God promises renewal at every point.

Here are some important renewals that span both Testaments: a new covenant to replace the one based on strict obedience to law (Jeremiah 31:31–34), a new heart (of flesh) to replace the rock-hard heart of rebellion (Ezekiel 36:26), new life to replace the life destined to end in death (Romans 6:4), and the new mind to replace the old one which fails to recognize God's mercy (Romans 12:2).

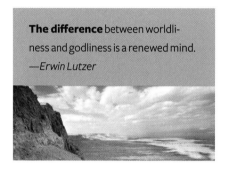

The difference between worldliness and godliness is a renewed mind.
—*Erwin Lutzer*

Of supreme importance, Jesus is Himself the author of renewal (Hebrews 10:20), as He opens the way to God's blessing. Faith in Jesus is compared to a "new self" that looks like the humanity God always intended (Ephesians 4:24). The new self or new you, relating to God through Christ in a new and living way, is responsible to follow a new command (1 John 2:8; 4:7): Love one another. So one's own renewal spills over into many other renewals as love beats back fear and greed.

These many points of renewal lead on the last day to a new heaven and new earth (2 Peter 3:13). Clearly God's project of renewal is not only the turn of one's life from an orientation of greed to service. The full extent of the project leads to new "resurrection" bodies (1 Corinthians 15:52) that will live forever with God in new places of wonder, too awesome to contemplate (1 Corinthians 2:9).

In the book of Ecclesiastes, the Teacher moans: "All things are wearisome. . . . There is nothing new under the sun" (1:8–9). The Bible answers: "Because of the Lord's great love we are not consumed, for his compassions never fail. They are new every morning; great is your faithfulness" (Lamentations 3:22–23). The psalms urge all people to "sing to the Lord a new song" for that, too, is part of the new spiritual life God offers (Psalm 98:1). If even your life appears stuck, problems mounting, resources eroding, tragedies and losses threatening, God promises renewal (Isaiah 42:9).

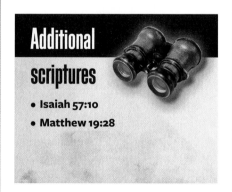

Additional scriptures

- **Isaiah 57:10**
- **Matthew 19:28**

Repentance

To repent, a person must turn from disobedience to grateful and eager acceptance of God's new life. This turning happens as part of a deep and personal awareness of one's need to be reconciled to God. Repentance was an important point in Jesus' teaching.

Jesus answered them, "It is not the healthy who need a doctor, but the sick. I have not come to call the righteous, but sinners to repentance."
—Luke 5:31–32

From the earliest accounts of humans' response to God, the record is mixed, and the weight of the record leans heavily toward the sin side. Disobedience and indifference show up more often in the record of humankind than does worship. How contrary to God's intention and interest is this! A fix must be found.

The Bible is largely the story of the fix—the mending of the relationship between holy God and sinful humanity. God takes the lead. But humans are not robots, programmed, automated, or manipulated. To mend the tear of sin, humans must repent—turn from their sins and admit their failures—and turn toward God and accept His solution.

Years of repentance are necessary in order to blot out a sin in the eyes of men, but one tear of repentance suffices with God. —*French proverb*

The Old Testament prophets were all about repentance. When Assyria and later Babylon had crushed Israel, the prophets pointed out the failures of the people, and especially Israel's leadership, to trust and obey God. They urged the people to renew faith in light of God's mercy. For John the Baptist, the last prophet whose preaching introduced Jesus, repentance was a major theme. Baptism was to be an outward sign of repentance, but the "turning" from sin and to God was not just inward remorse and water. John required that people act in accord with their change and make no lame excuses (Luke 3:7–8). Deeds had to follow words, or words were hollow.

Jesus began to preach in public about the time John the Baptist was arrested. His message was a call to repent and believe the good news because the kingdom of God was near (Matthew 4:17). It was as if royalty were approaching, and the garden weeds needed pulling. Lives, attitudes, and ambitions needed "turning" for the approach of God. This coming of the kingdom was a time for soul-searching and humility, not arrogance (Luke 14:11). Not that

God was a demanding ruler; rather, the very kindness of God leads people to repent (Romans 2:4). While repentance is urgent, it cannot be rushed. The patience of God waits for all to repent (2 Peter 3:9).

Modern persons might think repentance is such an ancient expectation. Today one must push, succeed, and be self-affirming. Indeed, people of every era must have recoiled at repentance— "Who me? I'm okay!" To this sense of independence from God, the book of Revelation says, Repent, return—or God's coming will mean bitter news, not good news (2:5). The prophet Joel urged his listeners to "return to the LORD your God, for he is gracious and compassionate. . . abounding in love" (Joel 2:13). When people repent, it is to a loving God that they turn. Repentance moves us from death to life, as it were, from darkness to light (Hebrews 6:1).

Additional scriptures

- Isaiah 30:15
- Joel 1:13
- Matthew 3:8
- 2 Corinthians 7:9

Resurrection of Christ

R

On the first day of the week following Jesus' crucifixion, the Bible reports, a nuclear bomb exploded in the form of a world-changing event: Jesus rose from the dead.

*The angel said, "Don't be alarmed. You are looking for Jesus of Nazareth, who was crucified. He isn't here! He is risen from the dead! Look, this is where they laid his body." —*Mark 16:6 NLT

Not everyone, then or now, believed that an event as unprecedented or impossible actually occurred. But two parts of the Bible's report address skeptics' understandable reluctance to believe. First, the tomb was empty. If disciples had made false claims of Jesus' resurrection, the first place to go to dispel the myth would have been the tomb. Second, eyewitness accounts of Jesus' post-resurrection appearances work against the "stolen bones" theory. Sightings by many work against the notion that a cabal successfully stole the corpse. Neither of these reports proves to the unconvinced that Jesus rose from the dead, but they do present evidence that discounts skeptics' suspicions.

Clearly the doubters expressed themselves even in the first century. Paul wrote in 1 Corinthians 15 and in 1 Thessalonians 4 concerning the importance of the resurrection, summarizing the gospel in 1 Corinthians 15:4, "He was raised on the third day." Yet some did not believe in resurrection per se. To these, Paul presented the evidence again and adds this strong concession: "If Christ has not been raised, your faith is futile" (1 Corinthians 15:17). Paul would not permit a "gospel" of mere moral values or honorable, dead teachers. The resurrection was God's sure sign that Jesus had conquered sin and death, and as He led, so His people would follow. "Encourage each other with these words," Paul told the church (1 Thessalonians 4:18).

> **Without the resurrection** there will not be a Christianity—Christianity stands or falls with the resurrection, and this single factor makes Christianity remarkably one of a kind.
> —Steve Kamar

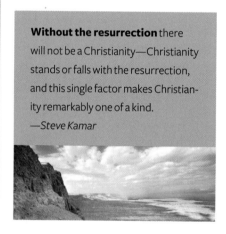

"Friday's here, but Sunday's coming!" is a modern way of pointing to the Bible's consistent and revolutionary teaching that "Christ has indeed been raised" (1 Corinthians 15:20). Following the four Gospels, the rest of the New Testament speaks of Christ as conqueror, firstborn among many brothers and sisters, intercessor at the right hand of God, high priest beyond the veil, and coming King. These active descriptors all assume a risen Christ— a resurrected God-man who was both recognizable yet magnificently different in body and physical capacity. Students of the resurrection suggest that when Jesus returns—"in a flash, in the twinkling of an eye" (1 Corinthians 15:52)—all His people will be raised in the same form and composite that Jesus exhibited—"raised in glory. . . raised in power" (1 Corinthians 15:43). Such a body eternally resists decay and never dies.

Note that nowhere does this future hope permit indifference to injustice, poverty, depletion of the environment, or ignorance concerning the gospel. Instead, Paul brings his teaching on resurrection to a close by insisting that "labor in the Lord is not in vain" (1 Corinthians 15:58). In other words, get busy, serve God eagerly, help people, and spread the Word. Jesus taught that His followers must work while we have daylight, for the night comes (John 9:4)! Christ's resurrection should motivate loving, thoughtful, and effortful service.

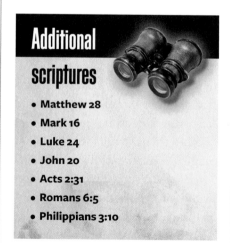

Additional scriptures

- **Matthew 28**
- **Mark 16**
- **Luke 24**
- **John 20**
- **Acts 2:31**
- **Romans 6:5**
- **Philippians 3:10**

Resurrection of Christians

Despite all appearances that dead people stay dead, the Bible advances the audacious claim that Christ rose from the dead. All who die "in Christ" will also be raised to eternal life.

We were therefore buried with him through baptism into death in order that, just as Christ was raised from the dead through the glory of the Father, we too may live a new life. If we have been united with him like this in his death, we will certainly also be united with him in his resurrection. —Romans 6:4–5

If you follow the Bible's central story—God loves and saves humankind—then resurrection of all who God saves is a natural climax. If Jesus is raised from the dead, all for whom Jesus died will also be raised. But the very idea of resurrection—new life after death—is so miraculous (and therefore improbable) that it is barely discussed in the Old Testament, and in the New, only in isolated passages. When Jesus was confronted with questions to show how tricky resurrection would be, He did not answer directly, but referred to the awesome character of God, whose authority covers both the living and the dead (Mark 12:18–27). The interrogators, members of the Jewish elite called the Sadducees, were

convinced that resurrection was folly.

If the Bible were organized as a textbook with readers' "most important questions" getting the longest chapters, this one—life after death—would surely be lengthy. As it is, the Bible clarifies but does not elaborate. The New Testament teaches this:

1. Jesus rose as "the firstborn from among the dead" (Colossians 1:18). Of the other records of resurrection (such as the child Elisha raised in 2 Kings 4:18–37, the widow's son Jesus brought back to life in Luke 7:11–16, the child in Matthew 9:18–26, and Lazarus in John 11), eventually they all succumbed to death to await the final resurrection. Jesus was raised at God's command and did not die again. His resurrection was to demonstrate eternal life—God's most amazing promise.

2. After death and prior to the resurrection, the "dead in Christ" (1 Thessalonians 4:16) enjoy conscious life in an environment of happiness and peace (John 14:2–3; Philippians 1:23). The Bible sometimes calls this period "sleep," but describes it not as blissful action. To be "in Christ" is to be covered by Jesus' sacrifice and reckoned as one of God's family. All the promises of God follow—wholeness, health, joy, relationships.

3. When Christ reappears at His second coming, the dead in Christ and those living will be given resurrection bodies like the one Jesus had (Romans 8:11; Philippians 3:20–21). This resurrection and renewal will be part of God's

bringing heaven and earth together, reclaiming the beauty of creation, and setting all records straight in a final judgment. The veil between heaven and earth will drop; all will be one eternal community of love and peace.

> **What reason** have atheists for saying that we cannot rise again? Which is the more difficult, to be born, or to rise again? That what has never been, should be, or that what has been, should be again? Is it more difficult to come into being than to return to it?
> —*Blaise Pascal*

4. The resurrection of Christ is the central event of history, the central hope of Christian faith (1 Corinthians 15:17). The Bible assures that resurrection awaits all who trust God through faith in Jesus.

Additional scriptures

- **Matthew 11:5**
- **1 Corinthians 15:12–29**
- **1 Thessalonians 4:17**
- **Hebrews 6:2**

Revelation

The act of God disclosing Himself or truths about Himself, the world, His purposes, plans, and will. Because God is personal and not hidden, He has revealed Himself to us, so we can know about Him; we can know Him.

They know the truth about God because he has made it obvious to them.
—Romans 1:19 NLT

R

Resurrection
of Christ

Resurrection
of Christians

Revelation

Reward

Righteous/
Righteousness

Righteousness
of God

According to much of the world, if God even exists, He is distant, impersonal, and unknowable. And in our rationalistic society, human reason is said to be the only reliable source of truth. With that worldview, any statement or claim of God breaking into human existence must be dismissed or explained away. But Christians, and the Bible, assert the opposite. Not only *can* God reveal Himself, but He, in fact, *has*—we can know about Him; we can know Him. And that's great news.

The first and most basic way that God has revealed Himself is in nature. That is, we can learn about the Creator by looking at His creation. And this is the thrust of the passage above and most of Romans 1 and 2. Paul states, "For ever since the world was created, people have seen the earth and sky. Through everything God made, they can clearly see his invisible qualities—his eternal power and divine nature. So they have no excuse for not knowing God" (Romans 1:20 NLT). The Bible affirms this in several other places (see Psalm 10:11; 14:1; 19:1–6; Acts 14:17). This is called "natural" (because of nature) or "general" (as opposed to specific) revelation. That is, we can know certain truths about God—power, creative abilities, sovereignty—by observing trees, flowers, oceans, birds, bees, fish, stars, weather, and human beings. This God-information is true but a bit fuzzy at times. But God doesn't leave it there.

God's revelation goes even further—He has revealed Himself in His Word. This is called "special" revelation, and, as we might expect, it is much more specific. In speaking of the Old Testament, Jesus made the point that everything written in the scriptures would be accomplished (Matthew 5:18). And He promised the disciples total recall of Him and His teachings (John 14:26). The Bible is very clear that the prophets and apostles spoke God's Word as He enabled them (Jeremiah 1:4–19; 1 Corinthians 2:13; 2 Peter 1:16–21). Both Old and New Testaments contain God's written revelation; thus the Bible is without error in its original manuscripts. And God's Word can tell us everything we need to know for faith and life (2 Timothy 3:16–17). Note: The last book in the Bible has the title "Revelation" because it *reveals*, through a vision to the apostle John, God's plans for the future. But the entire Bible is

[God] is not silent. That is the reason we know.... He has told us true truth; about himself—and because he has told us true truth about himself—that he is the infinite-personal, triune God—we have the answer to existence. —*Francis A. Schaeffer*

God's "book of Revelation."

God has also revealed Himself *perfectly* in Jesus. When some of the disciples asked Jesus to show them the Father, He responded, "Anyone who has seen me has seen the Father." (John 14:9) The Word became flesh (John 1:14–18), at the right time (Galatians 4:4–5), expressing "the very character of God" (Hebrews 1:1–3 NLT). The ultimate purpose of scripture is to reveal Christ (John 5:39; 1 Corinthians 15:3). If we want to know what God is like, the Bible tells us, we can look at Jesus.

Of course, the next part of that equation can be quite convicting for us Christians ("Christ-ones"): If people are to see what Jesus is like, they should be able to simply look at His followers, at us (John 13:34–35). What do our lives reveal about God?

Additional scriptures

- **Luke 2:32**
- **John 10:34–38**
- **Acts 10:43**
- **Acts 17:22–29**
- **Galatians 1:12**
- **1 Thessalonians 2:13**

Reward

Why follow God? What's in it for you? The Bible takes seriously these reasonable questions. But the answer may startle, for the reward of following God, the Bible reports, is God.

For the Son of Man is going to come in his Father's glory with his angels, and then he will reward each person according to what he has done.
—Matthew 16:27

When God crowns our merits, it is nothing other than his own gifts that he crowns. —*Augustine of Hippo*

Rules and guidelines for proper living are found throughout the Bible. From the earliest records to new and yet future events, rewards and punishments are woven into Bible instructions. The Old Testament in particular promises God's blessings for following His law, and the opposite for flaunting it (Psalm 19:11).

But all the Bible's laws (for instance, the Ten Commandments) and moral guidelines finally come down to what Jesus taught as the great commandment: to love God and one's neighbor as oneself (Matthew 22:36–40). Jesus becomes the Great Interpreter of what God wants and how God will reward the obedient.

Jesus recognized a reward of reputation and honor, but He advised that His followers seek a deeper reward. Don't make grand public announcements over your good deeds, Jesus said. If you do that, honor will come. But if you do good in a humble posture, without seeking public honor, the joy of participating in God's kingdom will go deeper, last longer, and be more satisfying. The proper reward for doing good is partnership with God (Matthew 6:1–4).

The correct attitude toward rewards is to not expect them. Don't do good for purposes of self-interest. For example, when planning a party, Jesus taught, don't base your guest list on return invitations. Instead, practice disinterested goodness (Luke 14:12–14). A person who does good without calculating rewards trusts God for whatever goodness God will give.

There is no moral contract. Rewards are not distributed on the basis of effort, length of service, or benefits gained from good service (Matthew 20:1–16). God will reward on a schedule no one can calculate but Him, who is to be fully trusted and not bargained with.

Most important, God Himself is our reward. Jesus' central point in describing the good life is that it is lived in the presence of God (Matthew 5:8). During your life, and at the final judgment, the great reward is friendship with God. The early church leader Augustine, said about rewards, *ipse praemium* ("He Himself is our reward"). This is a crucial insight that governs the Bible's vision of a future distribution of rewards (Revelation 22:12). Those who know God now will be supremely happy to abide with Him in the new heavens and new earth. While Jesus referred to mansions (or "rooms") in heaven (John 14:2), even a child will tell you that a large house without good company is boring and lonely. Life now and heaven later will be nothing like "boring and lonely" to those who know, serve, and love God. Knowing God now and loving God later are linked together in a life that pleases God.

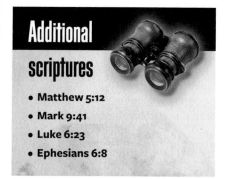

Additional scriptures

- **Matthew 5:12**
- **Mark 9:41**
- **Luke 6:23**
- **Ephesians 6:8**

Righteous / Righteousness

To modern ears, the term speaks of haughty self-assurance, but in the Bible this complex term is used to describe the quality that restores one's relationship to God.

For just as through the disobedience of the one man the many were made sinners, so also through the obedience of the one man the many will be made righteous.
—Romans 5:19

R

Resurrection of Christ

Resurrection of Christians

Revelation

Reward

Righteous / Righteousness

Righteousness of God

Note the emphasis on "made righteous" in this key verse from Paul. Being righteous is not something people do or perform in order to find God or win God's admiration. Rather, God is the one acting, doing, and declaring that people are made righteous (or to use a legal term, "justified"), and freed from sin's penalty. This common New Testament meaning of "righteous" is called the forensic meaning—God declares it, so it is done.

Old Testament believers held quite a different view. To them, the covenant terms presented by God were to be obeyed, and in case of failure (a frequent enough situation), repentance was required. Obedience leads to blessing, and blessing is a sign of righteousness. Persistent disobedience produces judgment—the opposite end-game to righteousness.

The prophet Amos describes righteousness as doing justice (Amos 5:7).

Hosea, whose marriage is itself a sermon, emphasizes righteousness as loving-kindness and mercy (Hosea 2:19). Micah sees God's righteousness as His defense of Israel against her enemies (Micah 6:5). Isaiah sees righteousness as decisions born of justice (Isaiah 1:26).

Righteousness is just rightness. Sometimes we make it too theological as a biblical word. Rightness is not easy of definition, but everybody knows what it is. We are conscious of rightness even if we cannot adequately define it. —*Harry Lathrop Reed*

Jesus understood the Old Testament and taught His listeners to conform their behavior to God's will as the right response to God's righteous kingdom. To participate in that kingdom requires an ethical obligation, just as God's covenant required it under the Old Testament commandments.

This ethical side of righteousness was noted in early preaching (Acts 10:35) and emphasized in the book of James. So strong is it there that a quick reading might appear to put James and Paul at odds (as Luther thought). James famously teaches that faith without works is worthless (James 2:20). To be truly justified before God, a person claiming faith must give evidence his or her faith is real by ethical behavior. Paul would agree, noting the distinction in his writing between righteousness as an act of God's grace, and righteousness as an obligation of the believer to follow God's will (Romans 4:1–5).

If the frequency of a word's appearance in the Bible indicates its weight to the author's argument, then Paul, by overwhelming numbers, is the Bible's primary expositor on the meaning of righteousness. In his letters, the righteousness all people need for salvation is not won by ethical behavior but by the death of Jesus Christ, God's Son, our Savior. By faith in Him, His righteousness is given to the undeserving. In gratitude for this gift, God's children ought to live righteously. This life is neither piety nor Puritanism, but the transforming of the mind (Romans 12:1–2) reflected in grateful obedience.

God will see the righteousness of Christ in each believer at the Last Judgment. That righteousness—given and exercised—makes forgiven sinners "shine like stars" (Philippians 2:15).

Additional scriptures

- **Genesis 6:9**
- **Ezra 9:15**
- **Psalm 11:5**
- **Psalm 34:19**
- **Matthew 23:35**
- **Hebrews 11:4**

Righteousness of God

Of the many qualities the Bible ascribes to God, righteousness is among the most prominent. It points to God's holiness, justice, and perfection. If God is righteous, His will and ways are good, true, and life-affirming.

I will give thanks to the LORD because of his righteousness and will sing praise to the name of the LORD Most High. —Psalm 7:17

In the Old Testament, God's righteousness shows in His faithfulness to the covenant with Israel. God makes the covenant, keeps His side of it, and the people are blessed. Thus, righteousness was much more than an abstract concept but a living reality on which people depended for survival and prosperity. Without God faithfully fulfilling His promises to guide, protect, and keep, that little nation would be swallowed by its powerful neighbors—exactly that happened in the fifth and eighth centuries BC. Then the people gasped—their historical visions of God's righteousness had to reckon with a new political reality of exile in Assyria and Babylon.

The Old Testament prophets answered. The righteous God had been abandoned by His own people who had corrupted worship with idols and spoiled justice by oppression of the weak and poor. God righteously judged them for their careless indifference to His will. This is the Bible's painful story of the relationship between holy God and sinful people: The promise is given, the people temporarily show gratitude and true worship, then the people fall away. Proud leaders and greedy clerics abandon God. God judges the nation. How would this sad, repetitive cycle end?

God's character is righteous, but His righteousness blends justice, mercy, kindness, effort, even sacrifice. God's righteousness is an active reach-out, a lifeline to save and restore fellowship.

Decisively, the righteous God Himself became a human being. In Jesus Christ, God Himself, the Son, second person of the Trinity, righteous and holy, became a man. The mission of Jesus was to embody righteousness as He announced and taught the approach of the kingdom of God. And then Jesus would die, bearing the sin of the world and completely satisfying God the Father's righteous demands. The gospel—the core of the Bible's message—is the righteousness of God made into a gift for all people through faith in Jesus Christ.

To receive the gift is to be changed, transformed, born anew in God's Spirit. Now God's righteousness is a quality of life to learn and enact. Making righteousness a priority, the Bible promises, means that all other priorities of life will be cared for. God has so promised that He cares for us as we care about Him (Matthew 6:33). Worry and anxiety are completely set aside in the light of God's righteousness at work in each person who believes. At the end of history, those promises will be more apparent, obvious, visible, and pure in the new heavens and earth, which the Bible endearingly calls "the home of righteousness" (2 Peter 3:13).

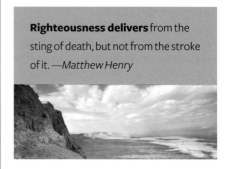

Righteousness delivers from the sting of death, but not from the stroke of it. —*Matthew Henry*

Additional scriptures

- **Psalm 7:11**
- **Psalm 65:5**
- **2 Corinthians 5:21**
- **2 Peter 1:1**

Sabbath / Lord's Day

A day, once a week, set aside to worship God and to rest from normal labor.

Remember the Sabbath day by keeping it holy. Six days you shall labor and do all your work, but the seventh day is a Sabbath to the LORD your God.
—Exodus 20:8–10

The Old Testament word "sabbath" means to cease and desist. In a labor-intensive environment such as the ancient world, endless work was required simply to survive. Farm plots tended meant food. Water gathered meant life. There was no end to it. But a pattern of refreshment was set in the account of creation itself, when God "rested" on the seventh day.

Genesis 2:3 tells that God "blessed the seventh day and made it holy." The language cannot imply that God experienced fatigue, or that the previous six days were in some way not holy (with the implication that only rest is holy, not work). Nonetheless God declared a special day at the end of the work involved in creation. This day of rest was later formalized in the fourth commandment. Whereas several commandments in Exodus 20 are stated as short, simple sentences, the fourth is elaborately explained and its most common excuses explicitly forbidden. The fourth command is the first of the life-in-the-world commandments. To rest and worship are important.

The command seems to be without controversy throughout the Bible. Unlike most commands, which were frequently violated or debated in Israel's history, to rest and worship became widely practiced and socially accepted. Apparently there were fewer dissenters to the command to rest than for any other. At the dawn of the New Testament era, Jesus entered the synagogue on the seventh day, "as was his custom" (Luke 4:16). Following Jesus' resurrection on the first day of the week (Luke 24:1), Christians began to practice the "Sabbath" on that day, rather than the last weekday. Thus most churches (Seventh Day Adventists are one notable exception) assemble to worship on Sunday, which is a common day off in parts of the world where the Christian church is influential. As Christians look forward to the great day of Christ's return, no day of the week is specified; yet John began his Revelation on the Lord's Day, the Christian Sabbath (Revelation 1:10).

Sabbatarian practice varies widely

The Lord's Day is the shadow of Christ on the hot highway of time.
—*Robert E. Speer*

today. The Bible offers little guidance beyond the instances cited here. Various practices have been adopted by churches attempting to withstand the pressures of commerce, sport, and entertainments, and at the same time honor the tradition of the command. Strict Sabbatarians still forbid work and many pleasures on the Sunday observance, while the mega-church movement has adopted its Sunday schedule to an increasingly distracted culture, adjusting the "Sabbath" to Saturday evening or sometimes a mid-week evening. Many Christians today interpret the Bible's Sabbath command to require regular weekly gatherings and rest from commerce, without a legalistic attachment to any particular day of the week. Hearing church bells ringing on Sunday, however, is still the norm in Christian lands.

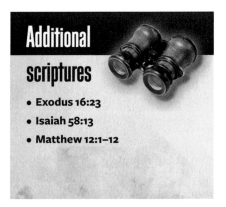

Additional scriptures

- **Exodus 16:23**
- **Isaiah 58:13**
- **Matthew 12:1–12**

Sacrifice / Offering

Blood sacrifice was the proper way to show homage to God during Old Testament times. Since Jesus' death was the final and sufficient sacrifice, the Bible does not require animal sacrifice now. But "sacrifice" still appears in the New Testament in terms of allegiance and service to God.

Through Jesus, therefore, let us continually offer to God a sacrifice of praise—the fruit of lips that confess his name. And do not forget to do good and to share with others, for with such sacrifices God is pleased.
—Hebrews 13:15–16

The Old Testament instructs followers of God to observe a complex set of sacrifices. Various animals or other property were required for special occasions or designated rituals. In most cases, the point and purpose of the sacrifice was to confess sin and cleanse oneself (or groups, or the nation as a whole) from the penalty of sin. Bulls, rams, lambs, and goats—males and healthy—were used in sacrificial rituals. The poor could substitute birds. Fish and wild animals were not sacrificed; only domestic animals that were owned. In that way, a person making the sacrifice would *feel* the cost of sin. The idea was never food for the gods, practiced by many ancient peoples, but the best

175

for God as a response to blessing or to find forgiveness. Grain offerings were also part of Old Testament piety (all of this is detailed in the book of Leviticus). Today we may question the worth or even the fairness of killing animals to cleanse people from sin. In the Old Testament, this was as clear and plain as apple pie—simply the right thing to do.

The coming of Jesus changed all this (except for Jews, who continued the Old Testament system). Jesus is described as the true Passover lamb (1 Corinthians 5:7) and the final sin offering (Romans 8:3). Jesus is frequently identified as the Suffering Servant of Isaiah 53 and the Messiah of Daniel 9. Several rather arcane words are used to describe Jesus' all-sufficient and final sacrifice. "Atonement" points to His repair of the breach that sin has caused. "Propitiation" puts emphasis on release from God's anger against sin. "Redemption" is a legal term suggesting that the prisoner (sinner) is released on payment of a ransom or bond (though the Bible does not carry the analogy further). The book of Hebrews frequently describes Jesus as our sacrifice for sin (Hebrews 2:9) and fulfillment of the covenant sacrifices outlined in Exodus 24 (Hebrews 9–10).

The Lord's Supper (1 Corinthians 11:23–26) is a reminder—but more than that, a sacrament—connected to Jesus' sacrificial death. Churches have pondered whether Jesus' blood must continually be sacrificed (as in the Mass) or if, as Protestants practice, the one death of Christ is sufficient. Over this issue much biblical intelligence has be spent, and some actual blood during times of religious conflict. Suffice it to say that when Christians take the Supper, they identify in the deepest way with the Savior on whom they totally depend for

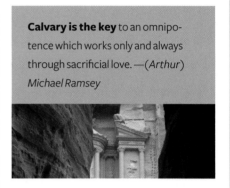

Calvary is the key to an omnipotence which works only and always through sacrificial love. —(*Arthur*) *Michael Ramsey*

cleansing from sin. The actual taking of the meal symbolizes and memorializes the nearly imponderable spiritual transformation of sins forgiven, grace received—our welcome into God's family.

Additional scriptures

- **Genesis 22:2**
- **Exodus 20:24**
- **1 Samuel 15:22**
- **Romans 12:1**
- **Ephesians 5:2**

Salvation

In the Old Testament, salvation is described as God picking up someone stuck in a muddy valley and setting that rescued person on a stable plateau. In the New Testament, a spiritual reality replaces that picture: Saved persons are moved from darkness to light, from outside of God's kingdom to inside, from isolation to fellowship, from death to life.

My God is my rock, in whom I take refuge, my shield and the horn of my salvation. He is my stronghold, my refuge and my savior—from violent men you save me. —2 Samuel 22:3

A central idea throughout the Bible is that salvation is the all-important transition from death to eternal life made possible by Jesus Christ on the cross. Its enactment depends first on the *willingness* of the one who is able to save and, second, on people accepting the gift of salvation.

On the first point, God is eager to save (2 Peter 3:9). This willingness goes beyond duty (God is not obliged) and springs from the very heart of God, in which loving-kindness and holiness merge together. God wants His creation to be restored and those who bear His image (people) to be restored to fellowship with Him. God ever helps His people to find Him and to love Him (Isaiah 41:14).

On the second point, God calls

humankind to respond to salvation by doing His will (James 1:22) and by listening to God's word (2 Peter 1:16–21). In this way, followers of Christ increasingly display the virtues that honor God and witness to God's power (2 Peter 1:5–11). Those who refuse are urged to believe (Hebrews 3:15).

> **The way to** be saved is not to delay, but to come and take. —*D. L. Moody*

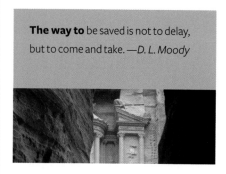

Salvation is rooted in Old Testament history. In this way, a Bible *idea* is given concrete expression. Before salvation makes its appeal to the mind and heart, God shows His power in saving the Hebrews from Egyptian servitude (the Exodus), saving Saul's leadership from the Philistines (the David vs. Goliath incident is famous), and saving a faithful remnant from the Babylonian exile after Judah fell in 587 BC. Each case is an instance of God lifting His people from peril to reconstituted blessing (Psalm 18:19), from the pit to the spacious place.

Finally in Jesus Christ, the Bible says, salvation has come to all kinds of people. Christ's death on the cross enabled the forgiveness of sin and the start of eternal life to all who believe

(John 11:40). Healings, promises to bless and prosper, and rescues from danger, are included in the New Testament's stories of salvation, as they are in the Old. But focus now is on the forgiveness of sin and adoption into God's family which Christ enables.

Salvation faces toward the future. Jesus said that the kingdom of God is near, has come, and is present. He also taught His followers to pray, "May your Kingdom come soon" (Matthew 6:10 NLT). Salvation points ahead to the future coming of Christ in power and worldwide recognition. This will be the time of Final Judgment and the time of the new heavens and new earth, which will fully restore all of creation's glory and then some (the details await the day). The book of Revelation uses magnificent images to try to approach apt descriptions.

In the meantime, God provides to all who believe the capability of knowing His salvation and growing closer to Him while life on earth lasts (2 Peter 1:3).

Additional scriptures

- **Psalm 62:2**
- **Isaiah 33:2**
- **Isaiah 52:7**
- **Acts 4:12**
- **Romans 1:16**

Sanctification / Transformation

These two weighty words—ominous in length and abstraction—describe the Bible's most important process: God's desire that all people know Him and live in fellowship with Him, shedding sin, embracing love and joy, worshiping wholeheartedly, and showing mercy to those in need.

Sanctify them by the truth; your word is truth. As you sent me into the world, I have sent them into the world. For them I sanctify myself, that they too may be truly sanctified. —John 17:17–19

(listing continues on p. 185)

Literally, the word "sanctify" means "to make holy, to set aside for special use." Why would any person want to be holy? The very idea rings of "holier than thou" or living by rigid rules of morality. But the Bible's call to holiness, or sanctification, is much more dynamic than the stereotype. To be sanctified is to follow the lead of an admired friend—in this case, Jesus Christ.

The Old Testament way of holiness was largely compliance to an elaborate system of rituals and sacrifices, each intended to bring one aspect or season of life into harmony with God. Designated priests supervised these rituals, and priests had their own set of procedures to ensure that God's designs, given to Moses, were followed. Interested Bible readers can enjoy the full scope of this system by reading the latter half of Exodus and all of Leviticus. Today such compliance might seem laborious. Indeed, during the Old Testament era, many failed to submit to it. But it was the law of God nonetheless. Those who forgot or ignored it could not enjoy the benefits of knowing God.

> **Sanctification** is glory begun. Glory is sanctification completed.
> —F. F. Bruce

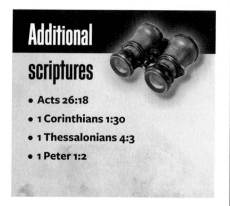

The New Testament changes the means and methods, while underscoring the goal and its reward. Jesus preached that the kingdom of God was near. No longer would priests mediate animal and grain sacrifices. Instead, Jesus is the new high priest whose own death is the final and full sacrifice. The New Testament way of sanctification (becoming holy) is to follow Jesus' lead in serving others. Now intimacy with God means learning His Word, praying, and trusting daily that God is with us. The Holy Spirit urges us onward, the church provides focus for worship, and the life experience of Christian communities shows the splendid (and sometimes soiled) ways that Christians pursue sanctification. Clearly the goal of Jesus' great prayer (John 17) is our sanctification.

Does this require special rules that others need not follow? Some communities will pursue holiness in distinctive ways, requiring abstinence of "x" and observance of "y." In what every way sanctification is taught and practiced—varieties are as plentiful as the cultures of the world—this the Bible teaches to all: The final goal of sanctification is to know Jesus Christ (Hebrews 2:10), to see God (Hebrews 12:14), and to live and work toward the fulfillment of "your Kingdom come" (Matthew 6:10 NLT). The Holy Spirit enables this growth (2 Thessalonians 2:13) and those who follow it recognize that it is a better way (Hebrews 10:19–25).

Additional scriptures

- **Acts 26:18**
- **1 Corinthians 1:30**
- **1 Thessalonians 4:3**
- **1 Peter 1:2**

Sanctuary

This is the place where God dwells. In the Old Testament, you could walk into it (at least parts of it). In the New Testament, the sanctuary is walking with you. Every person who trusts in Jesus is a place where God dwells.

Don't you know that you yourselves are God's temple and that God's Spirit lives in you? If anyone destroys God's temple, God will destroy him; for God's temple is sacred, and you are that temple. —1 Corinthians 3:16–17

Building a beautiful and permanent sanctuary was the dream of Old Testament worshippers. Their idea was that God must live somewhere and better if He lived in a very large and beautiful place. Most near-Eastern cultures had sanctuaries where their deities were alleged to live and their prescribed rituals to perform in that place. The Hebrew people went through four distinct stages with respect to their "house of God."

First was the sanctuary of the movable tent, called the tabernacle. Its construction is described in detail in Exodus 25–31 and 36–40. As ornate, colorful, and reverent as its description is, the tabernacle was never a permanent "home" for God. That place, the temple at Jerusalem, was conceived by David and built by Solomon at the height of Israel's national power and independence (1 Chronicles 22:19). Corruption and internal feuding among Solomon's successors led to a divided kingdom and eventually exile of the northern kingdom into Assyria and the southern kingdom to Babylon. By that time, the temple had been compromised by pagan worshipers, images of pagan deities, and other foreign altars. Nebuchadnezzar flattened it in 587 BC. Following the Babylonian captivity, a small band under Ezra and Nehemiah rebuilt the temple, absent the splendor and celebrations of the first. The ark of the covenant had disappeared in the looting of Jerusalem. It was never recovered.

When Jesus began to preach, "sanctuary" or temple took on a new meaning. Still a literal temple stood in Jerusalem, called Herod's temple, but the more significant New Testament teaching concerning sanctuary was metaphoric: The hope of a glorious temple was to be realized in the worldwide spread of the gospel and the establishment of churches. The church was not to be a place where God lived, but a place where God would be worshipped, where the truth of God would be taught. Indeed, God's temple was

to be the hearts and minds of faithful followers of Jesus, also called the body of Christ (Ephesians 4:12, 16). Paul describes this body-temple as a growing unity, an organism powered by the Holy Spirit.

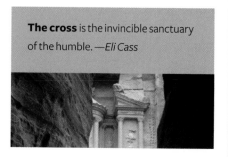

The cross is the invincible sanctuary of the humble. —*Eli Cass*

Revelation 21:22 pictures heaven without a temple. Instead, the new heavens and new earth are God's sanctuary, where God lives with all the saints (those who have been saved by faith in Christ). That temple will have continuous light and energy; no longer will people have to beg for God to forgive or remain with them; and the mood of the place will be very happy, very celebrative, very "up" (Jude 24).

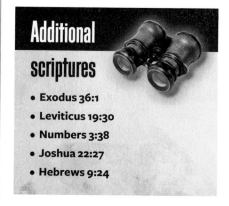

Additional scriptures

- **Exodus 36:1**
- **Leviticus 19:30**
- **Numbers 3:38**
- **Joshua 22:27**
- **Hebrews 9:24**

Satan / Enemy

S

Satan /
Enemy

Savior

Sign / Miracle

Sin /
Transgression

Slave

(listing
continues
on p. 195)

The name means adversary. In regions beyond our sight and often beyond our comprehension, the "prince of evil"—no cartoon phantom this time—seeks to discredit God's word, alienate God's people, and fracture every building block in the kingdom of God.

Be self-controlled and alert. Your enemy the devil prowls around like a roaring lion looking for someone to devour. —1 Peter 5:8

Satan's appearances in the Old Testament are infrequent. Satan appears in Job as a malevolent negotiator, cleverly uncovering the self-serving motives of obedience to God's will. He seems to challenge God, backing God in a deliciously adroit corner, until God relents and Satan vents his pent-up rebellion on Job (Job 1–2). In Zechariah 3:1, Satan is the accuser, and his arguments make perfect legal sense. But God is merciful, saving Joshua from a well-argued sentence. In Psalm 109:6, Satan stands "at his right hand"—a mysterious position of jeopardy and alarm.

In the New Testament, Satan plays a more central role. Jesus calls him the devil (John 8:44) and Beelzebub (Matthew 10:25); Paul describes him as the ruler of the kingdom of the air (Ephesians 2:2). Throughout the New Testament, Satan challenges the truth of the gospel and subverts its purposes. John explains that Satan has sinned from the beginning. Any sin committed by men or women is allegiance to Satan's rebellion. Jesus came to "destroy the devil's work" (1 John 3:8), which He did by exorcising, by healing, by forgiving sins, and, most emphatically, by rising from the dead.

"Spiritual warfare" is a term currently used to describe the Bible's description of the cosmic conflict between good and evil. God protects

Satan, who acts by an untiring power, and who will never let the saints rest till they are taken up to an everlasting rest in the bosom of Christ, is so powerful and subtle that he will often make the greatest and dearest mercies to become our greatest snares. —*Thomas Brooks*

183

believers (1 Corinthians 10:13), but believers are strongly obliged to action of their own. Stand firm in faith, Peter urges (1 Peter 5:9). Resist the devil, James teaches (James 4:7). Do not give the devil a foothold in your life (Ephesians 4:27), and put on the armor of God to battle him and his demons (Ephesians 6:11–13), Paul advises. All these defenses are required for so crafty an opponent, who may appear as an "angel of light" (2 Corinthians 11:14) but is really a prowling lion seeking prey to devour (1 Peter 5:8).

The devil is doomed (Revelation 20:10). His tenacity is futile. He is already judged (John 16:11) and will surrender someday to God (Romans 16:20). The job of the church is to tell all people "to open their eyes and turn . . .from darkness to light, and from the power of Satan to God" (Acts 26:18). That is another way of saying, "Come to Jesus, trust Him completely, and no longer act as if life is a crap-shoot and death a blank zone of nothingness. Life is intended to be full, deeply meaningful, a growing relationship with God."

For all his despair and complaints about unfair treatment, even Job confessed against the devil's claims, "I know that my Redeemer lives, and that in the end he will stand upon the earth" (Job 19:25).

Additional scriptures

- 1 Chronicles 21:1
- Matthew 4:10
- Luke 10:18
- 2 Thessalonians 2:9

Savior

The title of Jesus Christ as one who brings humans out of calamity from sin and into peace of reconciliation with God through the cross.

And we have seen and testify that the Father has sent his Son to be the Savior of the world. —1 John 4:14

The Bible is a story of God saving sinful people through Jesus; therefore, the title "Savior" is an apt title for Him (Luke 2:11; 2 Timothy 1:10), since a savior is a person who delivers an individual or group out of certain calamity. A synonym would be "rescuer." We can understand what it means for the Bible to call Jesus the "Savior" by considering the word's concept, its Old Testament use, and its Roman use.

Jesus Christ is a Savior because He came to save His people from their sins (Matthew 1:21). The sin of humans has placed a curse upon the earth (Romans 8:20) and requires a punishment from God upon those who sin. This punishment is death (Romans 6:23). Humans have no way to save themselves, for the sacrifices of animals could never bring forgiveness of sins (Hebrews 10:3–4).

Thus Jesus lived a perfect life and offered up His life as a sin offering for the people of God, both Jews and Gentiles (Romans 3:21–26). In this way, He is the Savior of the whole world (1 John 4:14). Jesus has reconciled sinners to God and has also reconciled the universe to God (Colossians 1:20). All those who place their trust in Christ receive this reconciliation, so the gospel message is the urging of the reception of this reconciliation (2 Corinthians 5:20).

In addition to the theological

meaning of this title, the idea of Savior evokes Old Testament imagery. "Savior" often appears in the Old Testament when referring to God (Deuteronomy 32:15; 1 Chronicles 16:35). God would deliver His people from calamity, both on the national (Nehemiah 9:27; Psalm 68:19; 79:9) and individual levels (Psalm 18:46). In fact, the prophets declare that God is the only Savior (Isaiah 43:11; Hosea 13:4). They also declare that the people are waiting for God to act as their Savior in the future (Isaiah 62:11; Micah 7:7). In proclaiming Jesus Christ as the Savior, therefore, the New Testament implies Christ's divinity, God saving His people. Mary cried out to God in this sense in Luke 1:47, but then Jesus was proclaimed as the Savior in Luke 2:11. In fact, Titus 2:13 uses both God and Savior as titles for Jesus Christ (see also Titus 3:4–6).

In addition to this Old Testament background of Savior, we should also note its background during Roman times. The term "savior" became part of the ruler cult of Rome, with particular reference to Augustus, the Roman Caesar during the reign of Jesus (Luke 2:1). Augustus was the savior because he brought peace to the Roman empire. While Augustus brought peace in Rome through conquest and oppressive rule, Jesus Christ brings peace with God (Romans 5:1) through serving others, giving His life as a ransom (Mark 10:45), and forgiving sins (Acts 5:31). So the New Testament proclaiming that Jesus is the Savior of the whole world (John 4:42) was a polemic against the Roman culture. This understanding is especially powerful in Philippians 3:20, a letter written to a Roman colony.

When we declare and confess Jesus as our Savior, we remember that our sins are forgiven but also that we are to obey Him as our God and our King as we wait for Him to come again (Titus 2:11–14), growing in our knowledge of Him (2 Peter 3:18). We also must never forget God's desire to be the Savior of *all* people, not just a few (1 Timothy 2:3–4), prompting us to pray that others might come to know Jesus as their Savior and to share the message with all whom we meet. Like Mary, our spirits should rejoice greatly because God our Savior has delivered us from our humble estate (Luke 1:46–49).

Additional scriptures

- **2 Samuel 22:3**
- **Psalm 42:5–6**
- **Isaiah 19:20**
- **2 Peter 1:1**

Sign / Miracle

A less common way of God working in the world that shows His power and causes people to understand who He is.

But if I do his work, believe in the evidence of the miraculous works I have done, even if you don't believe me. Then you will know and understand that the Father is in me, and I am in the Father. —John 10:38 NLT

S

Satan / Enemy

Savior

Sign / Miracle

Sin / Transgression

Slave

(listing continues on p. 195)

Christianity is a religion that rests upon miracles. The incarnation and resurrection of Jesus Christ are miracles; the revelation of God into human words in scripture is a miracle. Actually, a person cannot be a Christian without believing in miracles! Yet many find miracles difficult to believe. This reluctance may stem from faulty definitions of miracles such as "breaking the laws of nature," "a direct intervention of God," or "something impossible to explain." A better way to view miracles is as an unusual work of God in the world. Because God created the world, He established the "laws of nature," which He normally follows. But He can also work outside of those laws. So miracles are possible, though unusual, and with specific purposes.

The Bible uses three words to describe miracles, each reflecting something about the purpose of the miracle. The first is "sign," which means that the act is pointing to something else—God and His work. The second is "wonder," as the miracle leaves the audience astonished at what God has done. The third is "power" because the event shows the power of God. In light of these three words, one can see that the goal is to authenticate God and His messengers and to point to His saving purposes. We must be careful, however, because false prophets can perform "miracles," too (Matthew 24:24; Revelation 13:14). The message that accompanies the miracle must bring people closer to God and call for deeper worship of Him (Deuteronomy 13:1–11).

The Bible has three major clusters of miracles. The first is during the time of Moses because miracles authenticated his leadership (Exodus 4; 7) and helped free the Jews from Egypt (the plagues:

Exodus 7–12). The exodus event was a sign and a wonder (Deuteronomy 7:19), and it established the people of God.

The second cluster occurred in the ministries of Elijah and Elisha (1 Kings 17–2 Kings 7). These miracles affirmed these men as God's faithful messengers during a time of great spiritual apostasy in Israel (1 Kings 17:24; 2 Kings 4:9) and created a pattern for Jesus to follow, as they raised the dead (1 Kings 17:17–24; 2 Kings 4:18–37), turned little food into abundance (1 Kings 17:8–16; 2 Kings 4:1–7), and healed people from diseases (2 Kings 5:1–19).

> **A miracle is** not the breaking of the laws of the fallen world, it is the re-establishment of the laws of the kingdom. —*Anthony Bloom*

We find the third cluster in the ministry of Jesus and the apostles. While these miracles demonstrate Jesus' compassion, they showed that Jesus had the power (Matthew 8–9) to go along with His message (Matthew 5–7). Since Jesus restored things to the way that they were supposed to be, these works were also signs of the messianic age; the Messiah had come (Matthew 11:2–6)! Ultimately, these miracles were meant to lead people to faith in Christ (John 20:31). The apostles also performed miracles to prove that their message was the same as Jesus' message (Acts 3:1–10; Romans 15:18–19; 1 Thessalonians 1:5).

Many wonder if miracles happen today. Passages such as James 5:16–18 show that Christians still expect God to intervene in the world. Within this expectation, though, we must not discount natural means; God usually works in non-miraculous ways and sometimes does not intervene in desperate circumstances. Furthermore, the point of miracles is to proclaim the gospel message, not bring glory to the messenger or simply make life easier. We must not test God by asking for a miracle; Jesus spoke against the generation that expected miracles (Matthew 16:1–4). Finally, we must remember that the ultimate miracle has come in the life and resurrection of Jesus Christ and our salvation. Christianity has a miracle-working God who has used and still uses miracles to bring sinners back into relationship with Himself.

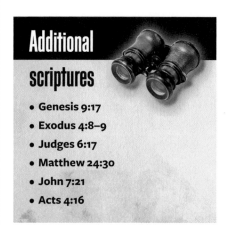

Additional scriptures

- Genesis 9:17
- Exodus 4:8–9
- Judges 6:17
- Matthew 24:30
- John 7:21
- Acts 4:16

Sin / Transgression

A deviation in word, thought, or deed, from the character, design, and will of God

For all have sinned and fall short of the glory of God. —**Romans 3:23**

In many ways, the concept of sin has disappeared in our world today; instead, many explain people's deviant behavior as a result of their scars as helpless victims or genetics as opposed to willful rebellion. In contrast, the Bible says sin involves acting contrary to God's will and character due to mistrusting Him; it is the corruption or absence of what God desires. We can understand sin better by looking at its classification, consequences, cure, and conquest.

Sin may be classified in many different ways. The sin of Adam and Eve in the garden shows them disobeying the commands of God; therefore, sin is lawlessness or disobedience (1 John 3:4). Jesus taught that even thinking out of accord with God's will is sin (Matthew 5:21–30); we can sin in word, thought, and deed. There are sins of *commission*—doing something that we shouldn't—and sins of *omission*—not doing what we should (James 1:22–25). The commands of God are a unified whole, so failure in one area constitutes failure to keep the whole law (Galatians 3:10; James 2:10); small sins and large sins both break the whole law.

The consequences of sin are dire. As promised in the garden (Genesis 2:17), death

comes through sin (Romans 6:23). This is both physical death (Ezekiel 18:4; Romans 5:12) and spiritual death (Ephesians 2:1) and, ultimately, eternal death (Revelation 21:8). An inclination to sin also passes on from human to human (Psalm 51:5), so that the body, mind, and will of humans are bent on sin. Thus, all humans sin and are unable to do any spiritual good in relationship to God in their own strength. Since nothing impure can be in the presence of God, humans are separated from God as long as they remain in this sinful state. In addition to the separation from God, sin also causes separation and alienation within the human race, as seen by Adam and Eve hiding from each other, and Cain killing his brother Abel (Genesis 3:7; 4:7–8).

While humans, in their own strength, are unable to get out of the hole that sin digs, God has made a rescue in Jesus Christ. Jesus, God in the flesh, died as a sacrifice for sin. He takes away the sin of the world by taking our sin and giving us His righteousness (2 Corinthians 5:21). We just need to believe in God's work in Christ. This does not happen through human understanding or will because God draws people to Himself and makes them alive in Christ. While Jesus talks about the sin that "will not be forgiven" (Matthew 12:31–32)—the sin of calling the work of the Holy Spirit the work of the devil—the only sin God does not forgive is the rejection of His offer of salvation in Jesus.

While the cure for sin has come, Christians still live in a conquest to defeat sin in their lives. In Romans 7, Paul documents the struggle of sin that remains in the life of a believer and then points to the key to fighting this battle—the ministry of the Holy Spirit—in

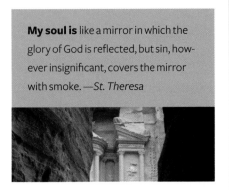

My soul is like a mirror in which the glory of God is reflected, but sin, however insignificant, covers the mirror with smoke. —*St. Theresa*

Romans 8. Although believers continue to struggle, we can be victorious over sin because of the Holy Spirit. We no longer have to live as slaves to sin. This victory over sin will only be complete at the return of Christ. Thus, Christians should not be afraid to discuss or confess their sins, for they are forgiven in Christ and have the Holy Spirit to fight sin until Christ returns.

Additional scriptures

- Ecclesiastes 7:20
- Isaiah 1:18
- Romans 6:6
- Ephesians 2:4–5
- 1 John 1:8–10

Slave

The idea of Christians being dependent and compelled to live and serve God, instead of sin, with their lives.

But thanks be to God that, though you used to be slaves to sin, you wholeheartedly obeyed the form of teaching to which you were entrusted. You have been set free from sin and have become slaves to righteousness.
—Romans 6:17–18

Throughout the course of history, people have fought against each other and oppressed others, often through slavery. The forms of slavery, however, differ from one culture to another. So when we read about slavery in the Bible, we must know how slavery worked in the civilizations of those times. Then we will be able to understand how the Bible confronts slavery and utilizes it as a metaphor.

Slavery was widespread in the Roman world, as scholars estimate that one out of five residents of Rome was a slave. The two most common ways people became slaves were being in debt or being a prisoner of war. At times, slaves would be paid and could purchase their freedom. But slaves were treated as property, not as persons. Since Roman culture placed a high value on freedom, losing one's freedom and becoming a slave was humiliating.

The Bible values every human being and promotes the release of slaves. Since God freed the Israelites from slavery in Egypt, they were to treat slaves with compassion and give them rest on the Sabbath (Deuteronomy 5:12–15). When individual Jews sold themselves into slavery, they were to be set free after seven years, though some chose to remain as slaves because they loved their masters (Exodus 21:2–6). While Israelites could keep non-Israelites as slaves, they could not kill them (Exodus 21:20) nor kidnap people and force them into slavery (Deuteronomy 24:7).

Meanwhile, the New Testament states that believers are equals—whether they are free or slaves (Galatians 3:28). In his letter to Philemon, Paul explained that the slave Onesimus was a brother to Philemon as a believer and, therefore, Philemon should release him. These words provided the foundation for the abolishment of slavery, though it was to utilize the established means of release. In the meantime, slaves were to see their service as being for God and to serve faithfully even if their masters were wicked (Ephesians 6:5–8; Colossians 3:22–24; 1 Peter 2:18). These commands serve to help employees in their relationships with their employers today.

Slavery also functions in the Bible as a metaphor. Unbelievers are enslaved to sin (John 8:34) and, therefore, have no inheritance in the family of God. This enslavement can also happen through false religious ideas. Slavery makes humans captive to fear, particularly of death. Release from this enslavement to sin happens through Jesus Christ taking the form of a slave (Philippians 2:7), as seen in particular in His washing of the disciples' feet (John 13). Believers, therefore, are no longer slaves of sin but children of God (Galatians 4:7). They are now to

Jesus Christ by his life and by his death released man from an obligation, a liability and a debt which otherwise he would have been bound to pay, and delivered him from a bondage and a slavery, by paying the purchase price of freedom which he himself could never have paid.
—*William Barclay*

be slaves to righteousness, using their freedom to serve God.

The gospel gives Christians freedom to promote the end of slavery both in the literal and figurative forms. While often forgotten, slavery still exists in many parts of the world; many Christians are seeking to bring awareness to this truth and freedom for these slaves, following in the footsteps of William Wilberforce and others. In addition, Christians should seek to eliminate the forces that lead to spiritual slavery, proclaiming the gospel of freedom. In doing so, though, Christians must remember that they can all too easily fall back into the conditions and mindset of slavery (Galatians 5:1) and need to continually look to the cross of Christ that sets the slaves free.

Additional scriptures

- **Genesis 44:10**
- **Psalm 105:17**
- **1 Corinthians 9:19**
- **Colossians 3:11**

Son of God / Son of Man / Only Begotten Son

S

Son of God /
Son of
Man / Only
Begotten Son

Soul

Spiritual Gifts

Suffering

The role of Jesus Christ in revealing the character of God and establishing His rule.

But these are written that you may believe that Jesus is the Christ, the Son of God, and that by believing you may have life in his name. —John 20:31

The church believes that Jesus Christ is the Only Begotten Son of God and the Son of Man. While Christians confess these truths, they might not understand the exact meaning of these biblical terms. For example, many think that the title "Son of God" refers to Jesus' divinity and "Son of Man" to His humanity, but this is not the full meaning of these titles. To understand these terms, we must remember that in the ancient world the son was the representation and likeness of the father. So the phrase "son of" would often be used to describe the character of people, such as "Sons of Thunder" (Mark 3:17) or "sons of disobedience" (Ephesians 2:2 NKJV), and show the quality of the person.

The title "son of God" appears in a variety of ways in the Old Testament that apply to Jesus. While the term could be linked to angels (Job 1:6), it also refers to Adam (Luke 3:38), Israel (Hosea 11:1), and the king (2 Samuel 7:14–15; Psalm 2:7). Thus, at times, the title "Son of God" might point to Jesus Christ as being the new Adam (Luke 4:1–11), the new Israel (Matthew 2:14–15), and the promised King (John 1:49). Because the Messiah was the Davidic king, this was also a messianic title. In God declaring Jesus His Son at His baptism (Matthew 3:17) and at the transfiguration (Matthew 17:5) and Jesus' statement of His special relationship to God the Father (Matthew 11:27), we realize something is greater to Jesus being the Son of God, as it shows that

Jesus is God (John 5:18). Thus, the Father and Son live in complete unity with each other so that they cannot be separated (John 1:18; 5:23) and to deny the Father is to deny the Son (1 John 2:22). Thus, the title Son of God points to Jesus' divinity as well as roles as king, Messiah, and the obedient Adam and Israel.

A closely related title to Son of God

Christians believe that Jesus Christ is the Son of God because He said so. The other evidence about Him has convinced them that He was neither a lunatic nor a quack. —*C. S. Lewis*

is "only begotten" (NIV translates this as "one and only") which can cause confusion (John 1:14, 18; 3:16, 18; 1 John 4:9). "Begotten" might seem to indicate that Jesus had a beginning, but the Greek word, *monogenos*, literally means "one of a kind," so this term indicates that Jesus is God's Son in a way that believers, who are also sons of God, are not. This is because He is of the same substance as God; He, too, is God, the second member of the Trinity (John 1:1).

The title "Son of Man" was Jesus' favorite term for Himself and also comes from its appearance in the Old Testament. It can be a generic term for a human being (Numbers 23:19). But it is also a special figure in Daniel 7:13 who became associated with the Messiah in the intertestamental period. Jesus, therefore, employed this title as a bit of a riddle, referring to Himself, but also pointing to Himself as the Messiah (Matthew 16:13–28). While describing His authority (Matthew 9:6) and return in glory (Matthew 19:28), Jesus also connected it to His suffering and resurrection (Matthew 17:12); Jesus is the Messiah who dies for His people.

In proclaiming Jesus as the Messiah, the Son of Man who suffers even though He is the Son of God, we remember that He came to make us children of God. Since Jesus calls us brothers (Hebrews 2:11), we can call God our Father. This prompts us to be obedient like Jesus, knowing that those who obey God are members of His true family. Just like Jesus, this might include suffering as the children of God; but through the work of Jesus, we know that we, too, will inherit a greater kingdom than we could ever imagine.

Additional scriptures

- **Mark 15:39**
- **Luke 1:32**
- **Luke 12:8**
- **Luke 22:69–70**
- **John 3:16**

Soul

The immaterial part of a human that lives after the death of the body and is reunited with the body at the future resurrection.

Don't be afraid of those who want to kill your body; they cannot touch your soul. Fear only God, who can destroy both soul and body in hell.
—Matthew 10:28 NLT

Many people believe that physical forces can explain everything, including human behavior, but the Bible teaches that humans have a material and an immaterial aspect. Sometimes this immaterial aspect of humans is labeled as a soul and sometimes as a spirit. Since both terms appear in 1 Thessalonians 5:23 and Hebrews 4:12, some differentiate between the soul and the spirit, with the soul as a person's consciousness and the spirit as the part that communes with God. This distinction between soul and spirit can cause a separation of the spiritual life from the physical or intellectual life and lead to anti-intellectualism. A better option is to view spirit and soul as synonyms for the immaterial aspect of humans, as the passages where they appear together do not require them to be distinct. Thus, humans are both material and immaterial, body and soul.

Part of being made in the image of God is the presence of the soul. In the creation account, God breathed into Adam to bring him alive; in doing so, He separated humans from animals and bestowed the image of God in him. The emotions and inward thoughts of humans are ascribed to the soul (Matthew 26:38; Luke 1:46–47). In fact, the soul is so integral to human life that the word can denote life itself (Luke 12:20 NKJV).

The soul is more honorable than the substance of the body, seeing that it is God's image and inspiration. Still, the body is its instrument and its colleague in all that is best. —*Cyril of Alexandria*

At physical death the body and soul separate, with the soul (spirit) departing from the body (John 19:30; Acts 7:59); the human body is not alive without this immaterial part of humans (James 2:26). In contrast, the soul lives on after death, as seen in Jesus' statement to the thief on the cross that he would soon be in paradise (Luke 23:43). In heaven, John saw the souls of saints who had died (Revelation 6:9), showing that they still lived even after being separated from the body. Thus, it seems that at death, the believer's soul lives in the presence of God (2 Corinthians 5:8; Philippians 1:23–24). This is not the final state, though, as both the righteous and unrighteous will experience a resurrection of the body (John 5:29), at which point all will be judged.

The scriptural teaching concerning the reality of the soul is different from other common understandings of soul and body. In contrast to the ancient belief that the soul was "imprisoned" in the body, the Bible affirms the importance of both the body and the soul; the goal is not to live as a disembodied soul but in a resurrected body (1 Corinthians 15:35–49). In addition, the biblical view differs from seeing humans as purely physical beings—we are not simply the products of our genes and environment.

Recognizing that humans have a soul affects how we should live in the world because both the physical life and the mental life of believers matter. Jesus emphasized both aspects in the Sermon on the Mount. Also, we should not simply seek physical desires and wealth but be concerned for our souls' futures. In addition, people do not cease to exist when they die; they continue to live on, waiting for the resurrection. This truth gives encouragement at the death of believers and should motivate us to share the gospel with those who do not believe. Finally, we recognize the mystery that exists in the world; some things are true that we cannot see and we cannot explain all things in physical terms, as we are more than physical beings.

Additional scriptures

- Deuteronomy 4:29
- 1 Samuel 1:15
- Psalm 6:3
- Matthew 16:26
- 2 Corinthians 5:1–4

Spiritual Gifts

A special ability in the life of the believer that comes through the empowerment of the Holy Spirit to serve the church.

A spiritual gift is given to each of us so we can help each other.
—1 Corinthians 12:7 NLT

S

Son of God /
Son of
Man / Only
Begotten Son
Soul
Spiritual Gifts
Suffering

In saving people for His own glory, God creates a community in which every member is essential. This is true because each Christian has received spiritual gifts (sometimes translated as "manifestation of the Spirit") that he or she ought to use to strengthen the church and share the gospel with the world. So we need to understand the nature of spiritual gifts, specific examples of gifts, and guidelines for employing these gifts.

The Bible uses multiple terms and examples to explain spiritual gifts. One term is *charisma*, which literally means "gift" (Romans 12:6; 1 Corinthians 12:4), showing that these gifts are expressions of grace. A second word is *pneumatikos*, which literally means "spiritual thing" (1 Corinthians 12:1; 14:1), showing that the gift is from the Holy Spirit. So spiritual gifts are different from natural skills or talents in that the Spirit gives and empowers them. The Old Testament describes particular people being empowered by the Spirit such as the judges (Judges 11:29) and builders of the tabernacle (Exodus 31:1–11), but looked forward to the day when the Holy Spirit would be upon all

(Joel 2:28–29). This happened at Pentecost (Acts 2:15–21). As a result, every Christian has a gift (1 Peter 4:10). The Spirit distributes these gifts throughout the church so that no one Christian has every gift and there is no one gift that every Christian has. But Paul tells the Corinthians that as a church they have all gifts (1 Corinthians 1:7) and should minister to the church with their gifts (1 Corinthians 14:12, 26).

Each of us, as members of the Body of Christ, has been given at least one spiritual gift. —*Bruce Kemper*

Passages such as Romans 12:3–8, 1 Corinthians 12:1–11, and Ephesians 4:7–13 give examples of types of gifts. These lists, however, differ, and some focus on the action while others focus on the person. They seem to be illustrative, not exhaustive lists, of gifts. While these gifts can be classified in many different ways, perhaps the most useful is that of gifts *of speech* and gifts *of service* (1 Peter 4:11). This distinction seems to reflect the distinction made between the ministry of elders and deacons (Acts 6:1–7). One type of gift is not greater than another; in fact, some that are not seen as important are, in reality, more important (1 Corinthians 12:22)! Since the proportions of each gift differ (Romans 12:6), believers with the same gift will vary in how they employ it.

The Bible also says that all gifts should be ruled by love for others—1 Corinthians 13 is nestled in the midst of Paul's discussion of spiritual gifts.

Furthermore, we should employ God's strength in using the spiritual gift, as it is for His glory. Since the believer is part of a larger body of the church, we use our gifts in complement with other gifted believers in the body.

Having spiritual gifts should encourage and challenge us. The encouragement comes in the fact that each of us has a vital role to play in the life of the church. The challenge comes in discovering our gifts and using them. Perhaps the easiest ways to identify a gift is by looking at what we are passionate about doing and seeing what skills and characteristics others affirm; the intersection of those two elements is the location of the gift. This gift might be in serving behind the scenes or leading the church in worship; both are needed as every gift is important for the church to bring glory to God and spread His glory in the world.

Additional scriptures

- **Romans 12:3–8**
- **1 Corinthians 12:1–11**
- **Ephesians 4:7–13**
- **Hebrews 2:4**

Suffering

To undergo pain and/or distress from the presence of evil and injustices in the present world in hopes of the future kingdom without suffering.

I consider that our present sufferings are not worth comparing with the glory that will be revealed in us.
—Romans 8:18

No person or religion can avoid discussing suffering because the world is filled with disaster, disease, violence, and injustice. Many people consider the reality of suffering and the problem of evil to be the biggest objection to Christianity; they wonder how an all-good and all-powerful God could allow suffering. The Bible is not a philosophical treatise designed to answer this question, but it does explain the cause and cure of suffering, helping Christians endure difficult times.

The ultimate reason for suffering is the curse upon the world caused by the sin of Adam and Eve (Genesis 3), though we must not always see sin as the cause of suffering in an individual's life. Sin has cursed all of creation, so it is the cause of natural disasters (Romans 8:18–23). In addition, sin has affected human hearts so that humans desire their own good, even at the expense of others. In the Old Testament, suffering came upon Israel because the nation broke its covenant with God and, therefore, experienced the curses promised by God (Leviticus 26; Deuteronomy 28). The New Testament also teaches that, at times, suffering happens as the result of disobedience; for example, a lack of respect for communion led to punishment of some members of the Corinthian church (1 Corinthians 11:28–30). The writer of Hebrews compares these sufferings to a loving father disciplining his wayward child (Hebrews 12:2–11). The poetic books of Job and Ecclesiastes, however, are reminders that suffering does not always relate to sin, as both the righteous and wicked suffer and Job had unparalleled sufferings even though he was an upright man. As Jesus pointed out with the examples of the man born blind (John 9:1–3) and the people who died at the tower in Siloam (Luke 13:1–5), mysterious purposes behind suffering are often tied to God's glory, not necessarily an individual's sin. One must be humble in saying why suffering happens—particularly in others' lives. Just as Job never received an explanation for his sufferings, so the reasons for our suffering often remain a mystery.

While the cause of suffering frequently remains mysterious, the cure for suffering is clear. God hears the groaning of His people on earth, as He heard the groans of Israel in its suffering of slavery (Exodus 2:24). In the suffering of Jesus Christ, (Isaiah 52:13–53:12), suffering is destroyed; as in the story of Joseph, God uses the evils of the earth for good (Genesis 50:20). This is because His suffering was for our sin (1 Peter 2:24), cleansing our hearts and ultimately bringing reconciliation to the fallen world. Therefore, the vision of the new heavens and new earth sees the complete end to suffering (Revelation 21–22).

While suffering will cease, Christians still suffer in the present. In fact, being a Christian seems to increase suffering, as believers should expect to be persecuted and suffer (2 Timothy 3:12). Christians can endure, however, by recognizing that through these sufferings, we develop character (Romans 5:3), the ability to minister to others (2 Corinthians 1:6), and the ability to overcome sin (1 Peter 4:1). We can look to the example of Jesus, recognizing that we are sharing in His suffering and, in

We often learn more of God under the rod that strikes us, than under the staff that comforts us.
—*Stephen Charnock*

doing so, are part of a community that suffers together. Beyond the example of Jesus' suffering in the past, Christians can also look to the great reward that awaits us after our sufferings on this earth (Romans 8:18). While suffering is real, it is also temporary, with the promise of no suffering and great joy in the future because of the sufferings of Jesus Christ (2 Corinthians 4:17).

Additional scriptures

- **Deuteronomy 28:53**
- **Ecclesiastes 2:12–17**
- **Isaiah 53:3**
- **Romans 5:3**
- **2 Timothy 1:8**

Trinity

One God eternally existing in three persons, (Father, Son, and Holy Spirit) who are equal in substance and power.

Therefore go and make disciples of all nations, baptizing them in the name of the Father and of the Son and of the Holy Spirit. —Matthew 28:19

While we can know God and have a relationship with Him, certain truths about Him puzzle even the brightest theologians. One such idea is the Trinity, which states that there is one God who exists in three persons. This doctrine is difficult to express since no analogy perfectly describes this concept. It is not that there are three gods, that God exists in three forms, or that God is in three parts; there is only one God, who exists in three persons, all of whom are fully God. While the word "Trinity" does not appear in the Bible, the concept emerges from passages that show that the one God is Father, Son, and Holy Spirit, who are all God and all distinct persons.

The Bible clearly teaches that only one God exists. Perhaps the plainest example of this is Deuteronomy 6:4–5, a prayer recited regularly by Jews that says God is one. Jesus affirmed the truth of this passage in Mark 12:29. The apostle Paul regularly declared only one God (1 Corinthians 8:4; Ephesians 4:5), and the point of Isaiah 44:6–45:25 is that the God of Israel is the only God.

In addition to passages affirming that only one God exists are passages that show the Father, Son, and Holy Spirit as all being God. Some passages put the Father, Son, and Holy Spirit in correlation to each other, implying a unity and equality among them (2 Corinthians 13:14). Other passages show that Father, Son, and Holy Spirit each have different tasks in the work of salvation (Ephesians 1:3–14; 1 Peter 1:2). Finally, some passages address the Father, Son,

The three persons in the Godhead are three in one sense and one in another. We cannot tell how—and that is the mystery. —*Samuel Johnson*

and Holy Spirit as God. Jesus' actions clearly indicated to those who watched that He thought He was God (Mark 2:7; John 5:18), and He accepted the declaration of the disciples that He is indeed God (John 20:28); the New Testament unequivocally declares the divinity of Jesus (John 1:1; Romans 9:5). The Holy Spirit is also called God (Acts 5:3–4) and is shown to possess attributes such as omnipresence (Psalm 139:7–8) and omniscience (1 Corinthians 2:10–11). Furthermore, the Holy Spirit is a person, not simply a force (John 14:16–17, 26); the Holy Spirit is a He, not an It. Therefore, the Father, Son, and Holy Spirit are each God.

The idea that God exists in three persons can be tricky, as we often think that being a person means having a body. The idea of personality, however, refers more to the fact that they are all distinct from each other; they are not different forms or manifestations of the same person but all exist at the same time. At the baptism of Jesus, all three members of the Trinity acted and existed simultaneously (Mark 1:9–11). They are distinct and of the same power, united in purpose with each performing different acts in the plan of salvation.

While words cannot exhaust the concept, the idea of the Trinity is practical. One realizes the unity and distinction in the Godhead and should value this in humans, whom the Triune God made in His image. Differences in genders and race display this diversity, as well as the different gifts of church members. Furthermore, God did not create human beings because He was lonely; He existed in a perfect relationship before the world began! God did not need us, but we need Him. While Christians might not completely understand how the Trinity works, they should relate to all three members, not over-emphasizing one and ignoring the other. God revealed the Trinity not so that we can fully understand His nature but so that we can fully enter into fellowship with Him in all three persons.

Additional scriptures

- **Matthew 3:16–17**
- **Ephesians 1:17**
- **Philippians 2:5–6**
- **1 Thessalonians 1:1**
- **1 Timothy 2:5**

Truth

A trait of God whereby He is genuine, real, faithful, and consistent, which humans are called to imitate.

For the law was given through Moses; grace and truth came through Jesus Christ. —John 1:17

Throughout history, people have asked the same question Pilate asked at the trial of Jesus: "What is truth?" (John 18:38) The Bible says that God is truth, as the Father (Psalm 31:5), Son (John 14:6), and Holy Spirit (John 14:17) all are connected to the truth. In saying that God is truth, we discover that He is real and consistent, and we should be as well.

Since truth is the opposite of falsehood, the fact that God is true shows that He is the only God. Only God fulfills the requirements needed to be God, so no other gods are real. Implied in this element of truth is that what God says is true; He cannot lie (Numbers 23:19). God defines reality; therefore, what He says is right and good and His law is truth. When Jesus came into the world, He spoke the truth (John 18:37), so the gospel message is the "word of truth" (Colossians 1:5).

An opposite of truth is inconsistency. When believers live hypocritically, they are not walking in the truth. God has no inconsistency; while humans are unfaithful, He is true. This means that God always acts in accordance with His character; He does what

He says. In fact, the Hebrew word for truth, *emet*, often is translated in English as "faithfulness."

Since God is the definition of truth, He asks humans to be true in their inward being (Psalm 15:2). This means

> **This coming to** know Christ is what makes Christian truth redemptive truth, the truth that transforms, not just the truth that informs.
> —*Harold Cooke Phillips*

that Christians are to reject lies, to speak truth to each other, and to wear a "belt of truth" (Ephesians 4:21–25; 6:14). Love and truth go together (1 Corinthians 13:6), which means that when Christians see other Christians wandering from the truth, they should confront them (James 5:19–20). This truly is love because knowing the truth leads to freedom (John 8:31–32). And the truth leads to holiness and the life that pleases God. In fact, truth is so integral to the Christian life that faithfulness is described as walking "in the truth" (3 John 3).

In contrast, the world does not want to know God or the truth. Unbelievers suppress the truth and prefer lies, as they follow Satan and are deceived by his counterfeit miracles. Some Christians even turn away from the truth and seek to lead others into these lies. At the end of time, people will turn further away from the truth and seek after lies (2 Timothy 4:3–4). Ultimately, judgment comes upon those who know the truth but reject it.

Christians chase after truth in a world that does not seek truth. This means that Christians renounce lies and deceitful ways and hate falsehood in a world that sometimes condones falsehood and deceit to advance one's agenda. In face of the postmodern world that sees truth as relative, Christians see truth as firm and unchanging since it is grounded in God. While this pursuit might be difficult, we must remember the ministry of the Holy Spirit, who is the "Spirit of truth." The Spirit will convict the world of its lies and will lead Christians into truth (John 16:7–15). Thus, God does not just demonstrate truth and demand truth in us but promises to help us find it when we seek after Him.

Additional scriptures

- **Isaiah 65:16**
- **John 17:17**
- **Romans 1:18**
- **1 Corinthians 13:6**
- **2 Corinthians 4:2**
- **Titus 1:2**

Wisdom

The ability to judge what is right and best and then do it.

The fear of the Lord is the beginning of wisdom, and knowledge of the Holy One is understanding. —**Proverbs 9:10**

The Bible is not just a book to be read but a book to be obeyed; it teaches what to know and also what to do. So the Bible is a book about wisdom. Every culture values wisdom and exhorts people to be wise; this is true of the Bible as well. In some ways, the biblical views of wisdom are the same, but a major difference is that wisdom in the Bible is a moral issue, with the opposite of wisdom being foolishness, which is godlessness (Psalm 14:1). Thus, failing to understand biblical wisdom leads to difficulties in this life and in the life to come.

According to the Bible, God embedded wisdom in the created order (Job 28:25–27); therefore, all people have access to wisdom. The book of Proverbs reflects this universal availability, being rich with examples from everyday life of how the world works (Proverbs 6:6–11). The book of James has many affinities to this sort of wisdom as well (James 3:1–12). The world, however, does not always work according to the principles established in Proverbs, as the wicked sometimes prosper and righteous suffer. So the books of Job and Ecclesiastes deal with the breakdown of these principles. While these books of wisdom often have appeal to Christians and non-Christians alike because of their practical content, they state that true wisdom only comes from fearing the Lord.

> **The wise man** is also the just, the pious, the upright, the man who walks in the way of truth. The fear of the Lord, which is the beginning of wisdom, consists in a complete devotion to God. —*Otto Zockler*

Humans live in rebellion against God and seek to know wisdom without God, and they have established a form of wisdom that opposes God and true wisdom (1 Corinthians 1:21). So we see a heavenly form and an earthly form of wisdom, with much of what the world thinks wise actually being foolish and what the world thinks foolish being wise. To be truly wise, we must begin with God and turn from evil. Wisdom is not an abstract force outside of God, but God Himself, as He has all wisdom and gives wisdom.

Ultimately, Jesus Christ is the personification of wisdom, so seeing Him is seeing true wisdom lived out.

Since wisdom and godliness are linked together, believers need to seek wisdom and live wisely. The pursuit of wisdom should be ongoing. We will never fully arrive at wisdom. In living on the path of wisdom, we must utilize the scriptures (2 Timothy 3:15) and other believers (Proverbs 13:20), but ultimately remember that only the Holy Spirit can impart the wisdom of God (1 Corinthians 2:13). Just as Solomon asked God for wisdom when he become king (1 Kings 3:9), so we should ask God for wisdom in difficult circumstances (James 1:5). Although Solomon became the wisest man who ever lived, he let his love for foreign wives turn his heart away from God and to idols (1 Kings 11:1–6). We see, then, that the wisdom of yesterday is no guarantee of wisdom for today or tomorrow. We must continually remember that seeking wisdom is seeking God and guarding our hearts (Proverbs 4:23).

Additional scriptures

- **Genesis 3:6**
- **1 Kings 4:29**
- **Proverbs 4:5**
- **Romans 11:33–36**
- **Ephesians 3:10**

Witness

Proclaiming to others
the work of God done
in Jesus Christ.

*But you will receive
power when the Holy
Spirit comes on you; and
you will be my witnesses
in Jerusalem, and in all
Judea and Samaria, and
to the ends of the earth.*
—Acts 1:8

The Bible often uses imagery from the judicial world and the term "witness" is a prime example. We use the word "witness" today to refer to someone testifying in court with relevant information for the case. In a similar vein, God calls His people His "witnesses," as they are to testify to the world about the truth of the gospel message, convincing them of its truth.

The purpose of God's people to proclaim His works to the world runs throughout the story of the Bible. In calling Abraham, God promised to make him a blessing to the other nations, as he would reveal God to them (Genesis 12:1–3). Israel was called to be a living testimony to the world about God (Deuteronomy 4:5–8) as God blessed them so that all the earth might fear Him. Israel did not live up to this purpose, as they actually offered false testimony about God and blasphemed His name among the nations (Romans 2:24). Instead of Israel testifying to the world, God testified against Israel and judged them. In sending Christ, though, God has once again called a people to be His witnesses.

The New Testament commands the church to be witnesses and shows them doing so. Jesus' final words to the apostles were for them to be His witnesses both among the Jews and among the Gentiles. The disciples did not go alone into the world, however, as their testimony came through the Holy Spirit. They also did miracles like Jesus did to show the authenticity and continuity of their message with his message. In this way, their work fulfilled the Old Testament requirement of the testimony of two or three witnesses (Deuteronomy 19:15).

While the church is a witnessing body, this task can be extremely difficult. Jesus promised that this testimony would incur opposition (John 15:18–25). This opposition would lead to the death of many Christians. In fact, the word "martyr" comes from the Greek word for witness. The idea of dying as a witness was common in the early church, as Stephen (Acts 22:20) and Antipas (Revelation 2:13) reveal. Believers, however, are to testify despite this opposition.

The Bible also gives encouragement in this task. First, believers must remember that a great cloud of witnesses (Hebrews 12:1) faced the same struggle that they have and only overcame and moved forward through faith. Second, believers should remember the awesome power of God's grace in the gospel; seeing what God has done in Christ compels believers to speak for Him (Acts 4:19–20). Related to this principle is understanding that this earth is not our home and that God is more powerful than anyone who can persecute, harass, or even kill us (Matthew 10:28). A final encouragement is

that believers are not alone when they testify, for God promises the Holy Spirit to be at work in these circumstances. In fact, we must remember that the power

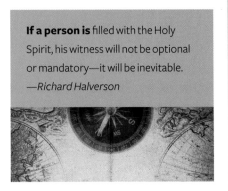

If a person is filled with the Holy Spirit, his witness will not be optional or mandatory—it will be inevitable.
—*Richard Halverson*

comes from God, not us. At times, the persecution of the church has been the seed for its spread—showing the authenticity and power of the message; God's grace is strong in our weaknesses. We cannot control undergoing persecution, but we can testify even in the face of it. In doing so, the truth of the gospel goes into all the world and we will join witnesses from every tongue, tribe, and nation testifying to the grace of God.

Additional scriptures

- **Proverbs 12:17**
- **Isaiah 44:8**
- **John 1:8**
- **Acts 22:15**
- **Revelation 1:5**

Word

God's message spoken through His servants and ultimately embodied in Jesus Christ.

In the past God spoke to our forefathers through the prophets at many times and in various ways, but in these last days he has spoken to us by his Son, whom he appointed heir of all things, and through whom he made the universe. —**Hebrews 1:1–2**

Just as in human relationships, words play an important role in the relationship between God and humans. Indeed, only through words is a relationship possible. The fact that God can speak and communicate is one thing that separates Him from false gods (Jeremiah 10:5). God must explain the meaning of His actions with words, so the words of God are necessary to know Him—and we need to understand the characteristics, means, and access point of God's message.

The qualities of a message are directly related to the attributes of the one who gives it. This means that God's word is powerful; He speaks and it is accomplished (Genesis 1–2). God is true and cannot lie (Titus 1:2), and His words are flawless (Psalm 12:6). As the creator of the universe, what God says is authoritative for all times (Psalm 119:89). Therefore His word should be obeyed (James 1:22).

Creation speaks of God, but God is too great for humans to comprehend, and sinful humans resist God and do not want to hear what He has to say. Thus God has condescended to humans and has spoken in human language through human messengers. In the Old Testament, this was through prophets with Moses being a special prophet who spoke with God "face to face"

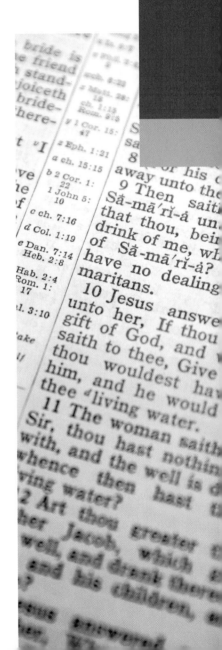

(Exodus 33:11) and communicated God's law to Israel. The ultimate revelation, though, comes through the one who is the Word—Jesus Christ (John 1:1, 14). The words that He spoke were the very words of God; they do not just interpret scripture but are equal to scripture. Christ's words call for obedience as was demanded by the Old Testament; whoever believes and keeps the words of Jesus has eternal life (John 5:24), while the one who rejects them does not have life (John 12:47). The gospel message, therefore, is known as the word of God (1 Peter 1:23–25), and the book of Acts chronicles how this message traveled and conquered the world.

Christians have access to God's word through the scriptures, which are God's words in written form. The writers of the New Testament understood the Old Testament to be God's words as the Holy Spirit spoke through and guided the writers of the Bible books. In addition, the New Testament writers put the words of Jesus and the apostles on par with the Old Testament writings, rendering the New Testament to be God's word as well. So the Bible is often called the Word of God because its words were God-breathed (2 Timothy 3:16). In the Bible, we hear God speak.

The fact that God has revealed Himself through the writings of scripture calls for Christians to delight in them (Psalm 1:1–2), love them (Psalm 119:97), and meditate upon them (Joshua 1:8). In understanding God's words, we will avoid sin and be able to confront the false teaching that bombards the believer. These words can be difficult at times, but eternal life only comes through God speaking to His people in Jesus and the Bible that speaks of Him. In studying the Bible, we must remember that the goal is not to simply know the words but to know the person who has spoken the words, the God who created us and brings us back into relationship with Him in Jesus Christ.

Additional scriptures

- 1 Kings 18:1
- Matthew 5:21–48
- John 14:10, 24
- 1 Corinthians 14:26

Worship

Proclaiming the character and work of God in word and deed.

Come, let us bow down in worship, let us kneel before the LORD our Maker; for he is our God and we are the people of his pasture, the flock under his care.
—Psalm 95:6–7

W

Wisdom
Witness
Word
Worship

God made humans to bring glory to Him and enjoy a relationship with Him; they are made to worship. Humans have rejected this purpose since the Garden of Eden, worshipping themselves and the created world instead of their creator. God's work of redemption creates a group of people who worship Him. Just as God led the Israelites out of Egypt so that they might worship and serve Him, He calls Christians to live for His glory (Ephesians 1:12) and the church to be a worshipping community (Hebrews 12:28). In doing so, Christians join in the worship of God happening in heaven (Revelation 4:8–11). The Bible teaches Christians how to worship God, with an emphasis on worshipping Him in the correct ways and in the correct mindset. We are to worship God in spirit and in truth (John 4:24).

Worshipping God in truth means worshipping in the ways God desires. The punishments that fell upon Aaron's sons (Leviticus 10:1–2) and Uzzah (2 Samuel 6:5–9) reflect how serious God takes irreverent worship. Thus, much of the Old Testament is a description of the ways that the nation of Israel should worship Him. Included in these regulations of the Old Testament worship were the Sabbath (Exodus 20:8–11), annual feasts like the Passover and the Feast of Tabernacles, the sacrificial system, purity laws, a proper place of worship (Jerusalem), and proper leaders of worship (the priests). The New Testament shows that Jesus fulfilled and transformed these requirements as he fulfilled the Law and is greater than the temple. So the church is not bound to things like the Jewish calendar, worship in Jerusalem, sacrifices, and purification and kosher laws; those things were a shadow and antitype of the things that came in Jesus (Hebrews 7–10). This does not mean that the commands of God have been loosened; instead, they have been transformed. For example, the Sabbath is a day to rest and a day to do good, and instead of offering daily sacrifices, we offer up sacrifices of praise (Hebrews 13:15–16) and live as sacrifices (Romans 12:1).

We also need to worship with the proper attitude. A common critique of Israel by the prophets was their hypocrisy in worship, as their hearts did not worship God (Jeremiah 7:21–26; Hosea 8:11–13; Amos 4:4–13). Jesus offered this same sort of critique in His ministry (Matthew 21:12–17). A similar concern emerges in Paul's writings, as he wants the church to do what is proper in practice (1 Corinthians 11), noting that worship should be orderly (1 Corinthians 14:33), and people should pay attention to their hearts (1 Timothy 2:8). Jesus' words in Matthew 5:23–26 show that an improper condition of a person's heart

> **Worship liberates** the personality by giving a new perspective to life, by integrating life with the multitude of life-forms, by bringing into the life the virtues of humility, loyalty, devotion and rightness of attitude, thus refreshing and reviving the spirit.
> —Roswell C. Long

hinders his or her worship.

Christians need to remember these principles as they gather for public worship. Ultimately, the services should focus on God and what He has done, not just the desires and thoughts of the people. The ultimate picture of God and His work is Jesus Christ, so worship should focus on Him. Furthermore, we do not just worship when we gather together with other Christians, sing, listen to preaching; worship is something that encapsulates all of life. In fact, a vital element of worship is service to God (Deuteronomy 10:12–13). Therefore, biblical worship happens by recognizing that the creator, not the creation, is to be worshipped in word and in deed and in spirit and truth; obedience to God is an essential part of worshipping Him, the very purpose for human existence.

Additional scriptures

- **Exodus 3:12**
- **Deuteronomy 29:18**
- **Psalm 100:2**
- **Luke 4:8**
- **Revelation 14:7**

Scripture Index

LEVITICUS 5
Confession

LEVITICUS 10:1–2
Worship

LEVITICUS 10:1–3
Ordain

LEVITICUS 19:15
Justice

LEVITICUS 19:30
Sanctuary

LEVITICUS 25:23–55
Redemption

LEVITICUS 26
Suffering

LEVITICUS 26:6
Peace

LEVITICUS 26:40–42
Confession

NUMBERS 3:3
Ordain

NUMBERS 3:38
Sanctuary

NUMBERS 6:22–26
Peace

NUMBERS 14:41–43
Apostasy

NUMBERS 16:30
Hell / Damnation

NUMBERS 18:7
Priest / Priesthood

NUMBERS 23:19
Son of God / Son of Man /
Only Begotten Son
Truth

NUMBERS 35:31–32
Ransom

DEUTERONOMY 4:5–8
Witness

DEUTERONOMY 4:29
Soul

DEUTERONOMY 5:12–15
Slave

DEUTERONOMY 6:4
God
Idol / Idolatry
Incarnation

DEUTERONOMY 6:4–5
Trinity

DEUTERONOMY 7:19
Sign / Miracle

DEUTERONOMY 9:9
Covenant

DEUTERONOMY 10:12–13
Worship

DEUTERONOMY 11:26–28
Blessed

DEUTERONOMY 13:1–11
Sign / Miracle

DEUTERONOMY 15:15
Redemption

DEUTERONOMY 17:7
Evil / Wicked

DEUTERONOMY 18:22
Prophecy / Prophets

DEUTERONOMY 19:15
Witness

DEUTERONOMY 24:7
Slave

DEUTERONOMY 28
Blessed
Suffering

DEUTERONOMY 28:53
Suffering

DEUTERONOMY 29:1
Covenant

DEUTERONOMY 29:18
Worship

DEUTERONOMY 32:15
Savior

DEUTERONOMY 32:22
Judgment / Wrath

DEUTERONOMY 32:43
Atonement

JOSHUA 1:8
Word

JOSHUA 22:5
Commandments / Law

JOSHUA 22:27
Sanctuary

JUDGES 2:17
Obedience

JUDGES 3:12
Evil / Wicked

JUDGES 6:17
Sign / Miracle

JUDGES 6:24
Peace

JUDGES 11:29
Spiritual Gifts

1 SAMUEL 1:15
Soul

1 SAMUEL 2:12–34
Ordain

1 SAMUEL 15:22
Sacrifice / Offering

1 SAMUEL 16:14–23
Deliverance / Healing

1 SAMUEL 20
Mercy

2 SAMUEL 6:5–9
Worship

2 SAMUEL 7:14–15
Son of God / Son of Man /
Only Begotten Son

2 SAMUEL 11
Perseverance

2 SAMUEL 12:1–10
Parable

2 SAMUEL 22:3
Salvation
Savior

PSALM 8:5
Glory

PSALM 9:17
Hell / Damnation

PSALM 10:11
Revelation

PSALM 11:5
Righteous / Righteousness

PSALM 11:7
Justice

PSALM 12:6
Word

PSALM 14:1
Wisdom

PSALM 15:2
Truth

PSALM 18:19
Salvation

PSALM 18:46
Savior

PSALM 19:7
Decree

PSALM 19:11
Reward

PSALM 20:6
Heaven

PSALM 24:7–10
Glory

PSALM 29:2
Holiness

PSALM 29:11
Peace

PSALM 31:5
Truth

PSALM 32:5
Confession

PSALM 33:11
Predestine

PSALM 34
Joy

PSALM 34:19
Righteous / Righteousness

PSALM 36:5
Love

PSALM 38:1
Judgment / Wrath

PSALM 38:18
Confession

PSALM 42:5–6
Savior

PSALM 49:7–9
Ransom

PSALM 51
Confession

PSALM 51:2
Regeneration

PSALM 51:5
Sin / Transgression

PSALM 62:2
Salvation

PSALM 65:5
Righteousness of God

PSALM 68:19
Savior

PSALM 76:8
Judgment / Wrath

PSALM 78:2
Parable

PSALM 78:24
Bread of Life

PSALM 89:14
Justice

PSALM 90:4
Millennium

PSALM 91
Demons

PSALM 92:4
Joy

PSALM 95:6–7
Worship

PSALM 96:10
Judgment / Wrath

PSALM 98:1
Renewal

PSALM 100:2
Worship

PSALM 103:3
Deliverance / Healing

PSALM 104:21
Predestine

PSALM 105:10
Decree

PSALM 105:17
Slave

PSALM 109:6
Satan / Enemy

PSALM 110:4
Priest / Priesthood

PSALM 118:15
Joy

PSALM 119:18
Commandments / Law

PSALM 119:72
Commandments / Law

PSALM 119:89
Word

PSALM 119:97
Word

PSALM 119:105
Commandments / Law

PSALM 126:3
Joy

PSALM 130:4
Forgiveness

PSALM 135:6
Predestine

PSALM 139
Hope / Blessed Hope /
Second Coming

PSALM 139:7
Filled with the Spirit

PSALM 139:7–8
Trinity

PSALM 139:16
Predestine

PSALM 140:12
Justice

PSALM 148:1–6
Decree

PROVERBS 4:5
Wisdom

PROVERBS 4:23
Wisdom

PROVERBS 4:23–24
Evil / Wicked

PROVERBS 4:27
Evil / Wicked

PROVERBS 6:6–11
Wisdom

PROVERBS 9:10
Wisdom

PROVERBS 12:17
Witness

PROVERBS 13:16
Doubt

PROVERBS 13:20
Wisdom

PROVERBS 29:4
Justice

ECCLESIASTES 1:8–9
Renewal

ECCLESIASTES 2:12–17
Suffering

ECCLESIASTES 7:20
Sin / Transgression

ISAIAH 1:2–4
Apostasy

ISAIAH 1:18
Sin / Transgression

ISAIAH 1:26
Righteous / Righteousness

ISAIAH 6:3
Holiness

ISAIAH 6:9–10
Parable

ISAIAH 9:6
Peace

ISAIAH 9:19
Judgment / Wrath

ISAIAH 10:10–11
Idol / Idolatry

ISAIAH 10:20–22
Remnant

ISAIAH 13:9–10
Day of the Lord

ISAIAH 14:24–27
Predestine

ISAIAH 19:20
Savior

ISAIAH 30:15
Repentance

ISAIAH 32:17
Peace

ISAIAH 33:2
Salvation

ISAIAH 40:5
Glory

ISAIAH 41:14
Salvation

ISAIAH 42:9
Renewal

ISAIAH 43:11
Savior

ISAIAH 44:6–45
Trinity

ISAIAH 44:8
Witness

ISAIAH 46:10
Predestine

ISAIAH 48:18
Peace

ISAIAH 52:7
Salvation

ISAIAH 52:13–53
Suffering

ISAIAH 53
Good News / Gospel
Prophecy / Prophets
Ransom
Sacrifice / Offering

ISAIAH 53:3
Suffering

ISAIAH 53:5
Atonement

ISAIAH 53:7
Lamb of God

ISAIAH 53:12
Prayer / Intercession

ISAIAH 57:10
Renewal

ISAIAH 58:13
Sabbath / Lord's Day

ISAIAH 59:17
Armor

ISAIAH 62:11
Savior

ISAIAH 65–66
New Creation / New
Heaven and New Earth /
New Jerusalem

ISAIAH 65:16
Truth

ISAIAH 65:17
Born Again

JEREMIAH 1:4–19
Revelation

JEREMIAH 2:1–9
Apostasy

JEREMIAH 7:21–26
Worship

JEREMIAH 10:5
Word

MATTHEW 10:28
Hell / Damnation
Soul
Witness

MATTHEW 10:29–30
Predestine

MATTHEW 10:38
Cross

MATTHEW 10:39
Cross

MATTHEW 11:2–6
Sign / Miracle

MATTHEW 11:5
Resurrection of Christians

MATTHEW 11:6
Apostasy

MATTHEW 11:27
Son of God / Son of Man /
Only Begotten Son

MATTHEW 12:1–12
Sabbath / Lord's Day

MATTHEW 12:31–32
Sin / Transgression

MATTHEW 13:1–50
Parable

MATTHEW 13:11
Mystery

MATTHEW 13:11–15
Parable

MATTHEW 13:18
Parable

MATTHEW 13:20–22
Perseverance

MATTHEW 13:31–32
Doubt

MATTHEW 13:33
Kingdom of God

MATTHEW 13:34–35
Parable

MATTHEW 13:36
Parable

MATTHEW 13:43
Parable

MATTHEW 13:45–46
Kingdom of God

MATTHEW 15:15
Parable

MATTHEW 16:1–4
Sign / Miracle

MATTHEW 16:12
Doctrine

MATTHEW 16:13–20
Messiah

MATTHEW 16:13–28
Son of God / Son of Man /
Only Begotten Son

MATTHEW 16:26
Soul

MATTHEW 16:27
Reward

MATTHEW 17:5
Son of God / Son of Man /
Only Begotten Son

MATTHEW 17:12
Son of God / Son of Man /
Only Begotten Son

MATTHEW 18:1
Disciple

MATTHEW 18:27
Mercy

MATTHEW 19:6
Marriage

MATTHEW 19:12
Marriage

MATTHEW 19:16
Eternal Life

MATTHEW 19:28
Regeneration
Renewal
Son of God / Son of Man /
Only Begotten Son

MATTHEW 19:29
Eternal Life

MATTHEW 20:1–14
Parable

MATTHEW 20:1–16
Reward

MATTHEW 20:28
Ransom

MATTHEW 21:12–17
Worship

MATTHEW 21:21–22
Doubt

MATTHEW 21:33–46
Parable

MATTHEW 22:30
Marriage

MATTHEW 22:36–40
Commandments / Law
Reward

MATTHEW 22:37–39
Love

MATTHEW 22:43
Inspiration / Scriptures

MATTHEW 23:35
Righteous / Righteousness

MATTHEW 24:6–7
Born Again

MATTHEW 24:14
Good News / Gospel

MATTHEW 24:22
Elect / Election

MATTHEW 24:24
Sign / Miracle

MATTHEW 24:30
Day of the Lord
Hope / Blessed Hope /
Second Coming
Sign / Miracle

MATTHEW 24:31
Elect / Election

MATTHEW 25:1–13
Bridegroom

LUKE 14:16–24
Parable

LUKE 14:25–27
Disciple

LUKE 15
Parable

LUKE 16:23
Hell / Damnation

LUKE 17:11–19
Deliverance / Healing

LUKE 18:1–8
Prayer / Intercession

LUKE 18:9–14
Parable

LUKE 19:11
Parable

LUKE 19:38–40
Messiah

LUKE 20:19
Parable

LUKE 21:29
Parable

LUKE 21:32
New Creation / New
Heaven and New Earth /
New Jerusalem

LUKE 22:19
Communion / Lord's Supper

LUKE 22:19–20
Communion / Lord's Supper

LUKE 22:55–62
Disciple

LUKE 22:69–70
Son of God / Son of Man /
Only Begotten Son

LUKE 23:43
Heaven
Soul

LUKE 24:1
Sabbath / Lord's Day

LUKE 24
Resurrection of Christ

LUKE 24:26
Glory

LUKE 24:28–35
Communion / Lord's Supper

LUKE 24:38
Doubt

JOHN 1:1
Son of God / Son of Man /
Only Begotten Son
Trinity
Word

JOHN 1:1–12
God

JOHN 1:8
Witness

JOHN 1:12–13
Adoption
Born Again

JOHN 1:14
Incarnation
Son of God / Son of Man /
Only Begotten Son
Word

JOHN 1:14–18
Revelation

JOHN 1:17
Grace
Truth

JOHN 1:18
Son of God / Son of Man /
Only Begotten Son

JOHN 1:29
Lamb of God

JOHN 1:36
Lamb of God

JOHN 1:41
Messiah

JOHN 1:49
Son of God / Son of Man /

Only Begotten Son

JOHN 2:1–11
Holiness

JOHN 3
Regeneration

JOHN 3:3
Born Again
Millennium

JOHN 3:3–8
Born Again

JOHN 3:7
Regeneration

JOHN 3:16
Cross
Doctrine
Eternal Life
Good News / Gospel
Incarnation
Love
Son of God / Son of Man /
Only Begotten Son

JOHN 3:18
Good News / Gospel

JOHN 3:27
Joy

JOHN 3:29
Bridegroom

JOHN 3:36
Eternal Life

JOHN 4
Messiah

JOHN 4:14
Eternal Life

JOHN 4:24
Worship

JOHN 4:25–26
Messiah

JOHN 4:26
Messiah

JOHN 4:34
Obedience

John 4:42
Savior

John 5:18
Son of God / Son of Man /
Only Begotten Son
Trinity

John 5:24
Eternal Life
Word

John 5:29
Soul

John 5:39
Revelation

John 6:31
Bread of Life

John 6:33
Bread of Life

John 6:35
Bread of Life
Communion / Lord's
Supper

John 6:38–40
Perseverance

John 6:40
Faith

John 6:48–51
Bread of Life

John 7:21
Sign / Miracle

John 8:31–32
Disciple
Perseverance
Truth

John 8:34
Slave

John 8:44
Evil / Wicked
Satan / Enemy

John 8:54
Glory

John 8:58
God

John 9:1–3
Suffering

John 9:1–6
Filled with the Spirit

John 9:1–36
Commandments / Law

John 9
Deliverance / Healing

John 9:4
Hope / Blessed Hope /
Second Coming
Resurrection of Christ

John 9:4–6
Deliverance / Healing

John 9:35–38
Deliverance / Healing

John 9:37
Messiah

John 9:38
Deliverance / Healing

John 10:10
Eternal Life

John 10:27–29
Perseverance

John 10:28
Eternal Life

John 10:28–29
Perseverance

John 10:34–38
Revelation

John 10:38
Sign / Miracle

John 11
Resurrection of Christians

John 11:27
Messiah

John 11:40
Salvation

John 12:16
Glory

John 12:41
Glory

John 12:47
Word

John 13
Slave

John 13:34–35
Revelation

John 14:1
Eternal Life

John 14:2
Reward

John 14:2–3
Resurrection of Christians

John 14:3
Heaven

John 14:6
Good News / Gospel
Truth

John 14:9
Revelation

John 14:10
Word

John 14:13–14
Prayer / Intercession

John 14:16
Holy Spirit / Comforter

John 14:16–17
Holy Spirit / Comforter
Trinity

John 14:17
Truth

John 14:24
Word

John 14:26
Holy Spirit / Comforter
Revelation
Trinity

John 14:27
Peace

John 15:9–11
Obedience

John 15:11
Joy

John 15:18–25
Witness

John 16:7–15
Truth

John 16:11
Satan / Enemy

John 16:22
Joy

John 16:22–24
Joy

John 16:33
Peace

John 17
Prayer / Intercession
Santification / Transformation

John 17:3
Eternal Life

John 17:12
Apostasy

John 17:17
Truth

John 17:17–19
Santification / Transformation

John 18:37
Truth

John 18:38
Truth

John 19:30
Soul

John 20
Resurrection of Christ

John 20:22
Holy Spirit / Comforter

John 20:24–28
Doubt

John 20:27
Doubt

John 20:28
Trinity

John 20:31
Sign / Miracle
Son of God / Son of Man /
Only Begotten Son

Acts 1:6
Hope / Blessed Hope /
Second Coming

Acts 1:8
Filled with the Spirit
Holy Spirit / Comforter
Witness

Acts 1:11
Day of the Lord
Hope / Blessed Hope /
Second Coming

Acts 1:21–26
Disciple
Fellowship

Acts 2:1–2
Holy Spirit / Comforter

Acts 2:1–4
Holy Spirit / Comforter

Acts 2
Body of Christ
Disciple

Acts 2:4
Filled with the Spirit

Acts 2:14–21
Prophecy / Prophets

Acts 2:15–21
Spiritual Gifts

Acts 2:17
Holy Spirit / Comforter

Acts 2:23
Predestine

Acts 2:31
Resurrection of Christ

Acts 2:38
Forgiveness
Messiah

Acts 2:38–39
Holy Spirit / Comforter

Acts 2:41
Baptism

Acts 2:42
Fellowship

Acts 2:47
Fellowship

Acts 3:1–10
Sign / Miracle

Acts 4:8
Filled with the Spirit

Acts 4:12
Salvation

Acts 4:16
Sign / Miracle

Acts 4:19–20
Witness

Acts 4:31
Filled with the Spirit

Acts 5:3–4
Trinity

Acts 5:19
Angels

Acts 5:29
Obedience

Acts 5:31
Savior

Acts 6:1–6
Ordain

Acts 6:1–7
Spiritual Gifts

Acts 7:41–43
Idol / Idolatry

Acts 7:52
Prophecy / Prophets

Acts 7:54–60
Filled with the Spirit

Acts 7:59
Soul

Acts 8:36–39
Baptism

Acts 9
Disciple

Acts 9:10
Disciple

Acts 9:26
Disciple

Acts 9:36
Disciple

Acts 10:35
Righteous / Righteousness

Acts 10:43
Revelation

Acts 13:2
Ordain

Acts 13:52
Filled with the Spirit

Acts 14:15
Idol / Idolatry

Acts 14:17
Revelation

Acts 14:23
Ordain

Acts 15:8
Holy Spirit / Comforter

Acts 15:19–20
Idol / Idolatry

Acts 16:1
Disciple

Acts 16:4
Decree

Acts 17:7
Decree

Acts 17:22–29
Revelation

Acts 17:26
Predestine

Acts 20:28
Atonement

Acts 20:28–35
Ordain

Acts 22:15
Witness

Acts 22:20
Witness

Acts 26:18
Evil / Wicked
Santification /
Transformation
Satan / Enemy

Romans 1
Revelation

Romans 1:5
Obedience

Romans 1:7
Grace

Romans 1:8
Grace

Romans 1:16
Salvation

Romans 1:16–17
Good News / Gospel

Romans 1:18
Judgment / Wrath
Truth

Romans 1:19
Revelation

Romans 1:20
Glory
Revelation

Romans 1:32
Decree

Romans 2:1–11
Judgment / Wrath

Romans 2:4
Repentance

Romans 2:11
Elect / Election

Romans 2:24
Witness

Romans 3:20
Commandments / Law

Romans 3:21
Prophecy / Prophets

Romans 3:21–26
Savior

Romans 3:22
Faith

Romans 3:22–24
Grace

Romans 3:23
Commandments / Law
Sin / Transgression

Romans 3:23–24
Eternal Life

Romans 3:23–26
Justice

Romans 3:24
Justification

Romans 3:24–26
Justification

Romans 3:25
Atonement

Romans 4:1–5
Righteous / Righteousness

Romans 4:5
Faith

Romans 4:7–8
Blessed

Romans 4:25
Justification

Romans 5:1
Justification
Peace
Savior

Romans 5:1–2
Commandments / Law

ROMANS 5–8
Death

ROMANS 5:3
Suffering

ROMANS 5:3–4
Perseverance

ROMANS 5:8–11
Reconciliation

ROMANS 5:10
Reconciliation

ROMANS 5:12
Evil / Wicked
Sin / Transgression

ROMANS 5:19
Obedience
Righteous / Righteousness

ROMANS 6:1–2
Grace

ROMANS 6:1–4
Justification

ROMANS 6:4
Grace
Renewal

ROMANS 6:4–5
Resurrection of Christians

ROMANS 6:5
Resurrection of Christ

ROMANS 6:6
Sin / Transgression

ROMANS 6:11
Death

ROMANS 6:15
Grace

ROMANS 6:16
Obedience

ROMANS 6:16–18
Holiness

ROMANS 6:17–18
Slave

ROMANS 6:19
Holines

ROMANS 6:23
Day of the Lord
Death
Justice
Reconciliation
Savior
Sin / Transgression

ROMANS 7
Sin / Transgression

ROMANS 7:4
Body of Christ

ROMANS 7:9–12
Commandments / Law

ROMANS 8:1
Judgment / Wrath
Justice

ROMANS 8:1–2
Commandments / Law

ROMANS 8
Angels
Holy Spirit / Comforter
Perseverance
Sin / Transgression

ROMANS 8:2
Eternal Life

ROMANS 8:3
Sacrifice / Offering

ROMANS 8:10
Justice

ROMANS 8:11
Resurrection of Christians

ROMANS 8:15
Adoption

ROMANS 8:15–16
Good News / Gospel

ROMANS 8:18
Suffering

ROMANS 8:18–23
Suffering

ROMANS 8:19
Filled with the Spirit

ROMANS 8:19–21
New Creation / New
Heaven and New Earth /
New Jerusalem

ROMANS 8:19–25
Deliverance / Healing

ROMANS 8:20
Savior

ROMANS 8:23
Adoption

ROMANS 8:26–27
Prayer / Intercession

ROMANS 8:28
Calling
Love
Prayer / Intercession

ROMANS 8:29
Heaven

ROMANS 8:29–30
Predestine

ROMANS 8:30
Heaven
Justification

ROMANS 8:32
Commandments / Law

ROMANS 8:35
Redemption

ROMANS 8:37
Love

ROMANS 8:37–39
Evil / Wicked

ROMANS 8:38
Death

ROMANS 8:38–39
Commandments / Law
Demons
Elect / Election
God
Love

ROMANS 9–11
Elect / Election
Mercy
Remnant

ROMANS 9:5
Trinity

ROMANS 9:16–17
Elect / Election

ROMANS 9:16–21
Predestine

ROMANS 9:23
Glory

ROMANS 10:9
Confession

ROMANS 10:9–10
Obedience

ROMANS 10:10
Confession

ROMANS 10:17
Faith

ROMANS 11:15
Reconciliation

ROMANS 11:25–32
Mercy

ROMANS 11:25–36
Mystery

ROMANS 11:26
Elect / Election
Remnant

ROMANS 11:33–36
Wisdom

ROMANS 12:1
Mercy
Sacrifice / Offering
Spiritual Gifts
Worship

ROMANS 12:1–2
Righteous / Righteousness

ROMANS 12:2
Regeneration
Renewal

ROMANS 12:3–8
Spiritual Gifts

ROMANS 12:4–8
Body of Christ

ROMANS 12:6
Spiritual Gifts

ROMANS 12:6–8
Calling
Disciple

ROMANS 12:14–21
Blessed

ROMANS 13:1–2
Obedience

ROMANS 14:11
Confession

ROMANS 15:13
Joy

ROMANS 15:18–19
Sign / Miracle

ROMANS 15:20
Good News / Gospel

ROMANS 16:19
Joy

ROMANS 16:20
Demons
Peace
Satan / Enemy

ROMANS 16:25–26
Mystery

1 CORINTHIANS 1:7
Spiritual Gifts

1 CORINTHIANS 1:18
Cross

1 CORINTHIANS 1:21
Wisdom

1 CORINTHIANS 1:30
Santification / Transformation

1 CORINTHIANS 2:8
Mystery

1 CORINTHIANS 2:9
Eternal Life
Renewal

1 CORINTHIANS 2:10–11
Trinity

1 CORINTHIANS 2:10–16
Holy Spirit / Comforter

1 CORINTHIANS 2:13
Revelation
Wisdom

1 CORINTHIANS 3:16–17
Sanctuary

1 CORINTHIANS 4:1
Mystery

1 CORINTHIANS 5:1
Marriage

1 CORINTHIANS 5:7
Sacrifice / Offering

1 CORINTHIANS 6:20
Redemption

1 CORINTHIANS 7:3–4
Marriage

1 CORINTHIANS 7:26
Marriage

1 CORINTHIANS 8
Idol / Idolatry

1 CORINTHIANS 8:4
Trinity

1 CORINTHIANS 8:4–6
Idol / Idolatry

1 CORINTHIANS 9:19
Slave

1 CORINTHIANS 10
Demons

1 CORINTHIANS 10:13
Satan / Enemy

1 CORINTHIANS 10:14
Idol / Idolatry

1 CORINTHIANS 10:16–17
Bread of Life

1 CORINTHIANS 10:20
Idol / Idolatry

1 CORINTHIANS 11
Worship

1 CORINTHIANS 11:3
Marriage

2 CORINTHIANS 6:14
Marriage

2 CORINTHIANS 7:4
Joy

2 CORINTHIANS 7:9
Repentance

2 CORINTHIANS 8:4
Fellowship

2 CORINTHIANS 11:14
Satan / Enemy

2 CORINTHIANS 12:1–4
Heaven

2 CORINTHIANS 12:1–10
Deliverance / Healing

2 CORINTHIANS 12:4
Heaven

2 CORINTHIANS 12:9
Grace

2 CORINTHIANS 13:14
Fellowship
Trinity

GALATIANS 1:6–12
Good News / Gospel

GALATIANS 1:12
Revelation

GALATIANS 2:9
Fellowship

GALATIANS 2:16
Justification

GALATIANS 3:8
Blessed

GALATIANS 3:10
Sin / Transgression

GALATIANS 3:11
Justification

GALATIANS 3:20–22
Mediator

GALATIANS 3:24
Justification

GALATIANS 3:26–28
Mystery

GALATIANS 3:28
Slave

GALATIANS 4:4–5
Revelation

GALATIANS 4:6
Adoption

GALATIANS 4:7
Adoption
Slave

GALATIANS 5:1
Slave

GALATIANS 5:16–21
Idol / Idolatry

GALATIANS 5:22
Joy
Peace

GALATIANS 5:22–23
Calling

GALATIANS 6:8
Eternal Life

GALATIANS 6:12
Cross

GALATIANS 6:14
Cross

EPHESIANS 1:3–14
Trinity

EPHESIANS 1:4–5
Elect / Election

EPHESIANS 1:5
Adoption
Predestine

EPHESIANS 1:7
Forgiveness

EPHESIANS 1:7–8
Grace
Redemption

EPHESIANS 1:9–11
Mystery

EPHESIANS 1:10
Elect / Election

EPHESIANS 1:11
Elect / Election
Predestine

EPHESIANS 1:12
Worship

EPHESIANS 1:13
Filled with the Spirit

EPHESIANS 1:15–23
Prayer / Intercession

EPHESIANS 1:17
Glory
Trinity

EPHESIANS 1:19–21
Calling

EPHESIANS 2:1
Sin / Transgression

EPHESIANS 2:1–2
Demons

EPHESIANS 2:1–7
Elect / Election

EPHESIANS 2:2
Satan / Enemy
Son of God / Son of Man /
Only Begotten Son

EPHESIANS 2:4–5
Grace
Mercy
Sin / Transgression

EPHESIANS 2:5
Good News / Gospel
Regeneration

EPHESIANS 2:8–9
Elect / Election
Faith
Grace

EPHESIANS 2:10
Predestine

EPHESIANS 2:14–17
Reconciliation

EPHESIANS 2:14–18
Peace

HEBREWS 9:11–14
Redemption

HEBREWS 9:14
Filled with the Spirit

HEBREWS 9:15
Covenant
Mediator
Ransom

HEBREWS 9:22
Forgiveness

HEBREWS 9:24
Sanctuary

HEBREWS 9:27
Deliverance / Healing
Judgment / Wrath

HEBREWS 10
Atonement

HEBREWS 10:3–4
Savior

HEBREWS 10:18
Forgiveness

HEBREWS 10:19–22
Faith

HEBREWS 10:19–25
Santification / Transformation

HEBREWS 10:20
Renewal

HEBREWS 10:23–24
Calling

HEBREWS 10:25
Fellowship

HEBREWS 10:26–27
Judgment / Wrath

HEBREWS 10:34
Heaven

HEBREWS 10:35–38
Faith

HEBREWS 10:35–39
Doubt

HEBREWS 11
Faith

HEBREWS 11:3
Faith

HEBREWS 11:4
Righteous / Righteousness

HEBREWS 11:6
Faith

HEBREWS 11:13
Heaven

HEBREWS 11:16
Covenant

HEBREWS 12:1
Perseverance
Witness

HEBREWS 12:1–2
Calling

HEBREWS 12:2
Cross

HEBREWS 12:2–11
Suffering

HEBREWS 12:7
Obedience

HEBREWS 12:14
Santification / Transformation

HEBREWS 12:24
Mediator

HEBREWS 12:28
Covenant
Worship

HEBREWS 13:1–3
Fellowship

HEBREWS 13:4
Marriage

HEBREWS 13:15–16
Sacrifice / Offering
Worship

HEBREWS 13:17
Obedience

JAMES 1:2–4
Joy
Perseverance

JAMES 1:2–8
Doubt

JAMES 1:5
Wisdom

JAMES 1:6
Doubt
Prayer / Intercession

JAMES 1:12
Blessed

JAMES 1:13–15
Predestine

JAMES 1:22
Salvation
Word

JAMES 1:22–25
Sin / Transgression

JAMES 2:10
Sin / Transgression

JAMES 2:13
Mercy

JAMES 2:14
Faith

JAMES 2:18
Faith

JAMES 2:19
Demons

JAMES 2:20
Righteous / Righteousness

JAMES 2:24
Justification

JAMES 2:26
Soul

JAMES 3:1–12
Wisdom

JAMES 4:3
Prayer / Intercession

About the Writers

Mark Fackler, Ph. D.

Mark Fackler, Ph.D., professor of communications at Calvin College, Grand Rapids, Michigan, is coauthor of *Media Ethics: Cases and Moral Reasoning* among other works. He was general editor for *500 Questions & Answers from the Bible*. Mark also teaches and conducts research in East Africa. In the springtime of the year, he calls balls and strikes, safes and outs, for West Michigan high schools.

Brian Dennert

Brian Dennert is an ordained pastor in the Presbyterian Church in America and has served youth and adults in pastoral ministry. A graduate of Cedarville University and Trinity Evangelical Divinity School, he resides with his wife in the suburbs of Chicago and is a Ph.D. student at Loyola University.

Contributors

Writers:

Mark Fackler
Brian Dennert

Project Manager:

Dana Niesluchowski

Cover and Interior Designer:

Cheryl Blum

Compositor:

Cheryl Blum

Indexer:

Andy Culbertson

Additional help from:

Dave Veerman
Linda Taylor
Betsy Schmitt
Linda Washington
Larry Taylor
Ashley Taylor
Neil Wilson

Photo Credits

Sidebar photos: iStock.com

Page 13.   iStock.com
Page 15.   iStock.com
Page 17.   iStock.com
Page 19.   iStock.com
Page 21.   iStock.com
Page 23.   iStock.com
Page 25.   iStock.com
Page 27.   iStock.com
Page 29.   iStock.com
Page 31.   iStock.com
Page 33.   iStock.com
Page 35.   iStock.com
Page 37.   iStock.com
Page 39.   iStock.com
Page 41.   iStock.com
Page 43.   iStock.com
Page 45.   iStock.com
Page 47.   iStock.com
Page 49.   iStock.com
Page 51.   iStock.com
Page 53.   iStock.com
Page 55.   iStock.com
Page 57.   iStock.com
Page 59.   iStock.com
Page 61.   iStock.com
Page 63.   iStock.com
Page 65.   iStock.com
Page 67.   iStock.com
Page 69.   iStock.com
Page 71.   iStock.com
Page 73.   iStock.com
Page 75.   iStock.com
Page 77.   iStock.com

Page 79.   iStock.com
Page 81.   iStock.com
Page 83.   iStock.com
Page 85.   iStock.com
Page 87.   iStock.com
Page 89.   iStock.com
Page 91.   Photos.com
Page 93.   iStock.com
Page 95.   iStock.com
Page 97.   iStock.com
Page 99.   iStock.com
Page 101. iStock.com
Page 103. iStock.com
Page 105. iStock.com
Page 107. iStock.com
Page 109. iStock.com
Page 111. Photos.com
Page 113. iStock.com
Page 115. Photos.com
Page 117. Photos.com
Page 119. Photos.com
Page 121. iStock.com
Page 123. iStock.com
Page 127. Photos.com
Page 129. Photos.com
Page 131. Photos.com
Page 133. iStock.com
Page 137. iStock.com
Page 139. iStock.com
Page 141. iStock.com
Page 143. iStock.com
Page 145. Photos.com
Page 147. iStock.com

Page 149. iStock.com
Page 151. iStock.com
Page 153. iStock.com
Page 155. iStock.com
Page 157. Photos.com
Page 159. iStock.com
Page 161. iStock.com
Page 163. iStock.com
Page 165. iStock.com
Page 167. iStock.com
Page 169. Photos.com
Page 171. iStock.com
Page 177. iStock.com
Page 179. iStock.com
Page 181. iStock.com
Page 183. Photos.com
Page 185. iStock.com
Page 187. Photos.com
Page 189. iStock.com
Page 191. iStock.com
Page 193. iStock.com
Page 195. iStock.com
Page 197. iStock.com
Page 199. iStock.com
Page 201. iStock.com
Page 203. iStock.com
Page 205. iStock.com
Page 207. iStock.com
Page 209. Photos.com
Page 211. Photos.com
Page 213. iStock.com